The Baby Boomer
Encyclopedia

THE BABY BOOMER ENCYCLOPEDIA

Martin Gitlin

GREENWOOD

AN IMPRINT OF ABC-CLIO, LLC

Santa Barbara, California • Denver, Colorado • Oxford, England

Copyright 2011 by ABC-CLIO, LLC

All rights reserved. No part of this publication may be reproduced, stored in a retrieval system, or transmitted, in any form or by any means, electronic, mechanical, photocopying, recording, or otherwise, except for the inclusion of brief quotations in a review, without prior permission in writing from the publisher.

Library of Congress Cataloging-in-Publication Data

Gitlin, Marty.
   The baby boomer encyclopedia / Martin Gitlin.
      p. cm.
   Includes bibliographical references and index.
   ISBN 978-0-313-38218-5 (hard copy : alk. paper)—ISBN 978-0-313-38219-2 (ebook)
1. Baby boom generation—United States—Encyclopedias. 2. Middle-aged persons—United States—Encyclopedias. 3. United States—Social conditions—20th century—Encyclopedias. I. Title.
   HN59.G565   2011
   305.2440973'03—dc22   2010041021

ISBN: 978-0-313-38218-5
EISBN: 978-0-313-38219-2

15   14   13   12   11   1   2   3   4   5

This book is also available on the World Wide Web as an eBook.
Visit www.abc-clio.com for details.

Greenwood
An Imprint of ABC-CLIO, LLC

ABC-CLIO, LLC
130 Cremona Drive, P.O. Box 1911
Santa Barbara, California 93116-1911

This book is printed on acid-free paper ∞

Manufactured in the United States of America

Contents

Preface

The Baby Boomer generation comprises 80 million Americans who were born from 1946 to 1965. The Boomers were so named because they were the population boom after World War II in the United States and the generation with the most people born. They have made a tremendous impact on every aspect of American society, affecting everything from astronomy to zoology. Conversely, everything from art to astronomy has affected them.

The impetus for *The Baby Boomer Encyclopedia* was to broadly encapsulate the generation. Much has been written and discussed about how the generation influenced a particular area of American life or how it has changed in regard to certain issues and events. This encyclopedia informs later generations about their Baby Boomer parents and gives Boomers insight into their own generation. *The Baby Boomer Encyclopedia* covers a wide range of subjects, including politics and activism, entertainment, the economy, arts and culture, health, religion, lifestyle, events, family life, and sports. The entries deal with specific aspects of those topics, including influential people and moments of time that proved significant to the generation as a whole or where Boomers made an impact. The individuals, topics, and events featured represent all eras of Boomer existence from 1946 to the present.

The nearly 100 alphabetically ordered entries included in *The Baby Boomer Encyclopedia* were chosen based on relevancy to the generation as a whole. Individuals were selected who made an impact on Boomers in the world of literature, sports, politics, or pop culture and only if they influenced or were influenced by a significant number of people from the generation. The goal was to find an ideal balance in one volume, providing readers with knowledge of topics and people strongly relevant to the Baby Boomer generation in an accessible and engaging style.

The politically oriented entries focus on significant events in the history of the generation, including the assassinations of the Kennedys and Martin Luther King Jr., the Vietnam War and the antiwar movement, Watergate, the Iran hostage crisis, and the Iraq War.

The encyclopedia also features entries about several cultural revolutions, such as the civil rights movement, environmental movement, and women's movement, as well as long-standing philosophies that greatly influenced many Boomers for short periods of time, including the radicalism and idealism of the 1960s and early 1970s and the wave of conservatism of the late 1970s and early 1980s.

The arts and culture entries cover a wide range of individuals, including rock-and-roll icons the Beatles, Bob Dylan, the Rolling Stones, Led Zeppelin, and U2; literary greats Ken Kesey, Norman Mailer, and Dr. Seuss; entertainers Jack Nicholson, Dustin Hoffman, and Mary Tyler Moore; as well as influential and controversial television programs and movies.

General social topics such as racism, homosexuality, marriage and infidelity, and sex are illuminated. The personal lives and relationships of Baby Boomers are explored as well in entries on dating, parenting, religion and spirituality, career changes, and many others. Also falling into the category of personal choice are entries about the use of drugs such as marijuana, LSD, and cocaine as well as drinking and smoking. The changes in hobbies and activities in which Boomers have participated are examined in entries about games, shopping, the Internet, and fads.

Many of the entries have cross-references to related entries. The entries end with further reading suggestions in book, article, or website format for the reader to explore each subject in greater detail. A topical list of entries allows readers to quickly find subjects of interest. A chronology lays out many crucial dates and events in Boomer history. The Selected Bibliography is another source to pursue more in-depth reading. Finally, several photos complement the entries.

Introduction

Generalizations about Baby Boomers, born between 1946 and 1965, are rife. They were the ones protesting the Vietnam War. They took LSD. They frolicked in the mud at Woodstock. They turned their backs on their religious upbringings and became atheists or agnostics. They shed their pacifism and called for bombing Iran back to the Stone Age during the hostage crisis of 1980. They felt like hypocrites telling their kids not to use drugs after they had spent their college years in a haze of marijuana smoke.

The reality is, of course, much more nuanced. Millions of Boomers, particularly from small towns and rural areas, backed American involvement in Vietnam. Few from the generation tried LSD. Only a half-million attended Woodstock. Many maintained or even strengthened their religious beliefs or called for prudent measures to free the American diplomats in Iran. Millions were too busy studying and preparing for their careers to smoke pot in college whereas others could not afford college or were forced to work after high school to help their families. Furthermore, the lifestyles and actions of Baby Boomers born in the second half of the 1950s and beyond proved quite different from those of the generation that entered the world previously.

Indeed, Baby Boomers cannot be stereotyped. But greatly because of the circumstances and events of the times, some were more visible to the public eye and media scrutiny than others, particularly when the first wave was coming of age in the turbulent 1960s.

The first of the Baby Boomer generation was born in 1946, nine months after the first American soldiers and other military personnel returned from Europe and Asia as World War II was coming to a victorious conclusion. The huge number of couples that wed and committed to creating large families in a condensed period of time made the Baby Boomer generation the most populous in the nation's history. The population of the United States jumped dramatically during the two decades following the war, which is considered the timeline spanning all Boomer births.

Boomers have had a tremendous impact on the United States politically and socially. A number of questions must be asked about those Baby Boomers who made the generation one of the most publicized in the history of the nation. How were they raised in comparison to those from previous and future generations? What circumstances and events during the childhood and teen years played a role in their outlook and actions? How did the lifestyles and worldviews of their parents influence them?

The Baby Boomers who gained the greatest notoriety were those of the first wave of the generation from white, middle- and upper-class suburban neighborhoods and inner-city black backgrounds. Several factors entered into the general upbringing of the former, which proved quite different from that of previous generations and played a significant role in future events. Among them was the massive shift of American families from the cities to suburbia in the 1950s, which critics claim resulted in restlessness and discontentment. It has also been asserted that being raised in tremendous affluence in comparison to previous generations weakened the work ethic of many white, suburban Boomers and gave them a sense of entitlement. In addition, parents were swayed by experts in the field such as pediatrician Benjamin Spock, who suggested they provide less discipline and more open affection for their children.

The result was a sense of freedom and open-mindedness by Baby Boomers that included the questioning of everything that had been taught to them during their youths. When they were confronted with injustices such as racial discrimination and perceived wrongs perpetrated by their government such as increased military involvement in Vietnam, Boomers felt no obligation to support such institutions. They also felt no obligation to agree with their parents on any issue, including those regarding lifestyles.

The same could be said about young black Baby Boomers, who no longer felt a need to show patience and let the nonviolence movement take its course in eliminating racial discrimination. They too questioned the status quo and refused to sit idly by while the bureaucrats squabbled over the most prudent methods of ensuring equal rights. The result was the most violent spate of race rioting in American history from 1965 to 1968.

The Baby Boomers who received the most publicity in the 1960s and early 1970s were young and idealistic. They envisioned a world enjoying peace and a world population that rejected materialism and competition and placed an emphasis on fostering loving human relationships. They backed up their contentions with actions, which culminated in the harmonious Woodstock music festival of 1969 that defined the spirit of the generation.

Although Boomers put their own stamp on the events of the time, the events of future times and the realities of life would mark them in the 1970s and beyond. Idealism was replaced with realism in the personal lives and worldviews. Financial reality and a desire to maximize professional potential combined to motivate Boomers to forge careers, which in turn brought out their materialistic sides. Events in later years such as the Iranian hostage crisis in 1979 placed a greater sense of global realism into the hearts and minds of once idealistic Baby Boomers.

For instance, millions from the generation who had once abhorred conservative politician Ronald Reagan voted for him in the 1980 presidential election.

Boomers were criticized by some in the media for embracing materialism and seeking financial wealth in the 1980s, but they asserted that they were simply working to achieve the same American dream that others of previous generations had. Yet they were criticized nevertheless for what some perceived as retreating from the principles of idealism they had established two decades earlier.

Since that time, a greater understanding has been reached that the Baby Boomers who had earned tremendous notoriety for their attitudes and actions in the 1960s have merely melded into traditional American society. The generation is also more appreciated now for what it has brought to the nation, including among many a need to establish and maintain equality for all citizens; a thirst to end discrimination based on race, creed, gender, and sexual orientation; a healthy cynicism about the claims of appointed and elected government and military officials; and what many consider the rock-and-roll music that remains the best in the history of the genre in regard to talent and artistic creativity.

The Baby Boomer generation has been arguably the most scrutinized in U.S. history.

Chronology

1945	American soldiers return home from Europe and Asia after World War II.
1946	The first Baby Boomers are born.
	Pediatrician Benjamin Spock authors the book *Baby and Child Care*, which would be a primer for a generation of parents about how to raise their Baby Boomer children.
1951	Cleveland radio disc jockey Alan Freed coins the term "rock-and-roll," which would be the music that would define the Baby Boomer generation.
1955	The civil rights movement begins in earnest when Montgomery, Alabama, activist and seamstress Rosa Parks refuses to give up her bus seat to a white man, thereby launching a successful bus boycott.
1957	The Cold War continues to panic Americans as the Soviet Union displays its technological advancement by launching Sputnik into space.
	Jack Kerouac's book *On the Road* is published, giving impetus to the Beatnik movement and planting the seeds for the counter-culture of the 1960s.
1958	The Hula Hoop becomes an instant favorite for young Baby Boomers.
1959	The first Barbie dolls are produced and become a cherished toy for young Baby Boomer girls.
1960	The birth control pill is approved for sale by the U.S. Food and Drug Administration (FDA), setting the tone for the sexual revolution.

1962   Young Boomers and their fellow Americans are frightened by the Cuban Missile Crisis, the first legitimate threat of nuclear war, which is eventually stifled through negotiation with the Soviet Union.

The Students for a Democratic Society (SDS) is formed. The organization becomes popular on college campuses and eventually helps create the antiwar movement among Baby Boomers.

Rachel Carson authors *Silent Spring*, kicking off the environmental movement.

1963   The assassination of President John F. Kennedy shocks Baby Boomers and sends the nation into mourning.

Feminist Betty Friedan's *The Feminine Mystique* is published. The landmark book plants the seeds for the second wave of the women's liberation movement by claiming that women cannot realize their promise in current American society.

1964   British rock-and-roll quartet the Beatles arrive in the United States in February and capture the imagination of young Baby Boomers, influencing their fashions, politics, and lifestyles.

The Gulf of Tonkin Resolution, which claims that North Vietnamese military personnel fired on American boats, gives President Lyndon B. Johnson full power to use and expand the U.S. military presence in Vietnam, including the use of ground troops.

1965   Race riots break out in the Watts section of Los Angeles. The growing anger and militancy of young black Baby Boomers play a huge role in the insurrection, which sets off a four-year period of inner-city rioting throughout the country.

American military involvement in Vietnam increases, launching the antiwar movement.

Ken Kesey and his Merry Pranksters begin a series of "acid tests" by distributing LSD at parties in the San Francisco area and in Southern California.

The last of the Baby Boomers are born.

Bob Dylan breaks out an electric guitar during the Newport Folk Festival and is roundly booed, but helps popularize folk rock along with the Byrds and the Mamas and the Papas.

The Rolling Stones release "Satisfaction," which is often rated as the greatest song in rock-and-roll history.

1967   The Summer of Love in San Francisco brings national notoriety to the hippie movement.

A demonstration against the Vietnam War turns violent at the Pentagon, marking the first major clash between antiwar protesters and authorities.

Dustin Hoffman stars in *The Graduate*, which portrays young Boomers as idealistic and the older generation as corrupt.

Inner-city race riots reach their violent peak with dozens killed in Detroit and Newark.

1968   The assassination of civil rights leader Martin Luther King Jr. results in mass inner-city rioting and greater militancy among young black Baby Boomers.

Baby Boomers become involved in presidential politics for the first time. Many campaign for antiwar candidates Eugene McCarthy and Robert F. Kennedy.

The assassination of Robert F. Kennedy sends antiwar Baby Boomers into despair. Angry Boomers clash with Chicago police at the Democratic National Convention.

The Yardbirds morph into Led Zeppelin, which blossoms into arguably the greatest heavy metal band in rock history.

Norman Mailer wins a Pulitzer Prize for *Armies of the Night*, an account of the 1967 March on the Pentagon.

1969   The Stonewall riots in New York City launch the campaign for homosexual rights.

The women's liberation movement begins in earnest.

A nation torn apart by strife comes together for one moment as Neil Armstrong becomes the first man to walk on the moon.

The Woodstock Art and Music Festival defines the spirit of the Baby Boomer generation. A half-million Boomers enjoy three days of music and interact peacefully despite tremendous logistical problems.

Quarterback Joe Namath leads the New York Jets to a huge Super Bowl upset of the heavily favored Baltimore Colts on January 12 after boldly guaranteeing victory.

1970   Four students are killed by National Guardsmen on the campus of Kent State University in Ohio, prompting rioting on campuses all over the country, many of which are shut down. The students protest the perceived expansion of the Vietnam War into Cambodia.

The Mary Tyler Moore Show debuts on CBS and becomes one of the most highly acclaimed sitcoms in TV history.

The first Earth Day kicks off the environmental movement in earnest.

1971   Sitcom *All in the Family* debuts on CBS, revolutionizing the genre by delving deeply and humorously into a wide array of social and political issues.

Muhammad Ali returns to boxing after his ban for refusal to accept his draft into the armed forces and loses for the first time ever in a 15-round decision to Joe Frazier.

1972   Eighteen-year-olds are allowed to vote for the first time as Baby Boomers flock to the polls.

1973   The Supreme Court decision on *Roe v. Wade* legalizes abortion.

1974   The growing evidence against President Richard M. Nixon in the Watergate cover-up and his eventual resignation create greater cynicism among Baby Boomers and other Americans about their elected officials.

1975   The Vietnam War officially ends. Debate begins on whether antiwar Baby Boomers and the protest movement in general played a role in its conclusion and whether those efforts undermined the American ability to win the war.

The marketing of the home version of Pong starts the video game revolution.

Saturday Night Live debuts on NBC in October and becomes a nationwide phenomenon.

Hank Aaron slams his 715th career home run, breaking the all-time mark established by Babe Ruth.

1977   The disco music rage is at its peak as Baby Boomers hit the dance floor at clubs throughout the country.

1979   A conservative wave sweeps the United States, taking many one-time liberal Boomers along with it after Iranian radicals take American diplomats hostage.

1980   Baby Boomers, many of whom had strongly criticized conservative Ronald Reagan in the 1960s, help elect him president.

Boomers mourn as Beatles icon John Lennon is killed by a gun-wielding assailant in New York City.

1981   The growing AIDS epidemic marks an end of the sexual revolution.

1983   The last Baby Boomers graduate from high school. *Newsweek* magazine declares 1983 to be "the year of the yuppie" as many Baby Boomers embrace materialism and financial wealth.

1989	The fall of the Berlin Wall symbolizes the fall of Communism and the end of the Cold War.
1991	Baby Boomers and most other Americans applaud the efforts by the United States and other United Nations' countries in the liberation of Kuwait from Iraqi military control.
	Theodor Geisel, alias Dr. Seuss, dies. He is remembered for helping raise Baby Boomers through dozens of entertaining and moralistic children's books.
1992	The first Baby Boomer president is elected with great help from Baby Boomer voters as Bill Clinton wins handily over incumbent George H. W. Bush.
	Johnny Carson hands over *The Tonight Show* reins to Jay Leno.
1995	The fear of terrorism at home begins when right-wing extremists bomb a federal building in Oklahoma City, killing 168.
1997	Princess Diana is killed in a car accident in Paris. Millions mourn.
1999	A massacre of students at Columbine High School in Colorado by fellow students worries Baby Boomers about the safety of their children at school.
2001	Terrorist attacks on the World Trade Center and Pentagon kill nearly 3,000 Americans and shock the nation. Baby Boomers join other generations in calling for the rooting out and capturing or killing of terrorist leaders.
2008	Weary of the war in Iraq and a depressed economy, Baby Boomers and younger generations lead the way in electing the first African American president, Barack Obama.
2010	The first Baby Boomers reach the retirement age of 65.

Alphabetical List of Entries

Topical List of Entries

ARTS AND CULTURE

All in the Family
Alternative Lifestyles
Baldwin, James
The Beatles
Carson, Johnny
Cocaine Era
Computers
Consumerism
Dating
Divorce
Dr. Seuss
Dr. Spock
Drinking
Dylan, Bob
Fads
Family Life
Fashion
Games
Hippie Movement
Hoffman, Dustin
Homosexuality
Internet
Jackson, Michael
Kerouac, Jack
Kesey, Ken
Led Zeppelin
LSD
Madonna
Mailer, Norman
Marijuana
Marriage and Infidelity
*M*A*S*H*
Media Portrayal of
Moore, Mary Tyler
Movies
Namath, Joe
Nicholson, Jack
Racism
Rock-and-Roll
The Rolling Stones
Saturday Night Live
Sex
Shopping
Sontag, Susan
Steinem, Gloria
Talk Show Revolution
Television
Thompson, Hunter S.
U2
The Who
Will, George
Women's Movement
Woodstock

ECONOMY AND JOBS

Career Changes
Charity

A

AARON, HANK (1934–) Few Baseball Hall of Fame athletes have earned a reputation for courage and conviction off the fields of battle that have matched their brilliance on it. One that has is Hank Aaron, who displayed both attributes in the face of chilling death threats and vicious racism in the early 1970s as he chased after the most hallowed record in American sport—the career home run mark of 714 set by Babe Ruth in 1927.

To the oldest Baby Boomers, Aaron was a model of consistency and production on the diamond. To Baby Boomers who were too young to have experienced the civil rights movement, the pronounced and violent racism of the late 1950s and 1960s, and the heroism of Martin Luther King Jr., the prominent black figure from their early lives to show the greatest mettle against hard-core prejudice was Aaron.

Aaron learned all about bigotry growing up in Alabama, the heart of Jim Crow country, in the late 1930s and 1940s. He was raised in a ramshackle house without electricity in a strictly segregated Mobile neighborhood. When he informed his parents that he yearned to be an athlete, they replied that he had better perform better than the white boys if he wished to be successful.

He performed better than arguably anyone ever has. Although Jackie Robinson had broken down the color barrier in Major League Baseball several years earlier, Aaron began his career with the Negro League Indianapolis Clowns, but his talents were duly noted by Boston Braves scout Dewey Griggs, who outbid the New York Giants for his services. Aaron quickly established himself in the minor leagues, earning Rookie of the Year honors in 1952, and then snagging the most valuable player award in 1953 as the first black player in South Atlantic League history.

The meteoric rise continued when Aaron landed a spot on the Braves roster in 1954, thereby becoming the last Negro Leaguer to compete in the major leagues. Just a year later, at the tender age of 21, he blossomed into one of the premier players in baseball by batting .314 with 27 home runs and 106 runs batted in. In 1956, he captured the National League batting championship with a .328 average.

And the following year, he led the Milwaukee Braves, which had moved from Boston in 1953, to the National League pennant, earning most valuable player honors along the way. That season, he nearly won the rare Triple Crown, leading the league with 44 home runs and 132 runs batted in while finishing third with a .322 batting average.

Remarkable consistency and versatility marked Aaron's career. He slugged between 24 and 44 home runs in 19 consecutive seasons, a feat made more remarkable by the fact that he achieved it during the heart of the most pronounced pitcher's era in major league history against Hall of Fame hurlers such as Juan Marichal, Sandy Koufax, Don Drysdale, and Bob Gibson. He also developed into quite a threat on the base paths, recording double figures in stolen bases every year from 1960 through 1968. By the time he was done swinging the bat, Aaron had led the National League at least twice in runs, hits, doubles, runs batted in, home runs, and batting average. He not only earned a spot on the National League all-star team in 21 consecutive seasons for his ability as a hitter, but also became quite noted for his speed and sure hands as an outfielder.

It was not merely his baseball talent that made Aaron one of the most revered men of his generation. Even more so, it was his quiet grace that was complemented by his fearless willingness to speak out against what he perceived as injustice. Despite playing nine years in Atlanta, which even after the civil rights movement had subsided still housed many vocal racists, Aaron was outspoken in his criticism of Major League Baseball for its lack of black coaches, managers, and front office personnel. The Cleveland Indians finally hired Frank Robinson as the first black manager in Major League Baseball in 1975, the year before Aaron retired.

The hard-core racists who sent hate mail and even death threats to Aaron during his chase to break Ruth's record of 714 career home runs were not the only people who were rooting against him. Millions of Americans in 1974 did not want to see a black man break the prestigious record held by the beloved Ruth. Aaron has admitted that because of it he did not enjoy what should have been the thrill of the chase, but he did not allow the pressure of the media attention and the hate mongers to slow him down on the field. Despite the fact that he was 40 years old, he continued to march methodically toward what many had believed to be an unbreakable mark. Aaron tied the record on the opening day of the 1974 season against Cincinnati Reds pitcher Jack Billingham and then shattered it in front of a home crowd in Atlanta four days later by lining a pitch by Los Angeles Dodgers pitcher Al Downing over the left field fence.

Aaron finally slowed down later that year, which he finished with 20 home runs. He was traded in 1974 to the American League's Milwaukee Brewers, with whom he completed his career as a designated hitter. Upon his retirement in 1976, he joined the Braves as Vice President of Player Development before a promotion to Senior Vice President several years later. He was placed into the Baseball Hall of Fame in 1982 and awarded the Presidential Medal of Freedom in 2002.

Aaron was not in attendance when San Francisco slugger Barry Bonds broke his career home run record of 755 in 2006. Speculation arose that Aaron had snubbed Bonds, whose widespread unpopularity was based on the belief that he achieved the mark at least partially through the use of performance-enhancing drugs. But Aaron displayed the grace that marked his playing career by congratulating Bonds and never intimating that the new record was tainted.

See also Racism; Team Sports.

FURTHER READING

Aaron, Hank. *I Had a Hammer: The Hank Aaron Story.* New York: HarperCollins, 2007.

Stanton, Tom. *Hank Aaron and the Home Run That Changed America.* New York: William Morrow, 2004.

AGING Among the battle cries of the rebellious youth of the late 1960s was "Don't trust anyone over 30."

The number of those who embraced that statement dwindled as time marched on, greatly because by the late 1970s most Baby Boomers were over 30.

By July 2005, more than half of all American Baby Boomers had turned 50. In 2006 the first had reached 60. When the first Baby Boomers hit the age of 84 in 2030, the number of Americans of retirement age (65) and over will be greater than 20 percent of the overall U.S. population as compared with 13 percent in 2006.

Baby Boomers have been generally far more health conscious and learned about maintaining their physical well-being than have previous generations, including that of their parents, who did not even receive official warning of the dangers of cigarette smoking until the early 1960s.

The philosophy of aging has also changed. Baby Boomers have shown a greater propensity than their parents to at least dabble in more strenuous activity while aging in an attempt to achieve the benefits of the old adage—living life to the fullest. A 60-year-old Baby Boomer is more likely to sky dive out of an airplane, to use an extreme example, than was a similarly aged individual of previous generations.

Although technology has provided many more lures to keep Baby Boomers indoors as they age, including the ultimate inducement in the personal computer, participation in sports and other physical activities is common. The importance of exercise has motivated millions to partake in activities even as mundane as jogging or brisk walking. The information explosion provided by a wider variety of media sources has increased awareness of the many means of staying healthy and living a longer life.

Baby Boomers have examined the lifestyles of their aging parents to develop a philosophy about how they hope to live their senior years. The result is the first generation in modern times to reject the notion of slowing down during retirement. Although Baby Boomers and their parents have shown a desire to travel as time allows, the former have also displayed a longing to remain active physically and even professionally.

Financial struggles and the need to continue building a nest egg for the future have forced some Baby Boomers to stay in the work force. But many people in that generation have continued to work beyond traditional retirement years simply because it keeps them active mentally and physically. Others have become self-employed, starting businesses they had yearned to become involved in for decades, thereby creating a dream-come-true scenario for what could be their last working years. A study conducted by Merrill-Lynch in 2004 concluded that remaining mentally active was the primary reason Baby Boomers listed for continuing work beyond retirement age. Maintaining a physically active lifestyle was second followed by the need or desire to earn money.

Philosophies on the effects of aging run the gamut. Superficiality was frowned upon by the young generation of the 1960s and 1970s. It showed in the far more relaxed manner of dress and look. School-aged Boomers dressed down and wore little makeup. But the protest against perceived superficiality did not last. The explosion of the plastic surgery business in the 1980s and beyond indicated that many Baby Boomers became quite concerned with their outward appearance as they aged, although only those who could afford it took action. But there remained a large segment of the Baby Boom population that eschewed such cosmetic pursuits to seek inner peace as well as a healthy lifestyle. Despite the influx of products that eliminate gray hair, many have decided to let the gray stay. They have embraced the ideals encapsulated in the old expression "aging gracefully."

Although the era of technological gadgetry has helped produce some inactivity resulting in an estimated increase of obesity among Baby Boomers ages 55–64 from 31 percent from 1988 to 1994 to 39 percent from 1999 to 2002, Boomers are still expected to live longer than their parents because of an overall concern with health and continued advancements in medicine. The death rate for heart disease and stroke has dropped dramatically since the first Baby Boomers were born.

FURTHER READING

Barnes, Stephen F. "Retiring Retirement." San Diego State University. 2010. http://interwork.sdsu.edu/elip/bve/documents/ArticleRetiringRetirement_000.pdf

National Institute on Aging. http://www.nia.nih.gov/

Rowe, John Wallis. *Successful Aging*. New York: Dell, 1999.

ALI, MUHAMMAD (1942–) The impact of boxing champion Muhammad Ali on the Baby Boomer generation transcends his brilliance in the ring throughout the 1960s and much of the 1970s.

Ali gained iconic status not merely for revolutionizing the heavyweight class with a heretofore-unseen combination of elusiveness and punching power. He also emerged as arguably the most recognizable and respected athlete of his generation through his brash personality and the trumpeting of and loyalty to his political and religious beliefs.

The fighter originally known as Cassius Clay forever changed how Baby Boomers viewed athletes and their potential to use their fame as a platform to make a political or social statement or even change the world.

Ali fought his way into the American scene when he won the gold medal in the light heavyweight division of the 1960 Summer Olympics in Rome. But he displayed a keen social awareness and passion even at the tender age of 18 when he tossed that medal into the Ohio River after being refused service at a restaurant because he was black.

Ali's association with black Muslim leader Malcolm X, conversion to that faith, and name change to Muhammad Ali alienated and alarmed the older generation. But many Baby Boomers, angered by what they perceived as the slowness of change brought about by the civil rights movement and who embraced the new black militancy, cheered Ali. That was particularly true for young blacks that had grown tired of the advocacy of nonviolence espoused by Martin Luther King Jr. by the mid-1960s.

Ali became a greater hero to a large percentage of white Baby Boomers in 1967 when he refused to serve in Vietnam, claiming conscientious objector status on the basis of his religion. In one of his most famous utterances, he stated that he had no quarrel with the Viet Cong and that, unlike some whites in the United States, those fighting against U.S. troops in South Vietnam had never called him a nigger.

Those who were taught to stick to their convictions gained further respect for Ali when he appeared at his scheduled induction into the U.S. Armed Forces in April 1967 but refused to step forward when his name was called. Ali was stripped of his heavyweight title and had his boxing license revoked by the New York State Athletic Commission. Other state boxing commissions followed suit, which temporarily sidelined his career. Ali remained free on bail but was not allowed to fight during what would have been the peak of his career.

Ali served the burgeoning antiwar movement well during his hiatus from boxing. He toured college campuses to speak out against the war, making him a hero to students who by the late 1960s had embraced a more vigilant and sometimes even violent approach to the cause.

Ali's journey mirrored that of many Baby Boomers in that his views softened with time. He became far less of a polarizing figure by the 1980s and was cheered by most Americans in 1996 when he was selected to light the Olympic flame to launch the Summer Olympics in Atlanta.

Although those Baby Boomers who know little or nothing about boxing consider Ali an icon strictly for his activities outside of the ring, boxing fans will always revel in his talent and most shining moments, which include his unmerciful taunting and mocking of hapless opponents who vainly attempted to strike more than a glancing blow on him as he danced about the ring with grace never before witnessed in a heavyweight fighter. His description of his style in the ring ("Float like a butterfly. Sting like a bee") became legend.

Ali was thrust into the spotlight in a seventh-round knockout of heavily favored Sonny Liston in 1964 that preceded his religious conversion. But his most famous fight was his first defeat, which occurred in his return from forced exile in a match at New York boxing mecca Madison Square Garden against archrival Joe Frazier in 1971. In what was promoted as the "Fight of the Century," Ali was sent to the canvas by a vicious Frazier left hook to the jaw in the 15th and final round, marking the first time he had been knocked off his feet in any fight.

Nine months after Ali wrested the heavyweight title away from Frazier in early 1974, he defeated upstart George Foreman in a battle in the African nation of Zaire that became known as "The Rumble in the Jungle." Ali's last memorable

Heavyweight challenger Muhammad Ali in Miami Beach training for title bout with champion Joe Frazier in Madison Square Garden, March 4, 1971. (AP/Wide World Photos)

fight was a technical knockout of Frazier in temperatures that soared over 100 degrees in the Philippines in what was later called the "Thrilla in Manila." Ali secured that victory when a dazed and exhausted Frazier could not answer the bell for the 15th round.

Ali went from being a highly controversial figure to one of respect and sympathy when he was diagnosed with Parkinson's disease in 1984. He has since undertaken hundreds of humanitarian and relief efforts around the globe, which further improved his image.

Among his noteworthy moments since retirement was his selection to light the torch to signal the start of the Summer Olympic Games in 1996 in Atlanta. He was then given a second gold medal to replace the one he threw into the river 36 years earlier to protest racism in America.

It can be debated that other athletes of the Baby Boomer generation provided as many memorable moments and matched the athletic greatness of Ali, but it is highly doubtful that any made more of an impact on American society than the man who became the most recognizable sports figure in the world. It was his combination of athletic genius, charisma, and dogged insistence on sticking with his principles no matter how controversial or unpopular that made Muhammad Ali arguably the most important athlete of the 20th century.

See also Antiwar Movement; Malcolm X; Vietnam War.

FURTHER READING

Hauser, Thomas. *Muhammad Ali: His Life and Times.* New York: Simon and Schuster, 1991.
Remnick, David. *King of the World: Muhammad Ali and the Rise of an American Hero.*
   New York: Vintage Books, 1999.

ALL IN THE FAMILY Baby Boomers and television were born and raised together. Postwar United States gave birth to the generation and the medium. But if there was one product of American media that did not accurately convey the reality of the times, it was the sitcom.

And it was done quite intentionally. The networks believed the recipe for success consisted of escapism and wholesomeness, particularly in the 1950s and early 1960s. Societal issues were simply never discussed. Shows such as *Father Knows Best, Leave it to Beaver*, and *Make Room for Daddy* were squeaky clean.

Network executives believed the more problems society experienced, the deeper its television viewers wished to escape. Americans would watch its young killed in the fields of Vietnam on the nightly news. They would witness the assassination of President John F. Kennedy and two of its brightest young political and social leaders, Robert F. Kennedy and Martin Luther King Jr. They would cringe at the sight of riots in the streets and on college campuses. But two hours later, they could relax mindlessly and follow the exploits of a talking horse.

The 1960s offered sitcom hits starring a martian (*My Favorite Martian*), a flying nun (*The Flying Nun*), two ghoulish families (*The Munsters* and *The Addams Family*), a hillbilly Marine (*Gomer Pyle*), a witch (*Bewitched*), a genie (*I Dream of Jeannie*), and a wealthy New York attorney who throws it all away and becomes an inept farmer (*Green Acres*). On television, spouses slept in separate beds, toilets were never seen, all laughter was canned, and not a word regarding the social and political ills of a country being torn apart by them was uttered.

Then on January 12, 1971, the revolution quietly began when CBS aired a new program produced by Norman Lear called *All in the Family* after it had decided with little fanfare to give the show a 13-episide commitment as a midseason replacement. That the four central characters were a middle-aged couple (Archie and Edith Bunker), their daughter (Gloria Stivic), and her husband (Michael Stivic) was not controversial. But everything else about the show was. Not only did it take the nation by storm, but it was also the defining show of the Baby Boomer era.

The few that tuned in the first few weeks could hardly believe their ears. They heard the hopelessly bigoted Archie, whose job consisted of lifting crates on a loading dock, refer to blacks as "Coons" and "Spades," Hispanics as "Spics," and Jews as "Hebes." They heard him debate heatedly, ignorantly, and uproariously with Mike, the liberal college student, about race relations, gun control, and the Vietnam War. They heard Gloria complain about her period and embrace the fledgling women's liberation movement.

Soon millions were tuning in. And they laughed every week. They laughed every time Archie referred to the simple-minded, nonconfrontational Edith as a "dingbat" and to Mike as "meathead." They laughed when Archie argued with all seriousness that the way to end skyjackings was to arm every passenger. They laughed when he complained that Mike and Gloria would not be so happy that a black family was moving next door when the watermelon rinds started flying out the window.

Although every topic of social and political relevance was off limits to the sitcoms of the day, little was taboo on *All in the Family*. Sex, war, peace, racism, sexism, menopause, homosexuality . . . they were all fair game. The first belch and flushed toilet sound in television history were heard on *All in the Family*.

The impact of the show reverberated throughout the medium. The mindless, socially irrelevant sitcoms of the times were replaced. CBS understood that it had launched a new era in television and immediately dumped their triumvirate of albeit highly successful rural sitcoms—*The Beverly Hillbillies, Green Acres*, and *Petticoat Junction*. A new era of family shows such as *Eight Is Enough* that discussed such topics as drugs and sex began to dot the airwaves. Meanwhile, the success of *All in the Family* resulted in several spinoffs that also dealt with social and political issues, including *The Jeffersons*, based on the Bunkers' black neighbors, and *Maude*, about Edith's feminist cousin.

All in the Family had a significant social impact. Arguments raged about whether subjects such as race relations, gun control, and the Vietnam War should be debated on television. And, what proved disturbing to many, Archie Bunker became a hero to many bigoted working-class Americans who agreed with his views despite the ignorance on which they were based.

Many believe that when Archie mellowed, the show lost its edge. By the mid-1970s, the issues that had been hotly debated such as the war and civil rights were no longer primary topics in the United States. It was at that time on the show that Mike and Gloria moved next door and Archie had traded in his job on the loading dock for ownership of a local saloon and his anger and overt bigotry has softened to frustration and a bit more understanding. *All in the Family* never recovered after Rob Reiner (Mike) and Sally Struthers (Gloria) left the show in 1978. Soon the character of Edith was killed off and the show morphed into *Archie Bunker's Place*.

Although the youngest Baby Boomers were simply not old enough to fully appreciate the significant impact of *All in the Family* on television and on society, those born in the 1940s and the 1950s certainly did. The show forever changed the medium, opening the doors for plotlines dealing with issues of social and political relevance. And it also helped Americans to feel freer to discuss and express sometimes unpopular opinions on those same topics.

In the end, it was obvious *All in the Family* had been recognized not only for its impact on television and society, but for its brilliance as a comedy. It soared to the top spot among primetime shows in the Nielsen Ratings and remained there for six years, and it also won several Emmy Awards, including four for Outstanding Comedy Series. Some believe only its controversial subject matter prevented it from winning more.

In time, the American sitcom has lost a bit of its edge. The era of sensitivity and political correctness could never produce another Archie Bunker. But millions of Baby Boomers and others are comforted by the fact that his views, particularly on race relations, are now considered so far out of the mainstream that they have lost their place in the entertainment industry. How Archie Bunker would have reacted to the election of Barack Obama as president can only be speculated.

See also Antiwar Movement; Kennedy, John F.; Kennedy, Robert F.; Racism; Sex; Television; Vietnam War.

FURTHER READING

McCrohan, David. *Archie & Edith, Mike & Gloria: The Tumultuous History of* All in the Family. New York: Workman, 1988.

The Museum of Broadcast Communications. "All in the Family," http://www.museum.tv/ archives/etv/A/htmlA/allinthefa/allinthefa.htm

ALTERNATIVE LIFESTYLES The romanticism and idealism that drove some Baby Boomers to embrace alternative lifestyles in the 1960s and 1970s most often gave way to stark reality. Although some continued to eschew a more traditional existence, mostly through communal living, the vast majority quickly returned to a conventional lifestyle.

Many Baby Boomers who dabbled in alternative lifestyles and found them not only emotionally and mentally satisfying, but also more consistent with their belief systems, were nevertheless forced to give them up because they didn't coincide with the traditional financial and professional motivation toward success in the United States. Simply, they felt the need to earn money that would provide not only the necessities of life, but also the creature comforts they began to crave. Others discovered that communal living, for instance, did not allow them to fulfill professional dreams that eventually became a driving force.

The very nature of communal living prevented it from making a large imprint on society. The intention of those who embraced it was to remove themselves from the mainstream and to enjoy a simpler, less-pressured existence. They lived quietly in a small world based on sharing and self-sufficiency. Some living in communes expected millions in the United States to toss off the chains of consumerism and join them, but the more traditional American lifestyle had become too entrenched over the decades for such a dramatic shift to be a realistic possibility.

The popularization of communal living was a natural progression from the Beatnik period of the 1950s and hippie era of the mid-to-late 1960s. The Hippie culture and others that Baby Boomers were sometimes forced to confront as parents in later years (e.g., punk and Goth) played significant roles in shaping the lives of young people, but they did not generally constitute what can be termed as alternative lifestyles, nor could more modern styles of living based on choice or political leanings such as veganism, which eschews all use of animals in diet, dress, or any other purpose.

The sexual revolution of the 1960s did result in widespread experimentation that significantly altered ways of life, particularly among some married couples. Swinging, wife-swapping, and other forms of mutually agreed on infidelities became popular in the 1970s, although not extensively. The wave of conservatism that followed early in the following decade, as well as the advent of AIDS, brought back what was termed "traditional family values" and ended the era of pervasive promiscuity.

The environmental movement and economic distress in more recent years have combined to increase the number of Americans seeking alternative lifestyles. Nature-friendly communities such as ecovillages and communes have appeared throughout the country with varying degrees of success. Some believe they will become the wave of the future, although there is little evidence that the United States will revert to a greatly agrarian society anytime soon.

However, the recession late in the first decade of the new millennium did motivate many to reconsider their priorities and search for a simpler existence that placed less emphasis on gaining wealth and more on creating a less competitive lifestyle based on sharing and interdependency.

See also Hippie Movement; Marriage and Infidelity; Sex.

FURTHER READING

Metcalf, William J. "A Classification of Alternative Lifestyle Groups." *Journal of Sociology* 20, no. 1 (March 1984): 66–80.

Miller, Timothy. *The 60's Communes: Hippies and Beyond.* Syracuse, NY: Syracuse University Press, 2004.

ANTIWAR MOVEMENT   The two significant antiwar movements in the United States—against the Vietnam War in the 1960s and 1970s and against the Iraq War in the new millennium—were different in scope and passion.

College-aged Baby Boomers spearheaded the crusade against the Vietnam War, which intensified in step with the escalation of American involvement. The seeds were planted by the formation of the Students for a Democratic Society (SDS) in the early 1960s and mushroomed on college campuses throughout the country, particularly at left-wing activist hotbeds such as the University of California at Berkeley, Columbia University in New York City, and the University of Michigan. The antiwar movement exploded in 1967 and was punctuated by a march on Washington and a protest at the Pentagon, in which most of the participants were young Baby Boomers. By that time, more than 200,000 U.S. troops had been sent to Vietnam.

The moral and political outrage felt by Baby Boomers over the conflict halfway around the world eventually sparked the same from the older generations,

More than 100,000 antiwar protesters rally near the Lincoln Memorial on October 21, 1967, before marching across the Arlington Memorial Bridge to the Pentagon. The march was one of the first important anti–Vietnam War demonstrations. (Lyndon B. Johnson Library)

although the increasing number of young men shipped off to the war and the rising death tolls played a huge role in turning the overall tide of public opinion. By 1969, most Americans favored the end of U.S. involvement in Vietnam and 500,000 were turning out for rallies against the war.

But the more forceful and even violent approach to protest, otherwise known as "taking the war to the streets" or "bringing the war home," was conducted almost entirely by college-aged Baby Boomers. Peaceful demonstrations sometimes erupted into riots on college campuses. The most notorious clash between antiwar protesters and the law occurred at the 1968 Democratic National Convention in Chicago, where in what has been described as a "police riot" demonstrators were beaten and arrested in front of television cameras, which brought protest against the carnage into the homes of millions of Americans.

The Chicago incident radicalized some college students and other Baby Boomers. It resulted in the organizing of the Weathermen (or Weather Underground), an SDS splinter group that claimed that its ultimate goal was to end the war through a violent overthrow of the government, but few joined the cause. The Weathermen group gained nothing but condemnation for its actions, which included the bombing of public buildings, one of which killed a University of Wisconsin student.

The most tragic moment of the antiwar movement occurred on the campus of Kent State University in Ohio on May 4, 1970, when the Ohio National Guard killed four students during a demonstration. The incident caused college campuses, where protests against the war had become less frequent over the past year, to erupt again. Rioting protesters shut many universities down during what was supposed to be the final weeks of that school year.

By that time, the antiwar movement had grown to represent all age groups. But by the early 1970s it began to fizzle as American troops were returning from Vietnam in droves. Widespread activism among Baby Boomers was over and has yet to return despite the unpopularity of one future war in particular; that is, the war in Iraq, which was launched in 2003. Although opinion polls showed that Baby Boomers had grown disenchanted and even angry about American involvement in that conflict, which the George W. Bush administration claimed was motivated by Iraq's supposed cache of weapons of mass destruction and which took place after the terrorist attacks on the World Trade Center and Pentagon on September 11, 2001, organized protests were less frequent, less attended, and dispassionate compared with those that marked the Vietnam War era. Approval ratings for Bush's handling of the war plummeted well under those of Presidents Lyndon B. Johnson and Richard M. Nixon during the Vietnam War, yet many of the same Baby Boomers who actively protested in the 1960s and early 1970s sat silent as Americans died by the thousands in Iraq.

Critics complained that Baby Boomers had become far more self-absorbed and less politically aware and active over the years. They offered that the reason Baby Boomers protested so vehemently against the Vietnam War was that they themselves were at risk of being drafted and sent to fight. Although men today have been required to register for selective service, there is no draft.

Boomers counter that the Vietnam War did not threaten many of them personally because they were protected by college deferments that legally allowed them to escape the draft. However, some admit that they were more likely to act upon their moral outrage earlier in their lives, particularly in the more volatile environment of the times and in the dark shadow cast by the assassinations of President John F. Kennedy, civil rights leader Martin Luther King Jr., and antiwar presidential candidate Robert F. Kennedy.

One reason antiwar sentiment was simply not expressed by Baby Boomers as strongly as the Iraq War grew less popular was that fewer Americans were killed in that conflict. The reported total reached just over 5,000, representing approximately eight percent of the number killed in Vietnam. But many believe that for a generation that became known for taking a stand based on its principles, Baby

Boomers earned criticism for their lack of antiwar activity and public moral outrage nearly four decades later.

However, some Boomers simply moved to the right on the political spectrum. Many who even vehemently protested against the Vietnam War supported the incursion into Iraq, at least initially, although the numbers decreased when the perception grew that Bush and those in power misled the nation about the motivations to begin the war, including the phantom weapons of mass destruction.

Like all generations at the time, most Baby Boomers turned against the war effort in Iraq and were greatly silent about their opposition. The activism that marked their outrage over the Vietnam War had all but died. Americans of all ages were left to wonder why.

See also Kennedy, John F.; Kennedy, Robert F.; Vietnam War; War.

FURTHER READING

Arnove, Anthony. *Iraq: The Logic of Withdrawal*. New York: Metropolitan Books, 2007.
DeBenedetti, Charles. *An American Ordeal: The Antiwar Movement of the Vietnam Era*. Syracuse, NY: Syracuse University Press, 1990.
Mailer, Norman. *The Armies of the Night*. Bergenfield, NJ: New American Library, 1968.

ASSASSINATIONS American Baby Boomers had flooded the hallways and classrooms of every educational institution from nursery schools to high schools by 1963. And on November 22 of that year, every one of them was informed of a tragic event that had taken place in Dallas, Texas. Although few of the younger children understood the enormity or ramifications of the news, it was a moment many would remember for the rest of their lives.

The murder of President John F. Kennedy forever ended the United States' innocence and left an indelible mark on the generation. Many Baby Boomers have been asked "Where were you when you heard Kennedy was shot?"

The Kennedy assassination played arguably the most significant role in launching an era of cynicism in the United States, particularly among Baby Boomers, who were just beginning to gain political awareness.

Although there had been an undercurrent of pessimism and disillusionment about the American ideal in the 1950s, such attitudes did not become prevalent until that fateful November day. Certainly not all of it can be attributed to the tragic event, but the Kennedy assassination did launch the most divisive era in the United States since the Civil War. In fact, the Baby Boomer generation and others have wondered for decades how the 1960s would have changed had he lived and served out his first and likely a second term, given that the best the Republicans could offer in 1964 was radically right-wing Barry Goldwater, who was never embraced by most Americans.

Would the country have been bogged down in Vietnam in a war that tore the nation apart if Kennedy had lived? Would he have been more equipped to quell black anger and frustration that erupted in race riots in major cities throughout the country? Would the Democrats have remained in office into the 1970s, thereby sparing the nation the Watergate scandal that raised cynicism and mistrust of the government to its peak?

That cynicism was exacerbated by the growing perception that the investigation into the assassination that resulted in the "lone gunman" theory was tainted and that the assassination was part of a conspiracy. The event is as controversial today as it was nearly five decades earlier because although the Warren Commission report concluded that Lee Harvey Oswald was the only man responsible, far more than a shadow of a doubt remains. Several conspiracy theories have flooded the print and electronic mediums, leaving many still wondering whether a second gunman had shot Kennedy from a grassy knoll, or Cuban leader Fidel Castro had ordered the assassination, or the CIA had played a role.

The Kennedy assassination was only the first of three that rocked the nation in a five-year span. The other two occurred just two months apart in 1968. Civil rights leader Martin Luther King Jr., who preached love and nonviolence as a way of overturning centuries of racist thought and actions in the United States, was murdered on April 4, 1968, in Memphis, Tennessee. And Senator Robert F. Kennedy—President Kennedy's younger brother—was shot and killed on June 6, 1968, in Los Angeles, California, just moments after securing victory in the California Democratic primary.

Although it has been claimed that the younger Kennedy would have been the favorite to win the presidency in 1968, the King assassination proved more significant. The immediate reaction was a spasmodic explosion in the inner cities. The most violent black riots of the decade broke out in more than 100 ghettos from coast to coast. In addition, the nonviolent direction of the civil rights movement that King had attempted to lead and that had already been challenged by those who espoused greater militancy was forever lost. The civil rights movement was shattered. The Poor People's March to Washington that followed failed to capture the imagination of the nation, for which many blamed the loss of King and his leadership.

To many blacks, the notion of peaceful change died with King on that April day. His assassination helped legitimize greater militancy as represented by the Black Panthers and black power advocates such as Bobby Seale, Huey Newton, Eldridge Cleaver, and Stokely Carmichael. But although King lay dead, the morality and righteousness of his message could not be ignored. By the early 1970s, the last vestiges of institutionalized racism had been eliminated, even in the South. The admiration King earned from all races in the United States led to the institution of an annual memorial holiday in his name.

The assassination of Robert Kennedy also greatly affected the immediate future of American politics. The anger, frustration, and fear felt by millions of antiwar Baby Boomers played out with great justification. Robert Kennedy was the lone presidential candidate remaining with a legitimate shot at the White House who opposed continued American involvement in Vietnam. His murder at the hands of Arab Sirhan Sirhan, who was motivated by what was then the side issue of Kennedy's support for Israel, presented an open path to the Democratic nomination for Vice President Hubert Humphrey. Humphrey backed President Lyndon B. Johnson's policy of maintaining a large military presence in Vietnam, where more than 35,000 American soldiers had already been killed.

It has been speculated that a Robert Kennedy presidency would have shortened the war by at least three years. Antiwar activists saw little difference between the policies of Humphrey and Republican candidate Richard M. Nixon. And although Nixon did institute a "Vietnamization" program in which the South Vietnamese gained greater responsibility for the war effort while U.S. troops were slowly withdrawn, he also extended the bombing of North Vietnam, and Americans soldiers were not out of the country for nearly five years after he took office. Tragic events such as the killing of four antiwar protesters at Kent State University by the Ohio National Guard in 1970 would probably never have occurred had Robert Kennedy won the presidency.

The sights and sounds from all three assassinations in the 1960s are etched in the memory of Baby Boomers everywhere: John F. Kennedy slumped over onto First Lady Jackie Kennedy in the back seat of the dark blue Lincoln convertible after he had been hit. The colleagues of Martin Luther King Jr. pointing to where the shot had come from while he lay dying on the balcony of the Lorraine Motel in Memphis. The screams of horror in Los Angeles after bullets were fired in the Ambassador Hotel kitchen and news came down that Robert Kennedy had been shot.

No generation in American history has been forced to deal emotionally with as many tragedies involving prominent and beloved political figures as Baby Boomers. The repercussions of the three assassinations in the 1960s will never be fully understood.

See also Kennedy, John F.; Kennedy, Robert F.; King, Martin Luther, Jr.; Malcolm X; Vietnam War.

FURTHER READING

Ayton, Mel. *The Forgotten Terrorist: Sirhan Sirhan and the Assassination of Robert F. Kennedy*. Dulles, VA: Potomac Books, 2008.

Epstein, Edward Jay. *The Assassination Chronicles*. New York: Carroll & Graf, 1992.

Pepper, William F. *An Act of State: The Execution of Martin Luther King*. New York: Verso, 2003

B

BALDWIN, JAMES (1924–1987) Outside of the political arena, young black Baby Boomers of the 1960s needed somebody to give voice to the frustrations and anger they felt about the centuries of discrimination that left many of them utterly hopeless. One figure that arose to express those feelings was writer James Baldwin.

Baldwin was not a Baby Boomer and he spent many years outside of the United States, but his profound experiences growing up in the New York ghetto of Harlem in the 1930s and 1940s and his vast talents as a writer provided food for thought for blacks of future generations, particularly those who created upheaval in the segregated South and inner cities.

Born into a poverty-stricken family in 1924, Baldwin was the oldest of nine children. He developed a contentious relationship with his strict, religious father and sought ways early in his youth to escape physically and emotionally. He stated later in life that he understood that he was an intelligent young man. He spent much of his time in libraries immersed in books and realized that he had a passion for writing.

Although Baldwin clashed with his father, he followed in his footsteps to become a preacher. He spent three years in the pulpit as a teenager and was forced to deal with the despair and anguish of his fellow blacks. Baldwin credited that period of his life into transforming him into a writer. At the age of eighteen, during the first year of American involvement in World War II, he left the pulpit and landed work on a railroad in New Jersey.

After a short stint in that job, Baldwin moved to Greenwich Village, where he befriended and was inspired by respected black author Richard Wright. Baldwin spent several years as a freelance writer, working primarily as a book reviewer. In 1948, Wright secured Baldwin a grant that allowed him to support himself as a writer in Paris, where he could remove himself from American society in an attempt to write about his experiences in the United States with greater clarity and objectivity.

Baldwin penned several pieces that were published in various magazines before traveling to Switzerland to finish his first novel, *Go Tell It on the Mountain*, which

was published in 1953. The semi-autobiographical work described his life growing up in Harlem, which was a subject fellow author Claude Brown followed with
great eloquence a decade later with his autobiographical account of his Harlem
upbringing in *Manchild in the Promised Land*. The passion and depth with which
Baldwin characterized the struggles of inner-city blacks was new to the literary
landscape and later elevated the book to the status of an American classic.

Baldwin spent the rest of the 1950s traveling and writing. He moved from Paris
to New York to Istanbul, during which time he authored *Notes of a Native Son*
(1955) and *Giovanni's Room* (1956). The works dealt, respectively, with heretofore
taboo topics such as inter-racial relationships and homosexuality. He delved into
subject matter that few writers felt the courage to explore until two decades hence.
Baldwin also penned the eloquent book *Nobody Knows My Name* in 1961.

Much had changed in the United States when Baldwin returned in the early
1960s. The civil rights movement that he had only read about was in full bloom
and Baldwin felt an obligation to himself and to blacks fighting for their freedom
to play a positive role in it. He befriended civil rights leaders such as Medgar
Evers, Martin Luther King Jr., and Malcolm X; traveled around the segregated
South; and wrote *The Fire Next Time* (1963), a powerful book about black identity
and the state of the racial struggle. By that time, some among the growing number
of black militants criticized him for his pacifist leanings.

Despite the gains of blacks during the civil rights movement, Baldwin grew
disillusioned by the murders of King, Evers, and Malcolm X and the state of race
relations in the United States. He returned to France and wrote of his disenchantment in harsh terms in the book *If Beale Street Could Talk* (1974), which was
criticized as being filled with bitterness and anger.

Although it did express such emotions, Baldwin continued to preach love and
understanding throughout the latter stages of his life. Baldwin penned several fiction,
nonfiction, and poetry works in the late 1970s and 1980s, including the long essay *The
Evidence of Things Not Seen* (1985), which lamented the murder of 28 black children
in Atlanta early in the decade, and he remained a vocal advocate of racial equality.

Baldwin died at the age of 63 of stomach cancer while living in France.

See also Assassinations; Civil Rights Movement; King, Martin Luther, Jr.;
Malcolm X; Racism.

FURTHER READING
Baldwin, James. *Go Tell It on the Mountain*. New York: Dell, 1980 (reprint).
Baldwin, James. *Nobody Knows My Name*. New York: Vintage Books, 1992 (reprint).
Baldwin, James. *James Baldwin: Collected Essays*. New York: Library of America, 1998.

THE BEATLES The first Baby Boomers and the Beatles came of age at the same
time. The evolvement of the Beatles played as influential a role in the evolvement
of the first wave of Baby Boomers as any public figures.

The Fab Four from Liverpool, United Kingdom, did not merely march in step with
the social and musical revolution of the 1960s; rather, they led the way. They swept
the generation up and carried it along for the ride not only with what is generally

considered the finest and most creative music in rock-and-roll history but also through their fashions, philosophies, political stands, and social outlook. Paul McCartney, John Lennon, George Harrison, and Ringo Starr all featured distinctly unique personalities and worldviews, but Baby Boomers often lumped them together throughout the decade as the most powerful force in the music world and beyond. Boomers were too young to identify with such early rock stars such as Elvis Presley, Chuck Berry, and Buddy Holly. The Beatles gave them idols from that genre to embrace as their own.

The love affair between American Boomers and the Beatles began in earnest when their plane touched down for the first time in the United States on February 7, 1964. They arrived at Kennedy Airport in New York to the adoring screams of thousands of fans before performing in front of record television audiences on the *Ed Sullivan Show*. They took the country by storm with such early hits as "I Want to Hold Your Hand," "She Loves You," and "Can't Buy Me Love." When they arrived in the United States, the Beatles occupied the top five spots on the *Billboard* charts, which was an unheard-of feat.

But even in their "lovable moptop" period, the Beatles made an impact on the creation of a generation gap between Baby Boomers and their parents, most of whom did not appreciate rock-and-roll and especially did not appreciate that their teenage sons were growing their hair to lengths unseen in the United States since the days of Buffalo Bill Cody. Moms and dads would soon grow more fearful of "bad boy" groups such as the Rolling Stones, but many of them would still place the Beatles high on the list of negative influences for their kids.

That impression grew with time as the Beatles shed their comparatively wholesome image and led Baby Boomers into the psychedelic era with classics such as "Strawberry Fields Forever," "I Am the Walrus," and "Lucy in the Sky with Diamonds." The haunting "A Day in the Life" pushed the creative envelope on the landmark 1967 album *Sgt. Pepper's Lonely Hearts Club Band*, which greatly impacted the music industry and helped give the Beatles mainstream critical acceptance. Even the Grammy Awards, which had yet to embrace rock-and-roll, awarded it the Album of the Year. The days of rock hits being placed in a neat little three-minute package intended for 45s was over. Considered by many the most important album in its genre, *Sgt. Pepper's Lonely Hearts Club Band* ushered in the Summer of Love and FM rock radio.

By that time, the individual Beatles had strongly established their own identities personally and musically. McCartney wrote many of the popular pop songs, whereas Lennon emerged as the most daring songwriter and politically radical Beatle. Harrison, who embraced Eastern religion, was dubbed the "quiet Beatle." Some believed Starr was merely along for the ride, but his peers later deemed him one of the better drummers in rock-and-roll history.

The Beatles received competition for rock supremacy from the Rolling Stones, the British Invasion was in full swing featuring such endearing bands as the Who and the Kinks, and American groups such as the Mamas and the Papas and the Byrds had answered that explosion from overseas. But the Beatles remained unquestionably the most influential artists of the 1960s and, according to most music experts, of all time.

The Beatles perform at New York's Shea Stadium before a crowd of 45,000 on
August 23, 1966. (AP Photo)

That influence continued into the early 1970s. Later records such as the *White
Album, Abbey Road*, and *Let It Be* soared to the top of the charts, as did hit singles
"Penny Lane," "Hello Goodbye," and "Lady Madonna." the Beatles moved away
from psychedelia but remained the most creative force in the music industry. Lennon, in particular, became a highly influential spokesperson for the growing antiwar movement in the United States and throughout the world. He and future wife
Yoko Ono lured many of the top names in the entertainment and literary fields to a
greatly publicized "Bed-in for Peace" in Canada during the height of the Vietnam
War in 1969.

Several forces, including personal friction and creative differences, tore the
Beatles apart by 1971, but each of them enjoyed success musically and commercially as solo artists. Harrison struck gold with the album *All Things Must Pass*
(1970), which featured hits "My Sweet Lord" and "What Is Life?" McCartney
formed a band called Wings, which created a series of hits, including "Band on the
Run," "Jet," "Rock Show," and "Maybe I'm Amazed." Lennon remained less commercial, although he and his Plastic Ono Band did create hits "Imagine," "Mind
Games," and "Instant Karma." Starr showed his individual talent with "Photo-
graph," "It Don't Come Easy," and "You're Sixteen."

As the 1970s progressed, fans clambered for the Beatles to re-unite. The murder of Lennon by John David Chapman in New York City in 1980 not only killed
that hope but also traumatized Baby Boomers who idolized Lennon and embraced
their memories of the Beatles. Harrison died in 2001, but the Beatles live on not
just in the hearts, minds, and ears of Baby Boomers. Baby Boomers have passed

on their love for the Fab Four to their children and grandchildren. Beatles CDs are not only purchased by Baby Boomers, but by millions of fans that were not even alive when they called it quits forty years ago. In fact, when the compilation *Beatles 1* was released in 2000, it immediately shot to the top of the charts.

Though only McCartney and Starr remain, the legend and brilliance of the Beatles have lived on through their films, as well as their tribute bands and other performances that have honored them. Their early years were featured in *A Hard Day's Night* (1964) and *Help!* (1965). Their psychedelic era was captured in *Magical Mystery Tour* (1967) and *Yellow Submarine* (1968). Tribute bands such as Rain and 1964 have proven highly successful by imitating the Beatles not only through their music, but their appearance as well. Meanwhile, a 2006 theater production titled "Love" by Cirque du Soleil allowed a new generation to gain an appreciation of the Beatles.

See also Assassinations; Religion and Spirituality; Rock-and-Roll; The Rolling Stones; Vietnam War.

FURTHER READING

"The Beatles Biography," Updated from *The Rolling Stone Encyclopedia of Rock & Roll* (Simon & Schuster, 2001), http://www.rollingstone.com/artists/thebeatles/biography.

Kozinn, Allan. *The Beatles*. London: Phaidon, 1995.

Trynka, Paul. *The Beatles: Ten Years That Shook the World*. New York: DK Publishing, 2004.

C

CAREER CHANGES Most Baby Boomers recall the days of their childhood when their fathers would return home from work. Chances were great that it was a job at which dad had toiled since he had graduated from high school or college. Perhaps he did not work for the same company, but the line of work had likely not changed.

Mom stayed home to take care of the kids and the housework. The thought of a second income rarely entered either of their minds.

However, by the mid-1970s, the sexual revolution and several other factors had dramatically altered the work world. For those same reasons, mom, dad, and all adults were quite likely to alter their careers on several occasions in their lifetimes.

The most dramatic shift occurred with the massive influx of women into the blue-collar and white-collar working communities. Previously, most working women were single. Although some were strongly career-oriented with visions of maximizing their professional potential, most required an income to survive and eventually left the work world when they wed and began to raise families. The married women who did work were also career-oriented or did so to supplement the family income or help out in an emergency, such as their husbands losing their jobs or perhaps going on strike.

The movement of the early 1970s that convinced women that it was not only their right but also their duty to themselves to try to make the most of their talents resulted in millions of new job seekers. By the mid-1970s, there were more adults looking for employment than there were jobs available, which forced many out of their current positions and played a role in the massive unemployment of that era.

The addition of millions of women and young Baby Boomers into the work-force as well as the advancement in technology and the phasing out of many jobs that had become obsolete created an environment in which career changes were inevitable. The closing of factories, particularly in large midwestern cities, forced millions of workers to retrain for jobs in new technologies or become better educated to seek employment in white-collar professions.

The computer revolution played as important a role in the many men and women changing careers in the 1980s and 1990s as any factor. Millions of new jobs requiring computer skills were created in those decades, giving unemployed and underpaid Americans an opportunity to work in a field that promised security and longevity.

Advancing technology has proven to be just one of several motivations for career change. Another is the quintessential Baby Boomer desire to "do your own thing." Many of that generation have quit longstanding jobs to pursue new careers, even if it meant taking an immediate financial hit until the business began to flourish. Many have traded the suit and tie or business casual attire required in an office setting for the sweat pants and t-shirt of self-employment. Whether working out of their home, purchasing an existing business, or starting their own business, self-employment has given many Baby Boomers the satisfaction of creating their own successes and the freedom from answering to a boss.

The economic downturn that struck in the mid-2000s forced some who had forged their own businesses to seek employment elsewhere. Many family-run operations died quickly because of the poor economy and lack of consumer spending. Unemployment numbers that hovered near 10 percent in 2010 made it necessary for many to change careers simply to continue earning an income.

See also Family Life.

FURTHER READING

Love to Know: Baby Boomer Career Changes. http://seniors.lovetoknow.com/Baby_ Boomer_Career_Changes

CARSON, JOHNNY (1925–2005) Young Baby Boomers sometimes wondered after they went to bed at night what their parents were doing. Quite often they were watching *The Tonight Show* with Johnny Carson.

The king of late-night television talk shows remains one of the most hallowed figures in American entertainment history. Carson ruled the weeknight ratings, particularly in the 1970s and 1980s, as host with his monologues, homespun comedic characters, creative sketches, and famous guest stars.

Carson grew up in the American heartland of Nebraska and developed an interest in magic as a child before performing professionally at the local Rotary Club at age fourteen as "The Great Carsoni." Following a two-year stint in the Navy during World War II and four years as a radio-drama major at the University of Nebraska, Carson embarked on a career as an announcer and disc jockey before hosting his first television program on WOW in Omaha called *The Squirrel's Nest* in which he cracked jokes, staged wacky skits, and conducted humorous interviews, just as he would do with stunning success decades later.

A growing passion for and success in entertainment motivated Carson to move to Hollywood in the early 1950s. He was cast on a similar show, the low-budget *Carson's Cellar*, by CBS. His talent attracted the attention of such comedic stars as Groucho Marx and Red Skelton, who showed their patronage by visiting Carson on the show for free. Soon CBS launched *The Johnny Carson Show*, which was broadcast regionally in the western United States. Low ratings forced its cancellation, but Carson quickly landed a job as a writer on the *Red Skelton Show*.

Carson earned his way back in front of the camera in 1954 by hosting short-lived quiz show *Earn Your Vacation* while maintaining his job with Skelton, whose injury during a rehearsal thrust Carson into the spotlight as a substitute host. Impressed executives at CBS created a prime-time *Johnny Carson Show*, which featured a variety of entertainment, including comedy, music, dance, skits, and monologues. But the program lasted just one year before leaving the air.

However, another game show proved highly successful and gave Carson's career positive direction. He landed work as host of ABC's *Who Do You Trust?* in 1957. The daytime program earned high ratings, lasted five years, and allowed Carson to show off his quick wit and talent for humorous banter with his guests. Into the early 1960s, he also appeared in several musical comedy shows and game shows and even dabbled as an actor on Broadway and in live television plays. Carson's star rose to the point in which he received opportunities to substitute on occasion for Jack Paar as guest host on *The Tonight Show* on NBC. On October 1, 1962, Carson assumed the job on a permanent basis. It would be his for 30 years.

Within four months, ratings for *The Tonight Show* had surpassed those achieved by Paar by more than a half million. Audiences embraced Carson's controlled style, impeccable comedic timing, and pleasant personality. Within a 15-year period, *The Tonight Show* doubled its audience despite strong competition from highly popular talk show host Steve Allen.

In the volatile 1960s and 1970s, young Baby Boomers and their parents found watching Johnny Carson therapeutic. As disturbing events such as the assassinations of major political figures, the Vietnam War, race riots, and Watergate dominated the headlines, the enjoyment viewers received laughing at his monologues and skits gave them emotional comfort before bedtime. Carson touched upon the news of the day, but only in a lighthearted way.

Along with sidekick Ed McMahon, whose hearty laugh and easygoing personality proved to be an ideal complement and his trademark "Heeeeere's Johnny!" introduction before every show became legendary, Carson attracted viewers not only with his nightly monologue and big-name guests but also his creative characters that appeared every so often. The most popular was arguably Carnac the Magnificent, a turbaned psychic who would give a humorous answer, many of them corny puns, to a question hidden in an envelope.

Carson remained king of late-night television until his final show on May 22, 1992. Singer Bette Midler gave a final goodbye to a tearful Carson with her rendition of "One for My Baby." The Carson finale attracted an estimated 50 million viewers.

Ironically, Carson's soothing style as a comedian and interviewer belied a rather volatile personal life. He was married four times and his son Richard was killed in a car accident in 1991.

In 1999, a 74-year-old Carson suffered a severe heart attack in his Malibu, California, home. A lifelong smoker, he died on January 25, 2005, from respiratory arrest resulting from emphysema. He was 79 years old.

See also Television; Talk Show Revolution.

FURTHER READING

Cox, Stephen. *Here's Johnny: Thirty Years of America's Favorite Late Night Entertainer*. Nashville, TN: Cumberland House Publishing, 2002.

Leamer, Laurence. *King of the Night: The Life of Johnny Carson*. New York: Avon Publishing, 2005.

McMahon, Ed. *Here's Johnny!* New York: Berkley Trade Books, 2005.

CHARITY In 1967, during the heyday of the hippie, a group called the Diggers toiled busily around the San Francisco streets Haight and Ashbury where thousands of young Baby Boomers had congregated to celebrate the Summer of Love.

The Diggers distributed free food every day and opened a series of stores where hippies could pick out clothes and other necessities of life without paying a cent. The Diggers even founded the Haight-Ashbury Medical Clinic, which provided free care.

Such charitable work performed by the Diggers was a statement about the idealism of what at the time was the younger generation. It was, after all, the 1960s, before most hippies traded their transient, sometimes even nomadic, lifestyles for careers and their tie-dye shirts and beards for suits and ties and clean-shaven faces. It was, in fact, before few Baby Boomers were old enough to forge careers.

But by the mid-1970s, social and economic reality had combined with the aging process to place the generation squarely into the working world. And the same Baby Boomers who admired and even took advantage of such groups as the Diggers for its charitable work were now on the other end of the spectrum. It remained to be seen if they too would put their time, money, and effort into helping those less fortunate.

Significant charitable contributions were simply impossible for millions of other Baby Boomers. Those born into the lower and lower-middle economic classes have often remained there throughout their adult lives and have never been able to afford the luxury of giving money away to charity.

History sends a mixed message. According to a Pew Research Center study, Baby Boomers do more volunteer work and are more likely to join charitable community groups than generations past and future but are less likely to donate money. And according to an analysis of 2003 Internal Revenue Service data by New Tithing Group, an organization that studies charitable giving, older Baby Boomers at that time donated an average of less than three fourths of one percent of their investment assets, significantly less than those older and younger than them.

Many Baby Boomers and others have also changed their philosophy in regard to charity. The belief that some who seek charity have not been aggressive enough professionally in taking care of their families or are simply lazy became more prominent in the late 1970s and 1980s. Even some Baby Boomers who once sympathized with the plight of their fellow Americans have taken a harsher view over the years.

One can also claim that Baby Boomers have proven more frugal and less charitable, but circumstantial differences also play a role in such statistical data. Income has risen significantly since the 1950s and 1960s, but so has inflation. The cost of big-ticket items such as automobiles and homes and the increase in the price of necessities such as food and utilities often leaves Baby Boomers scrambling to pay the bills. The thought of giving what is left over to charity is often passed over by the notion of spending it on entertainment.

Moreover, whereas the expensive electronic gadget deemed necessary by the parents of Baby Boomers consisted of a color television set, most Baby Boomers came to believe by the 1990s that one simply could not survive without a computer, cell phone, and various game consoles for their kids. Income is also used to send grown children to college and support elderly parents.

Baby Boomers complain that they boast less disposable income than did their parents, on the basis of comparative cost of living. Critics argue that the generation simply has not lived up to the ideals of its youth, although some fail to realize that the Baby Boomer generation is not represented solely by those who took the same view of charity as did the Diggers in the 1960s.

Among the more recent trends has been the charitable work of those who, it can be argued, need the most help. A 2001 study by the W.K. Kellogg Foundation discovered that a growing percentage of those providing money to charities were minorities, including poor African Americans, Latinos, and Native Americans.

See also Consumerism; Hippie Movement.

FURTHER READING

Ellinger, Ann and Ellinger, Christopher. "Why Don't Baby Boomers Give More Money Away?" AlterNet. June 29, 2009. http://alternet.org/story/54804/

New Tithing Group. "Wealth and Affordable Donations in Uncertain Times." December 2003. http://www.newtithing.org/content/titles/content/tempresearch.html

Prichard, James. "Philanthropy Growing Among People of Color." Associated Press. January 13, 2001. http://library.generousgiving.org/page.asp?sec=28&page=462

CIVIL RIGHTS MOVEMENT A Baby Boomer retrospective on the civil rights movement of the 1950s and 1960s is affected greatly by age, location, and race.

The youngest of the generation were not even born when the U.S. Supreme Court ruled that segregated schools were inherently unequal in the landmark *Brown v. Board of Education* case in 1954, which set the wheels in motion for a litany of rulings and legislation that shredded the Jim Crow system in the South and ended all forms of institutionalized racism throughout the country.

Boomers were not born yet when brave Rosa Parks refused to give up her seat to a white man on December 1, 1955, launching in the process the Montgomery Bus Boycott, the movement itself, and the career of Martin Luther King Jr. as its unquestioned and impassioned leader.

Many Baby Boomers had yet to be born or were too young to remember the heart of the movement. They cannot remember the violence wrought by white segregationists in attempting to prevent nine black students from entering Central High School in Little Rock, Arkansas, in 1957, the wave of sit-ins at lunch counters by whites and blacks demanding the integration of public places in the South, the murder of three civil rights workers in Mississippi by Ku Klux Klansmen with help from local lawmen, or the sweeping legislation such as the Civil Rights Act and Voting Rights Act signed by President Lyndon B. Johnson in the mid-1960s that made all forms of racial discrimination illegal.

Yet the sounds and images of the civil rights movement have been burned permanently into the hearts, minds, and souls of all Baby Boomers. They have seen documentaries showing an angry white mob trailing an innocent young black girl whose only "crime" was that she was walking to Central High School in an attempt to attend classes. They have seen on television the rubble of the Sixteenth Street Baptist Church in Birmingham, Alabama, under which lay four black children who had been killed by a bomb in 1963. They have been awed by the eloquence of King as he uttered his "I Have a Dream" speech before 250,000 onlookers in Washington, D.C. And they have witnessed a group of civil rights marchers being pummeled by Alabama state troopers on the Edmund Pettis Bridge in 1965 in what became known as Bloody Sunday.

The Baby Boomers who were most influenced by the civil rights movement were those who were alive to experience it. Among them, those who lived in the South were the most deeply affected. They carry with them the personal memories of segregation—the Jim Crow "separate but equal" rules that resulted in tremendous inequality for blacks. They can recall the "Colored" and "Whites Only" signs over everything from bus terminals to drinking fountains to restrooms. They lived through the era of the shiny, clean modern schoolhouses for white children that rested just blocks away from the dilapidated shacks in which blacks attended classes. They remember the bombings of black churches and the violence perpetrated against blacks peacefully demanding the rights to vote and integrate with their fellow Americans.

The civil rights movement influenced southern black Baby Boomers born in the 1940s and early 1950s the most. They played a direct role in the drama. They were forced to attend vastly inferior and underfunded schools; were barred from frolicking at the public beaches, pools, and parks; and even feared for the lives of their parents, who could be whisked away at any time by white-hooded Ku Klux Klansmen and flogged or murdered. For more than any group of people, the civil rights movement changed life in the South for Baby Boomer blacks who, as a result, could hope to look forward to a future without discrimination. The opportunities for southern blacks of the Baby Boomer generation in comparison to those of the preceding generations were overwhelmingly greater thanks to the civil rights movement and the conscience it stirred among the people and political leaders of the United States.

Among those whose conscience was stirred by the civil rights movement were white Baby Boomers living through the period. Its successes motivated young men and women of the generation to become involved, including the Freedom Riders of the 1960s, who risked life and limb by traveling to the heart of the South, where racism had existed for centuries, in an attempt to force change.

However, many black and white Baby Boomers alike became disenchanted with the slow pace of the civil rights movement as pacifistic Martin Luther King Jr. led it. Leaders and groups who voiced more radical and militant options to gain equality such as Malcolm X and the Black Panthers in particular attracted many blacks. The primary instigators of the massive inner-city rioting that erupted in the

Freedom Riders enroute to Washington, D.C. from New York City hang signs from their bus windows to protest segregation. During the summer of 1961, hundreds of Freedom Riders rode in interstate buses into the prosegregationist South to test a U.S. Supreme Court decision that banned segregation of interstate transportation facilities. (Library of Congress)

mid-1960s and lasted for the next several years were those of the Baby Boomer generation. Their frustration and anger against institutionalized racism and discrimination were justified by the findings of a study by the Kerner Commission of 1968, which reported that those factors were the motivation for black rioting.

The civil rights movement arguably ended when King was felled by an assassin's bullet on April 4, 1968, but its impact has been felt by Baby Boomers ever since. Race relations in American society have improved dramatically during the last half-century, although pure integration, particularly in the areas of education and employment, has yet to be achieved greatly because of the vast economic discrepancies still existing between American whites and blacks. But the major influx of blacks into the middle and upper classes can be directly attributed to the civil rights movement.

The civil rights movement was successful because its goals were so obviously embedded in the American ideal of equality for all. And its legacy can be seen everywhere in the country, including the White House, where a black man who earned the presidency by a popular vote resides. Such an occurrence before the civil rights movement would have been impossible.

See also Assassinations; Idealism; King, Martin Luther, Jr.; Malcolm X; Racism.

FURTHER READING

CNN Interactive: The Civil Rights Movement: The Civil Rights Struggle in Modern Times.
    http://www.cnn.com/EVENTS/1997/mlk/links.html

History Now. The Civil Rights Movement. http://www.gilderlehrman.org/historynow/06_
    2006/index.php

Lewis, John. *Walking with the Wind: A Memoir of the Movement.* Fort Washington, PA:
    Harvest Books, 1999.

Williams, Juan. *Eyes on the Prize: America's Civil Rights Years, 1954-1965.* New York:
    Penguin, 1988.

CLINTON, BILL (1946–) Bill Clinton was the first Baby Boomer president.
That alone did not secure him a close tie with his generation, but his life experiences and policies during his time in office from 1993 to 2001 most often did.

Unlike many of his predecessors in the White House, Clinton was a virtual
unknown until a few years before he sought the presidency. He was born William
Jefferson Blythe III on August 19, 1946, in Hope, Arkansas. He never met his
father, who was killed in a car accident three months earlier. After the death of
her husband, Clinton's mother, Virginia Cassidy Blythe, moved to New Orleans
to study nursing and placed her son in the care of his grandparents, Eldridge and
Edith Cassidy, in Hope. They played a major role in raising Clinton. They taught
him racial equality in the segregated South, allowing blacks and whites to patronize their small grocery store and purchase on credit.

Clinton was reunited with his mother at age four when she had completed her
nursing degree in 1950. Soon, she had married car salesman Roger Clinton, and
three years later the family moved to Hot Springs, Arkansas, where the couple
secured work. After half-brother Roger Jr. was born, Clinton had his last name
legally changed to his stepfather's.

The teenage Clinton began a journey to the White House with which idealistic Baby Boomers could identify. During the presidency of John F. Kennedy,
who spoke hopefully about Americans working to help their country, Clinton
embarked on a trip to Washington, D.C., as a high school senior to partake in
Boys Nation, a youth leadership conference. He was among the first to shake
Kennedy's hand in the Rose Garden, which proved to be a memorable and
inspiring moment. It was then Clinton decided to dedicate his life to seeking the
highest office in the land.

Clinton was also moved by the historic "I Have a Dream" speech by civil rights
leader Martin Luther King Jr., which he watched on television. King quickly
became one of Clinton's heroes. He was impressed by King's ability to bring
people together for a common purpose.

Although Clinton thrived academically, he also embraced extracurricular
activities. He was an especially talented saxophone player. He performed in jazz
ensembles, attended a band camp in the Ozark Mountains, earned the first chair in
the state band's saxophone section, and received several music scholarship offers.
Clinton even played the saxophone on *The Arsenio Hall Show* in 1992 during his
presidential campaign.

Clinton's music and academic scholarships allowed his family to afford to send him to Georgetown University in Washington, where he could be close to the political scene and become involved in the school's top-rated foreign-service program. He earned his degree in International Affairs and interned in the office of well-respected Arkansas senator J. William Fulbright, whom he greatly admired. There, Clinton gained valuable experience in the political world and lifestyle.

That experience and his academic success earned Clinton a Rhodes Scholarship, which enabled him to study at Oxford University in the United Kingdom. He returned to study law at Yale University, where he met future wife Hillary Rodham. Upon graduation from law school, he joined the faculty at the University of Arkansas. Clinton took the first opportunity to run for office in 1974 when he campaigned for a congressional seat and lost to Republican incumbent Paul Hammerschmidt. Hillary helped him in his campaign. On October 11, 1975, Clinton and Hillary were married.

A year later, Clinton was elected Arkansas Attorney General, and in 1978 he became the youngest governor in the history of the state at age 32. Among his primary focuses was improving the state's horrendous standing in education.

In 1980, nine months after daughter and only child, Chelsea, was born, a conservative wave in the United States played a role in Clinton losing his bid for a second term as governor to Republican Frank White, but he ran a vigorous campaign two years later and regained the governorship.

Clinton remained in that office for two terms before embarking on a campaign to reach the goal he had embraced since shaking hands with Kennedy. He announced his decision to run for president in 1991 and emphasized several issues embraced by fellow Baby Boomers, including improving the health care system and bolstering the economy. He related to Baby Boomers with his grass-roots style, appearing on television talk shows and setting up town hall meetings in which the electorate could speak with him directly.

Although Baby Boomers and others scoffed at some of his claims, including that he only tried marijuana once and did not inhale, Clinton came out of virtual anonymity to secure the nomination, easily defeating incumbent Republican George Bush on November 3, 1992. The United States prospered during his first term, enjoying its lowest unemployment and inflation rates since the early 1960s. Meanwhile, home ownership rates increased, crime rates decreased, and the Clinton administration managed to achieve the first balanced budget in decades.

Although the economy remained strong, Clinton's second term was marred by his relationship with White House aide Monica Lewinsky, which he first denied, then was forced to admit. The resulting investigation led to his impeachment by the U.S. House of Representatives in 1998, but Clinton's presidency was saved by an acquittal from the impeachment charges after a three-week Senate trial.

The affair permanently stained Clinton's record, but the subsequent problems encountered by successor George W. Bush in regard to the war in Iraq and the struggling economy had many Baby Boomers remembering fondly the peace and prosperity enjoyed during the previous administration. Baby Boomers also embraced Clinton's charitable work with the William Clinton Foundation and his partnership with George Herbert Walker Bush and George W. Bush to raise money for victims of Hurricane Katrina in 2005, the 2007 tsunami in Southeast Asia, and the earthquake in Haiti in 2010.

However, Clinton was criticized for his role in the defeat of Hillary to eventual president Barack Obama in the 2008 campaign for the Democratic presidential nomination. Many Baby Boomers who worked or rooted for his wife believed he inadvertently harmed her campaign by his mere participation, which brought up memories and connections with the Lewinsky affair.

See also Charity; Kennedy, John F.; King, Martin Luther, Jr.; Marijuana; Marriage and Infidelity; Vietnam War.

FURTHER READING

Clinton, Bill. *My Life*. New York: Knopf, 2004.
Clinton, Bill. *Giving: How Each of Us Can Change the World*. New York: Knopf, 2007.
Harris, John F. *The Survivor: Bill Clinton in the White House*. New York: Random House, 2005.

COCAINE ERA Nothing defined the excesses and self-indulgence of the disco era and decade beyond more than a fine white powder.

The introspection and mind-expanding drugs such as marijuana and LSD that exploded into widespread use in the 1960s were replaced by hedonism and cocaine in the 1970s. Although marijuana became even more popular early in that decade, the drug of choice was cocaine by the time celebrities began dancing the night away at centers of American narcissism such as Studio 54 in New York City.

The byproducts of the epidemic were a war on drugs spearheaded by President Ronald Reagan and first lady Nancy, the cost of which made the war on drugs launched by former President Richard M. Nixon pale in comparison; billions of dollars earned by South American drug lords and millions by American drug dealers; and the advent of crack cocaine, which proved more addictive and far deadlier than the drug's less concentrated form.

The self-absorption prevalent in the cocaine era was borne out of the highly combustible 1960s, which was marked by war, riots, and assassinations, as well as out of the early 1970s, when the Watergate scandal and the resulting Nixon resignation raised mistrust of the government to its peak and caused millions of Americans to lose interest in politics and embrace escapism. The horrific events of the past decade motivated many to look for mindless fun in any form, and cocaine certainly fit the bill. The sexual revolution of the 1960s had flowered by the mid-1970s and cocaine was the ideal drug to get partakers in the mood and raise the level of sexual enjoyment. In fact, the cocaine high itself has been described as a full-body orgasm.

Users of cocaine ran the socioeconomic gamut, but many users at that time were young, affluent Baby Boomers who could afford to purchase it extensively. A gram of cocaine cost around $100, which was considerable for most Baby Boomers, including many who had just entered the work world. But addiction knows no boundaries and cocaine placed some Baby Boomers who could not afford it in dire straits. Money that needed to be spent on necessities of life such as food and rent went instead to buying cocaine.

With high demand, suppliers scrambled to keep up, causing a drug war and the war on drugs. By the mid-1980s, an estimated 150 tons of cocaine was entering the United States each year as, according to President Reagan, the number of Americans using the drug had reached somewhere between 4 and 5 million. The production and selling of cocaine became a multibillion dollar business. South American and U.S. drug dealers made fortunes. After all, cocaine cost just pennies to produce, yet could be sold, because of the demand, for a price far exceeding that. Addicted Baby Boomers or those simply partying alone or with others could spend hundreds or even thousands of dollars on the drug in one binge-filled night.

Cocaine addiction soon worsened when users began cooking it down to its base and snorting highly concentrated doses, thereby feeling the effects faster. The form of cocaine called crack was not only highly addictive, but it cost much less, which allowed those who previously could not afford cocaine to buy it in large quantities. Crack cost about $10–20 a rock—many times less than the powdered form. Crack addiction mushroomed into an epidemic among black inner-city and poorer white Baby Boomers. Casual cocaine use declined in the late 1980s as crack became the drug of choice in much of the United States.

During the cocaine era, some street dealers became wealthy, and the war against drugs inside and outside of the country turned into a game of cat-and-mouse. The flood of cocaine into the United States remained all but unabated until the demand decreased in the early 1990s. The war on drugs proved far more effective in its ability to educate kids and parents to the dangers of cocaine than in its ability to prevent it from being produced outside of the country and sold inside of its borders.

Some ridiculed Nancy Reagan's "Just Say No" program, which begged parents to wage an unyielding battle against drugs, but it proved effective in turning many kids off. The effect of the campaign trickled throughout society and helped lessen the demand for cocaine among Baby Boomers. By the time President George H. W. Bush picked up the baton in 1989, cocaine use in all its forms had lessened.

One factor in the diminishing use of cocaine in the late 1980s and the greater awareness of its harmful effects today has been the tragic and highly publicized deaths the drug has caused over the years. Among the victims whose untimely deaths have been at least partially attributed to cocaine have been *Saturday Night Live* legends John Belushi and Chris Farley, as well as basketball star Len Bias and rock-and-rollers Bobby Hatfield and John Entwistle.

See also LSD; Marijuana; Reagan, Ronald; *Saturday Night Live*.

FURTHER READING

De Grandpre, Richard. *The Cult of Pharmacology: How America Became the World's Most Troubled Drug Culture*. Durham, NC: Duke University Press, 2006.
Tervalon, Jervey, and Gary Phillips. *The Cocaine Chronicles*. New York: Akashic Books, 2005.

COMPUTERS The earliest recollections most Baby Boomers have of computers were from television shows and science fiction movies of the 1960s. The computers were about eight feet tall, looked as if they weighed eight tons, took up an entire room, made strange beeping noises, and blinded the observer with flashing lights.

The general consensus was that computer technology would continue to improve, but few realized the all-pervasive influence computers would have on future society and the everyday lives of Americans. By 2000, millions of Baby Boomers were using computers to achieve everything from paying bills to making hotel reservations to finding the woman or man of their dreams.

Some Baby Boomers who saw the revolution coming and invested in computer-related companies in the 1980s earned a tremendous profit. Most of the others simply rolled along with the advancements in technology and eventually purchased a personal computer when the advent of the Internet made the owning of one essential in their professional and even personal lives.

However, critics believe that Baby Boomers' dependence on computers has had more a negative than positive impact on themselves as well as on society. Many have complained the art of conversation has deteriorated, particularly among the offspring of Baby Boomers, and they lay the blame at least partly on the computer boom. The massive amount of time spent on computers in a home setting has created a greater communication gap between family members. They also argue that the many hours spent on the computer, particularly for entertainment purposes, has played a role in the poor overall physical condition of Americans because it takes away from the time they could be exercising. They further contend that time on the computer has helped in the depersonalization process they believe has made their communities and the country as a whole a less friendly place in which to live.

The same holds true for the children of Baby Boomers. Obesity among American youth reached epidemic proportions by the 1990s, and a distinct lack of exercise received much of the blame. Young kids and teenagers, like their parents, often plant themselves for hours in front of computers to entertain themselves, which is one major reason among many that one rarely sees a neighborhood filled with playing children anymore, such as what was a common sight when Baby Boomers were growing up. The attraction to playing inside on the computer also keeps kids close to home, where they are more likely to eat, which is another factor in the fattening of modern youth.

Baby Boomers and their children who use computers themselves in what is perceived as the proper perspective have certainly benefited. Among the advantages that computers have provided is the saving of time. E-mailing and paying bills online is certainly easier, faster, and cheaper than writing letters and filling out forms by hand. Online dating services have been touted as greatly successful in bringing divorced or single Baby Boomers together—far more so than scouring singles bars and joining more old-fashioned single's clubs. And the computer has allowed millions of Baby Boomers to start their own home-based businesses as primary work and as a means of attaining a supplemental income to an existing job.

Computers have certainly created wealth for many Baby Boomers, especially Microsoft founder, Bill Gates, and Apple Chief Executive Officer, Steve Jobs. Both have become billionaires by running companies during the computer and Internet boom.

More importantly, computers have resulted in millions of job opportunities for ordinary Baby Boomers, including many who were forced to retrain to become proficient. Computers have become a necessity for businesses in the post-industrial era. Baby Boomers know that without at least a basic knowledge of computers, they will be left far behind.

See also Career Changes; Family Life; Games; Toys.

FURTHER READING

HitMill. "History of Computers." http://www.hitmill.com/computers/computerhx1.html
Markoff, John. *What the Dormouse Said: How the Sixties Counterculture Shaped the Personal Computer Industry.* New York: Viking, 2005.
Wurster, Christian. *Computers: An Illustrated History.* Los Angeles: Taschen Books, 2002.

CONSERVATISM The philosophy that has driven conservative thought has not changed radically in generations, but its popularity has shifted with the times and prominence of particular issues.

Conservatism has been described as a belief in limited government involvement in regard to religious, cultural, and economic affairs.

The popularity of conservatism in the 1950s had dipped considerably by the time Baby Boomers had reached an age of political awareness. The unfairness of racial segregation in the late 1950s and early 1960s drew attention to what was perceived as the need for government intervention to provide opportunities for blacks and narrow the economic gap between rich and poor.

Segregation was actually legislated in the Jim Crow South, where racism was far more publicized and its brutality often resulted in the murder of blacks before and during the civil rights movement. But it was also a fact of life throughout the country, preventing many blacks from being given a chance to share in the American dream.

One Baby Boomer who steadfastly challenged the rationale behind government programs such as affirmative action is conservative columnist George Will. He argued that expansive government involvement in the economic well-being of individual Americans endangered the nation's financial health and is inherently unfair.

However, among most Baby Boomers, it was this issue that doomed conservatism, which espouses the maintenance of tradition and champions the notion that everyone receives an equal opportunity under the capitalist system. Will's argument includes the notion of "diminished competence" to describe those who benefited from government action, whereas others believe racism had kept them from attaining equal opportunities. The federal civil rights legislation of the mid-1960s, which eliminated segregationist policy and acknowledged the inequalities in American society at the time, seemed to justify anticonservative thought.

The same held true in regard to foreign policy later in the 1960s when conservatism became synonymous with support of American involvement in the Vietnam War. Although some in the Baby Boomer generation, particularly early in the conflict, backed the notion that the United States needed to stop the spread of Communism in Southeast Asia, most believed that was a philosophy of past generations and was no longer relevant. By the late 1960s, Baby Boomers flooding college campuses from Maine to California grew more vehement in their opposition to the war. Conservatism remained viable and even popular among older and even some younger people in much of the country, yet most Baby Boomers railed against it well into the 1970s.

The tide began to turn when Baby Boomers joined the work world by the millions and began to perceive that the same government intervention used to ensure equality for all for which many were clambering a decade earlier was resulting in competition for themselves, particularly in the world of employment. Programs such as affirmative action, which attempted to reverse past job discrimination, angered some Baby Boomers by giving blacks preferential treatment in the hiring process. In some cases, court-ordered busing forced the young children of that generation to be transported out of the neighborhood during the school day and into inferior educational facilities.

Conservatism reached its zenith among Baby Boomers during the presidential administration of Ronald Reagan in the early 1980s. The cynicism and economic recession of the 1970s, perpetuated by the Watergate scandal and hyperinflation, were replaced by a new-found belief among Baby Boomers in the righteousness of capitalism and a restoration of patriotism, the fire of which was lit by the year-long hostage crisis in Iran. Reagan, considered far too conservative to lead the United States less than a decade earlier, proved tremendously popular to most of that generation. Many Baby Boomers who had railed against economic inequality in the 1960s and early 1970s did not seem to mind that the disparity between rich and poor was dramatically widened during the Reagan years.

That era of conservatism was linked inextricably with such political and moral leaders as Newt Gingrich and Anita Bryant, as well as the Religious Right. They tackled such critical debates as abortion and the teaching of creationism in American schools, intimating that those who were pro-choice on abortion or defended the separation of church and state were going against God's will. The number of Baby Boomers who embraced that philosophy increased markedly in the late 1970s and during the Reagan administration.

By the 1990s, Baby Boomers represented American society as a whole in that they were thoroughly mixed on the issues of conservatism, both fiscally and in foreign policy. The terrorist attacks of September 11, 2001, elicited only a temporary increase in conservatism, greatly because it was fueled by anger. The failure of the George W. Bush administration to convince Americans that the war in Iraq was a necessary effort in the fight against terrorism, as well as what has been noted as the worst economic crisis in the United States since the Great Depression, pulled Baby Boomers away from the Republican Party, which has been considered the bastion of conservative philosophy since early in the 20th century.

Baby Boomers joined other age groups in helping Democrat Barack Obama win the 2008 presidential election in a landslide, but they proved less one-sided in their voting than did the generation represented by their children. Simply, the issues that once motivated Baby Boomers to rail against conservatism changed over the years. The number of once-liberal Baby Boomers who considered themselves conservatives by the turn of the century greatly outnumbered those who had taken the opposite journey in political and social philosophy.

The early period of the Barack Obama presidency resulted in a new era of conservatism, some of which was motivated by a lack of trust and belief in him as a patriotic American, as well as a perception that he was allowing the federal government to grow too big and intrusive. The Tea Party movement that began in 2009 included a large number of Baby Boomers. A *New York Times* poll taken in the spring of 2010 claimed that 46 percent of all Tea Party members were between the ages of 46 and 64 and that the vast majority of those included were men.

See also Gun Control; Reagan, Ronald; Terrorism; Vietnam; Watergate; Will, George.

FURTHER READING

Levin, Mark R. *Liberty and Tyranny: A Conservative Manifesto*. New York: Threshold Editions, 2009.

Tygiel, Jules. *Ronald Reagan and the Triumph of American Conservatism*. New York: Longman, 2006.

CONSUMERISM Baby Boomers gained a reputation decades ago for being far less materialistic than their parents, but that image was arguably faulty from the start.

Certainly many who were born in the early Baby Boomer era eschewed consumerism and materialism. It was part of a philosophy embraced by hippies and other young people in the 1960s and early 1970s. But an estimated 65 million people were born during the Baby Boomer era. Baby Boomers who rejected consumerism and the capitalist system in general were the oldest of the generation and were most often products of middle class and upper-middle class upbringings. Those who categorize Baby Boomers as a group that renounces consumerism and materialism tend to ignore the fact that millions who emerged from working class homes and millions of others born in the late 1950s and early 1960s did not hold the same view of consumers as did their older siblings and did not grow up with the same distaste for the traditional "American dream," which is based on purchasing power.

In addition, most of those same Baby Boomers who once decried the evils of consumerism have since been lured into its temptations. The perceived necessity of forging a career has brought with it the desire to spend money not just on housing, food, and clothing but on more frivolous goods and services that can prove quite enticing in a nation driven by commercialism.

The result is the further stratification of American society, a reality once railed against by many in that generation, who are now greatly affected themselves. Lower class and lower-middle class Baby Boomers are no less materialistic than their wealthier peers but simply cannot financially afford to fulfill their desires. They are equally affected by the commercialism that is so pervasive in print and electronic media in the United States. The result is that poorer Baby Boomers can only dream about what they want whereas richer ones can purchase goods and services that commercials and ads tell them they need.

The height of 20th-century consumerism resulting in a vast widening of the socioeconomic gap occurred in the 1980s. Baby Boomers with enough disposable income to invest their money successfully often used their earnings on big-ticket items such as homes, cars, and expensive vacations. Meanwhile, the poor simply remained poor and even homelessness became prevalent. The questionable value system of the generation in that decade was best expressed in the 1987 movie *Wall*

Street, starring Michael Douglas in an Oscar-winning role as a billionaire corporate raider and personalized by a comparatively young Baby Boomer, played by Charlie Sheen, who is driven by consumerism and the accumulation of wealth.

Like their predecessors, millions of Baby Boomers have fallen victim to advertising techniques such as keeping customers dissatisfied with what they have and yearning for "new and improved" products. Such an example is the four-blade shaving razor produced by one company. A *Saturday Night Live* fake commercial skit of the late 1970s poked fun at a fictional company that attempted to justify selling a three-blade razor by concluding that "you'll believe anything." After all, it is widely believed that it takes but one razor to shave.

Baby Boomers have not filled their college-age children with the same idealistic view of their futures as many of them carried with them into American universities in the 1960s and early 1970s. Studies show that whereas most Baby Boomers believed their primary concern as they headed off to college was becoming an authority in their profession and making the world and country a better place, that of their kids is to make as much money as possible.

The ideal of consumerism is to motivate everyone in society to strive for upward mobility. But critics complain that the promotion of materialism intellectually weakens society and results in superficiality and selfishness. Many Baby Boomers also believe that the push for individual wealth makes people far less community-minded and concerned about society as a whole.

See also Charity; Idealism; *Saturday Night Live*.

FURTHER READING

Abelson, Jenn. "Conscious Consumerism." *Boston Globe* online. May 31, 2009. http://www.boston.com/bostonglobe/magazine/articles/2009/05/31/conscious_consumerism/

Schor, Juliet B. *The Overspent American: Upscaling, Downshifting and the New Consumer*. New York: Basic Books, 1998.

D

DATING Few aspects of American life have evolved more rapidly and changed more drastically during the Baby Boomer era than the dating scene.

The images of young dating couples from educational films or staid television programs of the 1950s and early 1960s are etched firmly in the memories of millions from that generation. One scenario would have the young man in suit and tie sharing a malted at the shake shop with his date, who was invariably wearing a dress that revealed little. The couple was concluding a date that likely featured no more body contact than hand holding at the movie theater. Even the kiss goodnight would only be achieved if the young man was bold and the young lady quite willing.

Certainly the reality of dating in that era was not quite as innocent at the mass media led one to believe. In some cases, couples went beyond kissing on a first date or practiced sexual intercourse comparatively early in a relationship. But many also maintained the morals of previous generations and waited until they were married to have sex. The dating scene remained greatly conservative while the earliest Baby Boomers were still preteens or in their early teens. Attitudes about what was proper on a date were all but universal.

Everything had changed by the mid- to late 1960s, although the sexual revolution did not affect all Baby Boomers. Many in small towns, rural communities, or conservative backgrounds continued to steadily date one person and wait until marriage before having sex. But by the time Baby Boomers born in the late 1940s and early 1950s began reaching dating age, the notion of dating more than one person and enjoying multiple sexual partners had become mainstream.

Changing attitudes were only one reason for this phenomenon. Another major factor was the birth control pill, the use of which flourished in the early 1960s. It has been estimated that more than a million women were using the pill by that time, which freed them to become sexually active without the fear of pregnancy. Although the eras of widespread sexual intercourse with multiple partners and one-night stands that marked the late 1960s and continued thereafter had yet to begin, more women were agreeing to have sex with generally eager male partners well before what has been recognized as the sexual revolution.

The usually accepted view of dating as one man courting one woman became blurred in some circles by the late 1960s and early 1970s, greatly because for many the goals of dating had changed. The increasing number of divorces or at least the perceived poor relationships between married couples in their own lives had soured some Baby Boomers on the notion and sanctity of marriage. They opted to date not as a way to meet the ideal partner for marriage but simply to make a sexual or intellectual connection. The notion of living together as opposed to marrying gained in popularity and practice. With the goal of finding the right man or woman to wed no longer in consideration, Baby Boomers often began dating several people during specific periods in their lives. And sexual activity generally occurred far earlier and even more often in relationships, particularly when several different methods of birth control had become prominent and easily accessible by the 1970s.

Although more aggressive means of landing a mate such as newspaper and magazine advertising existed before the birth of Baby Boomers and well before the sexual revolution, advanced technology brought more effective methods of finding whatever one yearned for in a partner. Computer dating, which allowed unmarried people to put their dating futures in the hands of technology, took hold in the late 1960s and increased in popularity the following decade.

However, the dating scene and the sexual revolution took a drastic turn back toward conservatism in the 1980s when the AIDS epidemic struck. No longer could men or women trust those whose sexual history was unknown to them. One-night stands and sexual activity on first dates became dangerous practices. Even the use of condoms could not guarantee safety.

The greater conservatism throughout society during the Ronald Reagan presidency through most of the 1980s permeated into the dating scene. Although divorce rates continued to hover at approximately 50 percent, an increasing number of Baby Boomers began looking for a soul mate with the intention of finding the ideal one to marry. In addition, many decided it was time to settle down. The oldest Baby Boomers were reaching their mid-thirties by that time and the youngest were entering dating age with a far more conservative outlook.

Arguably the greatest change in dating for Baby Boomers has been the use of web dating sites. By the mid-1990s, many in that generation and beyond were basing their search for a mate on one or more of the many dating sites that allowed them to select potential matches without leaving the comfort and safety of their own homes. Singles bars remained popular, but millions of Baby Boomers preferred to meet fellow singles through sites that allowed them to e-mail one another or chat online.

Such opportunities did not take all the guesswork out of finding mates because of the exaggeration or downright lying perpetrated by those who joined Internet dating sites in their profiles. But millions of Baby Boomers found great success and appreciated the various services offered for a comparatively low cost.

The population explosion brought about by the Baby Boomer generation and the high divorce rate in the United States since the 1970s have placed a tremendous number of older singles into the dating scene. Some divorced Baby Boomers are seeking enjoyable times and even hedonism after their breakups; however, most begin looking again for a lifetime partner, including millions with the aid of online dating sites. Although many singles of subsequent generations continue the tradition of dating for fun with little intention of settling down right away, older and divorced Baby Boomers have generally sought emotional and financial security through finding a mate.

One aspect of the dating scene that has changed little during the Baby Boomer era has been the various activities enjoyed by couples. Dinner and a movie remain a standard, as has drinking and dancing at a nearby club. But the horizons have certainly expanded over the last half-century in regard to what is widely accepted as fair game when a couple returns home from a date.

See also Computers; Conservatism; Marriage and Infidelity.

FURTHER READING

Bailey, Beth L. *From Front Porch to Back Seat: Courtship in Twentieth Century America.* Baltimore: Johns Hopkins University Press, 1989.
Online Dating Sites—Lovesites. "History of Internet Dating." April 22, 2008. http://www
    .lovesites.com/history-of-internet-dating

DEATH The feelings of the rebellious youth of the 1960s were encapsulated by arguably the most powerful lyrics ever sung by the Who's lead singer, Roger Daltrey, from the 1966 Baby Boomer anthem "My Generation" that he hoped he would die before he got old.

As retirement and senior citizenry creep up upon the oldest Baby Boomer, most of those same folks who were screaming "right on!" to Daltrey's words would admit now that they vastly prefer to remain alive for as long as possible.

Baby Boomers boast a wider-ranging philosophy about the subject of death than have previous generations, particularly in regard to the possibilities of an afterlife. They have been more likely to question Biblical teachings centering on the existence of heaven and hell. Some have even adopted Eastern religions, such as Buddhism and Hinduism, or Islam, all of which feature far different philosophies from Christianity and Judaism about what happens to the soul after the body is dead.

Baby Boomers, like those in previous and subsequent generations, tend to become more religious as they age, and those who embrace the notion of God have also proven to be more skeptical about traditional beliefs in how they believe God judges people after they die. Many Baby Boomers feel strongly that a loving and understanding God would never send someone to burn in hell forever simply because that person did not believe in God. Nor do they accept the notion that God would pass final judgment on people on the basis of how often they commit particular sins or ask for forgiveness.

During the first several decades of life, the philosophies of most Baby Boomers about death remained unaffected by any personal experiences because those close to them such as parents and grandparents most often had remained alive. The deterioration and passing of someone near and dear to their hearts often changed the way they perceived their own mortality and eventual demise. In addition, youths generally feel so chronologically distant from the time of their own demise that the subject of their own mortality rarely enters their minds.

One premise about death that has changed over the years for many Baby Boomers revolves around the importance of maximizing potential. Among the central philosophies of the hippie movement of the 1960s was the unimportance of striving for professional achievement or making the most of one's talents because such striving was tied in with a sense of egotism. But many of those same Baby Boomers later changed their outlook in the belief that if one only has one life to live and the Grim Reaper could show up at any time, one should live life to the fullest, which translates into maximizing the talents and gifts inborn and learned so one can feel satisfied about a life lived.

As Baby Boomers age, they have given more thought to the various means of death. Now that all Baby Boomers are well into their forties, most have given thought to the way they would prefer to die. Although Baby Boomers have generally adopted the same desire for longevity as did their parents and grandparents, they have also witnessed the deterioration of the human body as those same parents and grandparents have reached old age. Many of them have decided they would rather die than suffer in agony or be overcome by senility in a nursing home while forcing their own kids to empty their savings accounts to pay for care that serves merely to keep their hearts ticking.

What Baby Boomers have learned is that death can be a relief from the suffering of old age. Their hope is that they will not be afflicted with maladies that could prevent them from living comparatively pain-free and in good mental health.

See also Aging; Religion and Spirituality; The Who.

Further Reading

Becker, Ernest. *The Denial of Death*. New York: Free Press, 1997.

Hines Sight. "Baby Boomers Confront the Big 'Boom,'—Death." April 10, 2008. http://hinessight.blogs.com/hinessight/2008/04/baby-boomers-co.html

DEMOGRAPHICS The majority of mostly white middle class Baby Boomers were one generation too late to experience the great demographic transformation in American society. The families of the remainder of the Baby Boomers have remained in place for many generations.

The parents and grandparents of many of the first Baby Boomers populated the United States' largest cities. But the end of World War II also signaled the end of the urban white middle class in the United States and the beginning of the mass movement to the suburbs. Throughout the United States, Baby Boomers were being raised on the outskirts of town and beyond in newly built homes that looked almost identical to the ones next door and across the street.

Such was not the case for others from that generation. Many white Baby Boomers were living in the same small towns and even the same homes as had their families for generations. However, the black demographic was created by quite different circumstances. Some were forced to move from the South to escape the chains of second-class citizenry entrenched by Jim Crow laws. But in the 1950s and 1960s, their lone alternatives were the sprawling inner cities from which neither they nor most blacks could afford to move. Black Baby Boomers born and raised in big-city ghettos were simply the most current of several generations living in dire straits and depressing neighborhoods.

Many from that generation who had spent at least their first years on a farm also experienced a change. The farm population, which had been decreasing for decades, continued to dwindle in the 1950s and 1960s. An estimated 6.8 million Americans lived on farms in 1935; that number had dropped to approximately 2 million by the mid-1960s.

Although some families moved on occasion or even quite often, mostly because of employment opportunities for the father, the demographics for suburban Baby Boomers growing up in the 1950s and early 1960s changed little. Their parents felt a sense of familiarity and comfort with their neighbors and their schools. Most early Baby Boomers recall that nearly all of their friends not only grew up in two-parent homes, but also remained there throughout their childhoods, although some traded one suburban setting for another.

Of course there were exceptions. Because of those exceptions, the populations of particular states leaped considerably. Beginning in the 1950s and continuing today, warm temperatures and job opportunities have lured millions of Americans to Florida, California, Texas, and Arizona. The population of all four states has jumped by at least 300 percent since 1950. In fact, California's population exploded from 10.5 million to 33 million from 1950 to 2000 whereas Florida's population increased from 2.8 million to 16 million during that same period.

The trends toward suburban living and relocating to states with a great deal of warmth and sunshine have continued as Baby Boomers aged and began making life decisions of their own. Among the most significant trends in the 1970s and beyond has been the mass exodus of black Baby Boomers from the inner cities into the suburbs throughout the country. Greater opportunities and the disintegration of institutionalized racism and discrimination have lifted the socioeconomic status of millions of blacks, which in turn have allowed them to move into middle class and upper-middle class neighborhoods. The result has been a further decline in the population of major cities, particularly in the former industrial hotbeds such as Pittsburgh, Cleveland, and Detroit.

The mass exodus has prompted a somewhat successful marketing blitz to bring folks back into the cities through new housing at lower costs, but the phenomenon has had little effect on Baby Boomers. The effort has proven more tantalizing to young singles who move into cities to save money on commuting to work or to be closer to what they perceive as a more exciting nightlife.

As more Baby Boomers reach retirement age, it would be expected that the populations of northeastern and midwestern metropolitan areas will continue to dwindle in relation to the growth of populations in states such as Arizona, Florida, and California.

Baby Boomer demographics shifted a bit in the mid-2000s with the collapse of the housing market, particularly in southern states such as Florida. But it remains to be seen if such changes are permanent or merely a temporary phenomenon motivated by the economic realities of that era.

See also Racism.

FURTHER READING

Bickford, Eric. "White Flight: The Effect of Minority Presence on Post-World War II Suburbanization." http://eh.net/Clio/Publications/flight.shtml

Myers, Dowell, and Lonnie Vidaurri. "Real Demographics of Housing Demand in the United States." 1996. http://www-rcf.usc.edu/~dowell/pubs/demohaus/demohaus.htm

DIANA, PRINCESS OF WALES (1961–1997) Diana Frances Spencer was neither portended for princesshood nor the status of commoner when she was born in Norfolk, United Kingdom, on July 1, 1961. She eventually blossomed into a Baby Boomer icon for embracing commoners as part of British royalty.

Affectionately known as Lady Di, her tumultuous years as princess were marked by her infidelity and that of Prince Charles, eating disorders, a passion for helping the downtrodden of the world, and affection from the British people that bordered on hysteria. Her life ended in tragedy and her death is one of the most controversial in world history.

Diana was among the last wave of English Baby Boomers. She was born into wealth but not stability. She felt unloved and lost, particularly after the separation of her parents when she was just six years old. She attended a series of preparatory schools where she was merely an average student and eventually moved in with her father, Johnnie Spencer, at the sprawling and impersonal family estate in Althorp. Among the many traumatic events of her childhood was when her father began dating and then married Raine Legge, whom Diana and her siblings despised.

Diana's life took a fateful twist in 1977 when she was introduced to Prince Charles through her sister Sarah, who had been dating him. Too young and shy, Diana shunned his early advances, although she admitted to being flattered and intrigued. Two years later, Diana moved with three roommates into a London flat purchased for her by her parents. She dabbled in work as a housekeeper, nanny, and kindergarten teacher's aide, but by that time her life revolved around her intensifying relationship with Charles and the media attention it attracted.

Diana was riddled with doubts about Charles's commitment to her. She was particularly suspicious of his relationship with his old friend Camilla Parker Bowles. Adding to her doubts was his comments that indicated ambiguity about his feelings when he proposed to her. Diana accepted anyway, and the wedding, which was held on July 29, 1981, was an American television phenomenon. Baby Boomer women who were about the same age as Diana were particularly enchanted by the event.

Little did they know that Diana and Charles were not enchanted with one another. Her suspicion that her husband was cheating with Parker Bowles proved justified after she had given birth to Princes William and Harry. Meanwhile, Charles reportedly grew jealous of Diana for her immense popularity that overshadowed his own reputation. Diana was mobbed and adored wherever they went. But the enormous pressure on her to fit in with the royal family and be what she perceived as a dutiful wife contributed greatly to her bulimia and depression. She

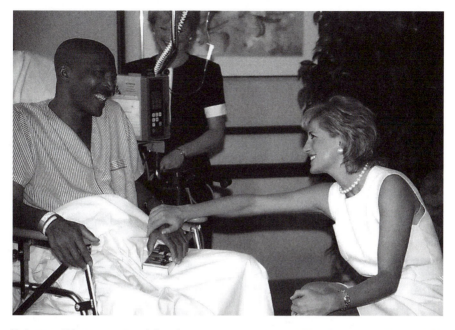

Princess Diana meets with a lung cancer patient at Northwestern Memorial's Hospice-Palliative Care Unit in Chicago, June 6, 1996. (AP Photo/Sue Ogrocki)

began having affairs of her own. By 1992, she and Charles were separated and four years later they were officially divorced.

By that time Diana had been established not only as a global icon, but also as one of the most caring and giving women in the world. Among her most passionate campaigns was against antipersonnel landmines, which still peppered the landscapes of war-torn areas in Africa and Bosnia. She undertook highly publicized trips to both regions and eventually helped convince some nations to sign the Ottawa Treaty, which placed a ban on antipersonnel landmines (however, many of those same countries have yet to earmark funds for their removal).

After her divorce, Diana became a tabloid target. She was shown on a yacht in the French Riviera with new boyfriend Dodi Al-Fayed in July 1997, after which both of them were hounded incessantly by paparazzi. Their desire to elude photographers led them on a high-speed chase through the streets and into a tunnel in Paris on August 31, 1997. The result was a crash that took both of their lives.

Millions lined the streets as Diana's body was transported from Westminster Abbey on September 6. The British public and much of the world grieved. Her impact was particularly felt by Baby Boomers. She had made a point of not trying to rise above the common people despite her status, and that was appreciated more by Baby Boomers who hated the haughtiness they associated with British royalty. Baby Boomers had and still do cherish her as one of their own.

See also Charity; Divorce; Marriage and Infidelity.

FURTHER READING
Clayton, Tim. *Diana: Story of a Princess*. New York: Atria, 2001.
Morton, Andrew. *Diana: Her New Life*. New York: Pocket Books, 1995.
Simmons, Simone. *Diana: The Secret Years*. New York: Ballantine, 1999.

DIVORCE The media portrayal of married couples from the 1950s and 1960s as blissfully content is most certainly false. No real-life husband and wife could possibly be as happy together as those on such antiseptic television shows as *Leave It to Beaver* or *Ozzie and Harriet*.

But to the minds and hearts of many early Baby Boomers, the relationship between mom and dad was close to perfect during those years. The threat of divorce was so far-fetched to most children of that generation that it rarely entered their thoughts. That one day their mother and father would not be sitting at the same dinner table with them was not even considered.

For most older Baby Boomers, such comforting thoughts about their parents were certainly justified. The divorce rate among men and women of the previous generation remained low through the turbulent 1960s. According to divorceinfo .com, about nine percent of women over 15 were divorced in 1960. The figure rose to 14 percent by the end of the decade and continued to rise.

Divorce rates began to skyrocket in the 1970s and peaked at about 23 percent in 1978, according to the same study. The rates stabilized and even curtailed a bit thereafter, and most estimates are 40–50 percent of all marriages have or will end in divorce. Several factors have played roles in the dramatic increase in the divorce rate over a relatively short period of time. One factor in the higher divorce rate was the marketing of the birth control pill, which not only gave couples a better opportunity for family planning, but also presented women with more sexual freedom. It was only natural that contraception designed for women would make some feel less committed to a marriage that might not have been working for them emotionally or sexually and more interested in exploring new relationships.

The explosive increase in the number of women seeking not only employment but also careers of their own in the 1970s proved a factor in the growing divorce rate. The trend gave many women financial independence and a sense of overall independence, both of which sometimes translated into dissatisfaction with the status quo. Although the primary result of the many women seeking careers was that unmarried women remained single for longer, the newly acquired feeling of independence in their professional lives also drove many married women to also seek freedom in their private lives.

The trends of the times also greatly affected the divorce rate. The sexual revolution launched by young Baby Boomers in the 1960s had permeated much of society by the early 1970s. The taboo of having multiple sexual partners had been removed and even the marriage vows were not deemed quite as sacred anymore. Extramarital affairs had previously been a comparatively rare occurrence. When they were discovered, the bonds of matrimony were often too strong to break up the marriage. In addition, in previous eras a lack of financial independence had kept wives by their husbands' sides through thick, thin, and infidelity. The outlooks on marriage had changed dramatically by the 1970s. Men and women were more likely to be unfaithful and seek divorce when infidelities were revealed. The times touted the advantages of being young, single, and hip, and even middle-aged married people fell into the trap. The so-called sanctity of marriage simply did not hold as much importance to them as it once did. Some couples decided to live with "open" relationships in which infidelity was allowed; others were overcome by jealousy and anger over cheating spouses despite the freedom of the times and the result was divorce.

The early Baby Boomers were now marrying by the millions and were swept up in the sexual and cultural revolution many of them had helped start. The divorce rate in the United States that had been inching up since the mid-1960s soared in the 1970s. An estimated 11 women per 1,000 were getting divorced annually in 1968. The figure increased steadily and drastically throughout the 1970s to the point at which it reached 23 per 1,000 women by 1979. The divorce rate had more than doubled in one decade.

Statistics cannot explain the emotional pain divorce has caused Baby Boomers over the years. Many have experienced grief when their parents broke up and again when their own marriages disintegrated. Hundreds of divorce recovery groups have been founded in more recent years to help Baby Boomers and others deal with the heartbreak and the sense of loss.

Divorce rates have remained high throughout the last few decades and there are no signs that they will ever diminish to the levels seen before the sexual revolution of the 1960s. Some studies have indicated that divorce rates have remained steady or have even slightly dropped since the early 1980s. At that time, conservatism and an emphasis on so-called family values became popularized. The notion of making a strong attempt to keep marriages together, particularly for the sake of the children, has been embraced by millions of Baby Boomers. The result has been the increased popularity of marriage counseling, which has allowed couples to attempt to work out their problems before they become irreconcilable. Although it is quite possible, even probable, that divorce will never be considered as grave a step as it once was, couples have generally become more interested in saving their marriages than they were a generation ago.

Many believe the key is surviving the first decade or two of matrimony. Baby Boomers who have done so are far more likely to remain together for a lifetime because they have proven their love and commitment to one another. Studies have shown that divorce rates have slightly declined for those born in 1955 or later, and those who were wed in 1975 or since enjoy better odds of reaching their 10th and 15th wedding anniversaries than those who were married the previous 20 years.

Time and the American culture of the future will determine future divorce rates, but history will indicate that Baby Boomers were in the middle of the storm that saw divorce rates rise to unprecedented heights.

See also Conservatism; Marriage and Infidelity; Sex.

FURTHER READING

Centers for Disease Control and Prevention. National Vital Statistics System. Marriages
    and Divorces. http://www.cdc.gov/nchs/mardiv.htm#state_tables
Riley, Glenda. *Divorce: An American Tradition.* Lincoln, NE: University of Nebraska
    Press, 1997.

DRINKING The effects of alcohol and the threat of alcoholism were foreign to
most Baby Boomers during their childhood. Even if dad asked for a martini when
he arrived home from work and both parents drank a cocktail or glass of wine
every once in a while, they were not usually stumbling around drunk, especially
in front of the kids.

Television in the 1960s and 1970s was full of couples or coworkers on such
sitcoms as *Bewitched* or *The Mary Tyler Moore Show* having a drink or two. The
electronic media placed drinking in the adult world squarely into the cultural
mainstream, although it had been part of American life for centuries before and
decades since.

The difference in more recent times has been that problem drinkers are far more
infrequently portrayed as comic characters. One noted example of past character-
izations was Otis, the town drunk on the *The Andy Griffith Show*, which dominated
the ratings throughout the 1960s. Viewers laughed when Otis stumbled into the
courtroom and locked himself into his jail cell as sheriff Andy Taylor and deputy
Barney Fife looked on. They laughed harder when a befuddled and crocked Otis
rode a cow down the main street of Mayberry in the mistaken notion that he had
been sold a horse.

The line separating casual and social drinking from alcoholism has been crossed
by millions of Americans, but the problem was not treated with what many perceive as appropriate seriousness, particularly by the mainstream media, until several years after the oldest Baby Boomers reached adulthood. The freewheeling
disco era attracted millions from that generation to nightclubs, where they not
only danced the night away but also often drank to excess. Whether it was beer,
wine, mixed drinks, or straight shots, the idea was often to lessen or lose one's
inhibitions, a goal perceived as a necessary tool to make a connection with a date
or an attractive stranger.

However, not all Baby Boomers were drinking. A trend toward healthy lifestyles strongly affected the generation in the early 1970s. Although some Baby
Boomers who had become actively health-conscious in terms of diet and exercise drank occasionally, they understood the physical ramifications of excessive
drinking. Many of those same people have made maintaining healthy bodies
a priority throughout their lives and do not drink at all or greatly limit their
consumption.

Although cocaine had gained tremendous popularity in the late 1970s and early
1980s, its cost precluded it from ever becoming the drug of choice for most Baby
Boomers. Rather, that distinction belonged to alcohol. Older Baby Boomers had
outgrown or tired of marijuana, and although younger ones also gravitated to pot,

they were much more likely to partake in alcohol than were teenagers in the late 1960s and early 1970s. Whether consumed socially and in controlled amounts or as a means of getting tipsy, alcohol had been the most popular drug for every generation in the United States. Baby Boomers have been no exception.

In more recent years, good news and bad news have emerged about alcohol consumption, both of which conscientious Baby Boomers have used to modify their drinking habits. The confirmation that red wine consumed in moderation promotes good heart health has increased the number from that generation who partake in an occasional or even daily glass of red wine; others simply drink red grape juice to receive the benefits.

The bad news about alcohol consumption continued to mount over the years, including new studies about its dangers to aging Baby Boomers. Studies have shown that the aging process brings with it greater sensitivity and less tolerance to alcohol, which can result in triggering or worsening serious medical problems, including high blood pressure, liver and heart disease, diabetes, and ulcers. Also indicated is that alcohol consumption can hasten memory loss and an inability to sleep, particularly when mixing with prescription or even over-the-counter drugs.

That alcoholism is a disease that must be treated as such became generally known and accepted early in the Baby Boomer generation. Baby Boomers also became quite aware that it can be hereditary, which allowed them to understand their own cravings and bent toward alcohol abuse. But such events in the lives of Baby Boomers as the loss of a spouse or other loved one, which can cause loneliness and grief, have sometimes triggered an unwise level of alcohol consumption that leads to addiction.

There is arguably greater awareness today than ever about the dangers of alcohol. Baby Boomers have been in the forefront of the education process, and millions of others have taken steps to cure their own ills in regard to drinking, including receiving substance abuse treatment. Treatment options such as joining Alcoholics Anonymous, which features its famed 12-step program, have gained popularity. The organization claims that its membership has soared from approximately 1 million in 1976 to 2 million by 2001.

According to findings published in 2003 by the journal *Drug and Alcohol Dependence* and based on data analysis from the National Household Survey on Drug Abuse, the Baby Boomer–dominated 50-and-over population in the United States will increase from 75 million in 2000 to an estimated 113 million in 2020. During that time, it has been estimated that the percentage of those in that age group seeking substance abuse treatment will rise from 2.3 percent to 3.9 percent. That statistic speaks volumes not only about the number of Baby Boomers who struggle with alcohol abuse, but also the greater awareness of the dangers of alcohol and the susceptibility to addiction with which many are confronted.

See also Heath and Health Care; Television.

FURTHER READING
Wortitz, Janet Geringer. *Adult Children of Alcoholics*. Deerfield Beach, FL: HCI Books, 1990.

DR. SEUSS (1904–1991) Most Baby Boomers would remember one children's book author with great affection: Dr. Seuss.

The works of Theodore Seuss Geisel served not only as bedtime stories for Baby Boomers into the early 1970s, but also played a significant role in teaching the entire generation to read. Moreover, they provided moral lessons that have helped guide Baby Boomers through their lives.

Geisel began his career as a freelance cartoonist. Prestigious magazines such as the *Saturday Evening Post* published his work before he landed a full-time job creating advertising campaigns for Standard Oil. He learned the art of animation producing training films for the U.S. Army Signal Corps during World War II before returning to civilian life. Editors from such publications as *Life* and *Vanity Fair* thought highly enough of his talent to publish his work, but book publishers were not convinced. The first book Geisel wrote and illustrated, *And to Think That I Saw It on Mulberry Street*, was rejected 27 times before being accepted by Vanguard Press. The book was replete with imagery of Geisel's hometown of Springfield, Massachusetts, for which he felt a strong fondness.

Geisel's book-writing career coincided chronologically with the flowering of the Baby Boomer generation. His rhyming prose and imaginative illustrations captivated children. He also wrote age-appropriate books at different levels, allowing kids to be raised on Dr. Seuss books. Baby Boomers learned to read through such classics as *Hop on Pop, Green Eggs and Ham*, and *One Fish, Two Fish, Red Fish, Blue Fish*. They moved on to such noted works as *The Cat in the Hat* and *Yertle the Turtle*, and then tackled more advanced books such as The *500 Hats of Bartholomew Cubbins*. When their parents read to them at bedtime, no book was more appropriate in lulling them into slumber than *Dr. Seuss's Sleep Book*.

Many contend that Seuss's books dealing with moral issues have raised the ethical level of the United States. Baby Boomers learned about the evils of prejudice and greed from *The Sneetches*, the value of every life from *Horton Hears a Who*, the meaning of Christmas from *How the Grinch Stole Christmas*, and how absolute power corrupts in *Yertle the Turtle*.

The passion many Baby Boomers have felt for Dr. Seuss works has translated into their parenting. Although Geisel died on September 24, 1991, before many children of that generation were even born, he continues to illuminate the minds of young people.

An estimated 200 million Dr. Seuss books have been sold in 15 different languages. The Dr. Seuss legend continues to grow. Not only was *How the Grinch Stole Christmas* converted into an animated television special in 1966 that is often aired around the holidays, but that book and *The Cat in the Hat* and *Horton Hears a Who* were far more recently turned into feature length films. Geisel's books have been the source of 11 children's television specials and a Broadway play titled *Seussical the Musical*.

See also Movies.

FURTHER READING

Dr. Seuss National Memorial: All about Dr. Seuss. http://www.catinthehat.org/history.htm

Seussville: http://www.seussville.com/lb/home.html/

DR. SPOCK (1903–1998) Dr. Benjamin Spock proved more influential to the upbringing of Baby Boomers than anyone but their parents. His 1946 book titled *The Common Sense Book of Baby and Child Care* was perceived by millions of American parents throughout the 1950s and 1960s as an infallible guide for child rearing. It sold more than 50 million copies worldwide, which placed it second in book sales to the Bible.

Spock, the most revered pediatrician of his generation and American history, was born in New Haven, Connecticut, on May 2, 1903. Five more siblings followed, which gave him an opportunity to experience child rearing first-hand. He even helped his parents—a prominent lawyer and housewife—perform such chores as changing diapers and babysitting.

A fine student at the Phillips Academy in Andover, Massachusetts, Spock followed his father's footsteps to Yale University, where he excelled in history and made his mark athletically by participating on the rowing crew that won a gold medal in the 1924 Summer Olympics. Spock then studied at the Yale School of Medicine for two years before transferring to the Columbia University College of Physicians and Surgeons. He graduated first in his class in 1929.

Spock was intrigued not only by the physical aspects of medicine, but also the psychological needs of children and their relationships with fellow family members. He delved into psychoanalysis for a six-year period, which provided him with a unique breadth of knowledge for his profession. The more he studied psychological and emotional components of childhood through interaction with kids and their parents, the more he came to believe that the current belief systems were faulty. He then revolutionized parenting.

Among Spock's progressive ideas about parenting was the belief in oneself rather than such childcare professionals as physicians. He stressed that nobody understood children with greater clarity than their own parents. For instance, he countered the prevailing belief that crying babies should be left alone so they do not become spoiled. Rather, he offered that they should be hugged and loved to increase their feelings of security. Spock also claimed that parenting should be enjoyable and that parents should forge a light-hearted and friendly relationship with their kids rather than establish one of strict authority. Among his specific teachings was that allowance should not be used as payment for chores and that spanking gives kids the impression that the bigger and stronger get their way, which could lead to bullying later in life. He advocated as normal and healthy the notion of little boys playing with dolls and little girls playing with toy cars.

The Common Sense Book of Baby and Child Care took the United States by storm and was accepted and even praised by doctors and other childcare professionals. Spock's reputation remained strong throughout the 1950s and 1960s, during which time he taught child development at Western Reserve University in Cleveland, Ohio, and penned many other books on the subject. He appeared as a guest on several national talk shows, particularly in the early 1970s, such as *The Tonight Show with Johnny Carson, The Merv Griffin Show, The Art Linkletter Show, The Mike Douglas Show,* and the *David Frost Show.*

Spock's link to Baby Boomers became more direct and was strengthened during the 1960s. He railed against nuclear testing early in the decade, claiming that it harmed children and nursing mothers. Spock was even more vigilant about the Vietnam War. He became sickened to hear and read about the children to whom he was so committed maimed or killed halfway around the world. He actively protested, sending letters to the White House, and then taking to the streets. In 1967 he joined a group delivering nearly 1,000 draft cards to the Justice Department in Washington. He was even arrested later that year for crossing a police line in front of an armed forces induction center in New York. Spock was convicted for aiding and abetting resistance to the draft, but a federal court later overturned it. His political activism also motivated him to run for president in 1972 on a third party ticket. He continued to speak out against perceived injustice, particularly during protests against nuclear weapons. By the time he reached the age of 80 in 1985, he had been arrested 12 times.

Spock took pride in keeping up with the times. He often revised *The Common Sense Book of Baby and Child Care* to update parents on new medical considerations and included writings on modern issues such as working mothers, single parenthood, homosexuality, AIDS, vegan and vegetarian diets, and daycare centers. He admitted that his early and widely accepted view that women should be most responsible for childcare no longer had a place in modern society.

Spock died after a long bout with cancer in 1998 at the age of 95.

See also Antiwar Movement; Health and Health Care; Political Participation; Talk Show Revolution; Vietnam War.

FURTHER READING

Dr. Benjamin Spock, 1903–1998. http://www.drspock.com/about/drbenjaminspock/0,1781,00 .html

Spock, Benjamin. *Dr. Spock's Baby and Child Care*, 7th ed. New York: Pocket Books, 1998.

DYLAN, BOB (1941–)   Bob Dylan was the musical poet for the first wave of mostly white, suburban Baby Boomers, although his influence extends beyond that realm. He was also the most impactful folk artist of his time, whose transition from acoustic to electric guitar caused consternation in the folk community but created a new genre called "folk rock" that spawned highly successful bands that became early Baby Boomer icons such as the Byrds and the Mamas and the Papas.

Dylan's imprint on the music scene can be felt today with acclaimed albums and frequent touring, although his popularity as a performer has dissipated over the last quarter-century. But he was in the forefront of returning folk music in the spirit of Woody Guthrie and Pete Seeger back into the mainstream. His influence in the early 1960s helped others (e.g., Peter, Paul, and Mary) find an audience.

Robert Allen Zimmerman was born on May 24, 1941, in Duluth, Minnesota. He grew up in the nearby town of Hibbing, where he dabbled in poetry as a child. He was self-taught in playing the piano and guitar and even formed bands called Golden Chords and Elston Gunn and His Rock Boppers as a teenager. He was enthralled with early rock-and-roll artists Elvis Presley and Little Richard, as well as country and folksingers such as Guthrie and Hank Williams. Dylan's adventurous spirit was displayed at the University of Minnesota, where he would perform at clubs and tell audiences of his desire to travel cross-country, as Guthrie had done, to get to know the United States. It was at that time he changed his name to Bob Dylan, which he thought sounded cool.

After having befriended bluesman Jesse Fuller and learning to play the harmonica, Dylan decided to become a professional musician. He dropped out of school in January 1961, and moved to New York not only to get into the business but also to meet his idol, Guthrie. He joined the burgeoning folk rock scene in Greenwich Village, where his reputation grew. He was greatly moved by his visits to a dying Guthrie at a New York hospital.

A glittering music review of Dylan's performance in the Village in *the New York Times* motivated Columbia Records to sign him to a contract. Dylan's self-titled album, a collection of folk and blues standards that contained just two original songs, was released in March 1962. His nasally voice gave him a unique sound, but it was not until he began writing with passion that he gained popularity and critical acclaim. His 1963 album *The Freewheelin' Bob Dylan* comprised all original songs and became immediately influential. His masterpiece "Blowin' in the Wind" was covered by Peter, Paul, and Mary and soared to number two in the charts.

Young Baby Boomers who began fermenting thoughts of societal change loved Dylan not only as a musician but also as a poet. And just as they began embracing

Bob Dylan and Joan Baez sing at the 1963 March on Washington. The pair were again featured in D.A. Pennebaker's 1967 documentary, *Don't Look Back*. (National Archives)

rock music, so did Dylan, who slowly moved away from his folk roots. His third album, *The Times They Are A-Changin'*, hinted at his disenchantment with Columbia promoting him as a protest writer and singer. So did his next record, *Another Side of Bob Dylan*, which included the song "It Ain't Me, Babe," which expressed a thinly veiled desire to move way from the folk scene.

Dylan began a romantic relationship with fellow folkie Joan Baez in 1965 and grew musically by adopting the electric guitar and providing the folk-rock megahit "Mr. Tambourine Man" for the Byrds. That year he also released the half-acoustic, half-electric album *Bringing It All Back Home*, which featured classics such as "It's All Over Now, Baby Blue" and "Subterranean Homesick Blues." Dylan caused an uproar in the folk community when he showed up to the 1965 Newport Folk Festival and began playing an electric guitar, which prompted dedicated folkies to boo him roundly. But Dylan was undeterred in his conversion to rock-and-roll—his 1965 *Highway 61 Revisited* album that featured the hit single "Like a Rolling Stone" was exclusively that genre.

The hits continued in 1966. Dylan's album *Blonde on Blonde* contained songs such as "Just Like a Woman" and "Stuck Inside of Mobile with the Memphis Blues Again" and sold 10 million copies. Dylan had reached the artistic peak of his career, but he was not one to continue on the same path if his visions took him elsewhere. After a motorcycle accident in July 1966, he returned a year-and-a-half later with a country rock album titled *John Wesley Harding*, which, although it reached number two on the charts, removed him from the rock-and-roll spotlight. His next offering, *Nashville Skyline,* featured the hit "Lay Lady Lay" and was even more country.

Although Dylan's political influence had waned by the early 1970s, he remained wildly popular. He sent three consecutive albums (*Before the Flood, Blood on the Tracks*, and *Desire*) to number one on the *Billboard* charts, marking the first time he had reached that milestone. The last record featured the protest song "Hurricane," which was about boxer Rubin Carter, who had been unjustly accused of murder and was languishing in jail.

However, Dylan was struggling in his personal life after breaking up with wife, Sara. He set out to find himself and announced in the early 1980s that he was a born-again Christian despite having been born Jewish. He released several Christian rock albums, all of which were panned. In 1988, he formed the group the Traveling Wilburys with former Beatle George Harrison, former Electric Light Orchestra leader Jeff Lynne, and rock legends Tom Petty and Roy Orbison. The band was highly popular but broke up quickly and never toured.

Dylan has remained active but has never regained the popularity or the direct influence he had in the 1960s and 1970s. Dylan did earn an Academy Award for Best Song in 2001 for "Things Have Changed" and received a presentation from the Kennedy Center Honors for artistic excellence. Although his performances have earned him tremendous acclaim and he is considered, along with the Beatles, as perhaps the most influential artist of the rock era, his greatest contribution to music was undoubtedly his writing. Songs he penned such as "Blowin' in the

Wind," "Mr. Tambourine Man," and "All Along the Watchtower," which was covered by Jimi Hendrix, have made Dylan arguably the greatest poet of the Baby Boomer generation.

See also The Beatles; Rock-and-Roll.

FURTHER READING

Cott, Jonathan. *Bob Dylan: The Essential Interviews*. New York: Wenner Publishing, 2006.
Dylan, Bob. *Chronicles: Volume One*. New York: Simon and Schuster, 2005.

E

ELECTIONS One motivation for young Baby Boomers in protesting the Vietnam War was that they were old enough to be killed halfway around the world but ineligible to help select American political leaders who could create foreign policies resulting in more young men dying on the fields of battle.

All that changed when the voting age was lowered to 18 just in time for the 1972 presidential election, won handily by Republican Richard M. Nixon over George McGovern, who was deemed too liberal. However, the Vietnam War was winding down by then.

Several factors have greatly influenced presidential and other elections during the Baby Boomer era. Changes in media coverage, critical issues (although the economy has most often proved to be front and center), and the mood of voters have all played important roles in determining the outcome of every election since Baby Boomers first began paying attention around 1960.

In 1960, the electronic media took a major leap forward in helping determine voter leanings when Democrat John F. Kennedy engaged in three nationally televised debates against Nixon during the presidential campaign. The events proved to the American people and to political candidates how important the medium of television could be. Although some believed that Nixon out-dueled Kennedy in terms of substance, the former was shown in front of millions of viewers sweating and appearing rather shady whereas Kennedy looked fresh, confident, and more honest. There is little doubt that the debates swung the campaign in Kennedy's favor, which, it can be argued, proved the difference in what turned out to be an exceptionally close election. Kennedy won by a mere 118,000 votes, although the electoral count was a bit more decisive.

The 1964 rout by Democrat Lyndon B. Johnson over Republican Barry Goldwater was the first in which Baby Boomers had become greatly aware of the issues. Although nobody in that generation was yet of voting age, some were becoming quite politically active, including those few who traveled to the South to help register blacks to vote and to further along integration. Although liberal-minded

Baby Boomers had yet to influence the American political landscape, the nation was beginning to shift to the left politically and the conservative Goldwater was no match for the moderate Johnson, who had promised that his "Great Society" plans would end discrimination and raise the nation up to live out its creed that all men are created equal. One Johnson campaign ad showed a little girl picking a daisy, followed by a countdown and an atomic bomb explosion. The obvious inference was that Goldwater was capable of using nuclear weapons and was therefore dangerous. The ad ran just once, but it proved highly effective. Johnson dominated the election outside of the Deep South and Goldwater's home state of Arizona.

All hell had broken loose in the United States by the 1968 presidential election, and Baby Boomers were at the forefront of the violence and controversy. Although millions of the generation were part of the "Silent Majority" who backed American involvement in Vietnam, a higher number opposed the war, particularly college students. Some became involved in the surprisingly successful early primary campaign of antiwar candidate Eugene McCarthy under the banner "Be Clean for Gene," which motivated Robert F. Kennedy to announce his intention to run and Johnson's shocking decision to withdraw his name from consideration. But when Kennedy, who appeared to be a shoo-in for the Democratic nomination, was assassinated after his California primary victory, all but handing the reins to Vice President Hubert H. Humphrey, the campaign was left without a candidate who planned to extract U.S. troops out of Vietnam. Millions of Baby Boomers across the country were disenchanted and infuriated.

They took out their frustration and anger, as did the Chicago police, during the contentious Democratic National Convention in late August 1968. Youth had little stake in the November election because neither Humphrey nor Nixon had any intention of staging an immediate withdrawal from Vietnam. Despite a late charge from Humphrey as the election approached, Nixon won by a painfully thin 500,000 votes, although again the electoral count was not nearly as close.

Although all Baby Boomers born before 1954 were eligible to vote in the 1972 presidential election, even the inclusion of a more liberal generation could not prevent Nixon's landslide victory, which was achieved through several factors, including the fact that he had the advantage of being the incumbent. McGovern lost credibility during the campaign when he dumped vice presidential candidate Thomas Eagleton, who had admitted that he had received psychiatric counseling, and replaced him with Sargent Shriver. And just days before the election, the White House announced that peace was in sight in Vietnam, which certainly took the wind out of McGovern's sails. McGovern only won Massachusetts en route to an ignominious defeat.

Skepticism of the American political system had peaked by the 1976 presidential election. The Watergate scandal had toppled Nixon the previous year, and, coupled with the still-fresh memory of the Vietnam War, Baby Boomers had become more discouraged about their country than ever. But many of them saw in Democratic candidate Jimmy Carter a fresh face and honest voice. Young voters helped end eight years of Republican rule in the White House by giving Carter a decisive victory. In fact, Baby Boomers ages 22–29 gave Carter 56 percent of their vote, approximately five points higher than he received overall.

However, it was at that point that the economy became and remained the dominant issue for voters. A massive recession fueled by hyperinflation and gas shortages doomed the Carter presidency, as did his inability to free American hostages who had been taken by radical Iranian students in 1979. Many Baby Boomers politically followed the rest of the nation to the right, which led to the 1980 presidential election of Ronald Reagan—the same Ronald Reagan whom young politically active Baby Boomers would have laughed about had he been suggested as a presidential candidate a decade earlier. Younger Baby Boomers ages 22–29 gave Michael Dukakis an equal number of votes as Reagan, which suggested that the liberalism of the 1960s and 1970s had yet to die out.

However, there was little doubt that widespread liberalism had been dead and buried by 1984. Reagan's election had ushered in an era of political and social conservatism that helped him become the first full two-term president since Dwight D. Eisenhower. His ability to return to Americans a sense of pride in their country allowed him to beat Democratic contender Walter F. Mondale in a landslide that year. It marked the first election in which Baby Boomers voted for the Republican candidate as heavily as did other generations. That trend continued through 2008. The old adage that people generally become more conservative with age was certainly gaining credibility.

Riding Reagan's coat tails in 1988 was Vice President George H. W. Bush. The age of conservatism had yet to fizzle, which allowed Bush to easily defeat Democrat Dukakis, who spun his wheels throughout the campaign. Bush characterized Dukakis as a prototypical northern liberal, a category from which no politician in the 1980s could benefit. Many Baby Boomers who embraced the welfare state and such tactics as affirmative action and school busing in the 1960s and 1970s as a means to narrow the economic and educational gaps in the country were now part of the political and economic mainstream and were far more likely to vote on issues on the basis of how they impacted themselves and their families rather than their effect on society and the suffering of those less fortunate.

Bush was generally applauded for his foreign policy, including his handling of Desert Storm, the first conflict requiring a significant number of American troops since the Vietnam War. But the economy struggled and two decades of nearly exclusive Republican residency in the White House had disenchanted millions of Baby Boomers, who were ready to elect the first presidential candidate to represent them—Bill Clinton.

However, Baby Boomers ages 25–49 surprisingly gave Clinton a slightly smaller margin than what he received from the rest of the electorate. But Baby Boomers did help give Clinton a landslide victory over Bush, who was seeking a second term. And despite the scandal involving Clinton and Monica Lewinsky, an aide with whom he finally admitted he had had an affair, he remained greatly popular. With solid Baby Boomer backing, Clinton had little trouble defeating Republican Robert Dole in 1996 to earn a second term.

By the turn of the millennium, the younger electorate had become more likely to vote Democratic than were Baby Boomers. In 2000 and 2004, those 18–29 favored Al Gore and John Kerry, respectively, albeit by small margins. Like many

Americans, Baby Boomers sat at the edge of their seats well into election night in 2000 as the painfully close vote in Florida that required the examination and re-examination of ballots decided the outcome. Many still believe that voter fraud played a role in the election of George W. Bush. However, fairly strong support from Baby Boomers allowed the conservative Bush to reside in the White House for eight years.

As the war in Iraq became increasingly unpopular and the American economy plunged into the depths of a recession, Bush grew increasingly unpopular among Baby Boomers and every American generation. That unpopularity played a role in dooming 2008 Republican presidential nominee, John McCain, who was swept aside by vibrant Barack Obama in what eventually became a not surprisingly lop-sided election. Although Baby Boomers solidly backed Obama, they had remained far behind the younger generations in voting for more liberal candidates. Voters between the ages of 18 and 35 leaned overwhelmingly in favor of the Democrat.

The trend in Baby Boomer voting speaks volumes about two critical points. First, the generation consists not simply of those who were most visible and active in the tumultuous 1960s and early 1970s. There might not have been a more con-servative silent majority among Baby Boomers, but there were millions from com-munities throughout the country who were marginally and strongly Republican. Second, the mass movement of formerly liberal Baby Boomers into the working world and parenthood indeed moved them politically to the right, although issues such as the civil rights movement and American involvement in Vietnam certainly played a role in their political liberalism.

See also Assassinations; Clinton, Bill; Conservatism; Kennedy, John F.; Political Participation; Reagan, Ronald; Thompson, Hunter S.; Vietnam War; War; Watergate.

FURTHER READING

Fund, John. *Stealing Elections: How Voter Fraud Threatens Our Democracy*. New York: Encounter Books, 2004.

Polsby, Nelson W. *Presidential Elections: Contemporary Strategies of American Electoral Politics*. New York: Free Press, 1991.

Thompson, Hunter S. *Fear and Loathing on the Campaign Trail '72*. New York: Grand Central, 1973.

ENVIRONMENTAL MOVEMENT *Silent Spring* author Rachel Carson (1907–1964) was not a Baby Boomer, but she launched the modern environmental move-ment, and Baby Boomers were the first to become passionate about preserving the environment.

Carson's *Silent Spring* was a 1962 bestseller focused on the dangers of pesti-cides to wildlife and humans. Harshly criticizing the chemical industry, it spurred an intense examination of other environmental concerns.

Carson had not intended to write a book when a friend concerned with the rap-idly decreasing bird population in her hometown asked her to investigate. Having toiled for the United States Fish and Wildlife Service, Carson had been concerned with the extensive use of pesticides, but she only intended to write an article. By

Rachel Carson, shown here giving testimony before Congress in 1963, was a noted biologist and ecology writer whose books played a major role in launching the modern environmental movement. Carson's book *Silent Spring*, published in 1962, became a best-seller and touched off a controversy that led to a fundamental shift in the public's attitudes toward the use of pesticides. (Library of Congress)

the time she had completed the project, she had written more than 200 pages of a book that would be credited with stirring Americans to action.

Silent Spring also motivated the chemical industry to fight back, which provided the opening salvos of the battle between the environmental movement and corporate America. The National Agricultural Chemicals Association spent a now-paltry $250,000 to discredit the book and its author. The Velsicol Chemical Company of Chicago threatened to sue the publisher, Houghton Mifflin. *The New Yorker*, which had been running excerpts from the book, was also threatened with a lawsuit but stood firm by insisting that everything in the book was accurate.

The importance of *Silent Spring* even stirred the conscience of President John F. Kennedy, who cited the book in announcing plans to research the effects of pesticides on humans and the environment. Carson testified in front of Congress on the issue and was interviewed on national television by renowned newscaster Eric Severeid. U.S. Supreme Court Justice William O. Douglas lauded it as a call to action and the most important publication of the 20th century for the human race.

The awareness of how various industries were damaging the environment extends back to the movement against deforestation in the middle of the 19th century. But *Silent Spring* and a general skepticism in regard to American industry led to a greater militancy in the 1960s. Baby Boomers led the moral charge against all forms of pollution and found sympathetic ears throughout the country. The campaign against dumping and littering led to one of the most remembered and beloved television commercials of the 1970s that opens with a Native American rowing a canoe looking sadly at pollutants emanating from a factory on a city skyline. His sadness grows after he emerges from the boat to see a garbage-filled shoreline and a person toss trash from a speeding car. A closeup of the man in full Native American regalia reveals a tear under his right eye. The underside of this ad was that the actor was an Italian American and the ad was placed by the organization Keep America Beautiful, which has been criticized as being a corporate "greenwash," with sponsors such as bottlers spending millions, for example, to defeat bottle bills and keep their environmentally unsound business practices unchecked, pushing responsibility onto consumers. (Excellent!)

Unlike other issues of the 1960s such as the Vietnam War that proved far more contentious, protecting the environment was a campaign embraced by Baby Boomers to which older and somewhat more conservative Americans could relate. Environmental issues became a mainstream concern by the late 1960s, which prompted the passage of the National Environmental Policy Act and the creation of the U.S. Environmental Protection Agency, although some have complained that the latter eventually provided more protection for industry than for the environment. The Clear Air Act of 1970 greatly strengthened antipollution standards.

Wisconsin Senator Gaylord Nelson created a political agenda, persuading Kennedy to embark on an 11-day conservation tour in September 1963. Although it created barely a ripple in placing the issue into a national spotlight, Nelson proceeded to speak around the country and discovered that the American people were far more interested and concerned about the environment than were their political leaders. Nelson believed that if politicians could become aware of that fact, a great deal could be accomplished. The result was the first Earth Day, which was held on April 22, 1970, in which an estimated 20 million Americans participated to call attention to various environmental issues such as air and water pollution, toxic waste, oil spills, pesticides, and extinction of wildlife. Baby Boomers who had been protesting the Vietnam War turned out in droves to throw their efforts into a potentially more dangerous, widespread, and long-term problem that threatened not just young American men, but the entire world.

The event certainly spoke volumes to American political leaders. Despite President Richard M. Nixon's veto, the Water Pollution Control Act passed in a landslide vote in 1972, followed by the Endangered Species Act a year later.

Although Baby Boomers as a group moved to the right politically with time, they remained at the forefront of the environmental movement. Being environmentally conscious became second nature to millions in that generation, and outrage over conservation and environmental abuses often led to action. But U.S. industries grudgingly accepted changes in environmental regulations, sometimes fighting every step of the way. Many have complained that conservative politicians have sided with industry in an ongoing battle to prevent environmental regulations from maximizing profit.

In more recent years, the issue of global warming has alarmed Baby Boomers and others, including scientists and a growing number in the political world. Some argue that the issue is a phantom, and others believe global warming has not been caused by human-made factors. Environmentalists have concluded that industrialization, pollution, and deforestation have combined to increase greenhouse gases that have trapped heat near the Earth's surface, resulting in warmer temperatures in the 1990s and 2000s than in at least 400 years. They further contend that Arctic ice, glaciers, and mountain snow are rapidly melting, which has and will continue to wreak havoc with wildlife and will eventually even threaten the very existence of coastal cities around the world because of rising sea levels.

Many Boomers are skeptical about such perceived dangers of global warming and remain apathetic or even hostile to environmental concerns, yet most have become sympathetic and many have taken active steps to help as a matter of course. Millions participate in recycling projects at community and individual levels. At individual and professional levels, Baby Boomers have spearheaded the effort to promote a greater awareness of the environmental dangers and scenic eyesores and toxicity caused by littering. They are passing on an environmental consciousness to their children and grandchildren, who have inherited the problems caused by previous generations.

FURTHER READING

Carson, Rachel. *Silent Spring*. Boston: Houghton Mifflin, 1962.

Nelson, Gaylord. "How the First Earth Day Came About." EnviroLink. http://earthday .envirolink.org/history.html

Shabecoff, Philip. *A Fierce Green Fire: The American Environmental Movement*. Washington, D.C.: Island Press, 2003.

EQUAL RIGHTS The goals of the women's movement launched in earnest in the late 1960s were as much perceptual as they were tangible. Its leaders understood that they would achieve nothing if they could not change the mindset of men and women whose attitudes regarding gender roles had been rooted deeply in American history.

Inspired by the success of the civil rights movement to stir the conscience of the nation and make palpable changes, their motivation was to achieve equal rights for women in all aspects of society.

Open-minded Baby Boomers of both sexes were more easily convinced that women should battle against their subservience in the workplace and at home. In fact, the oldest of that generation helped spearhead a revolution that quickly became known as the women's liberation movement.

The process would be slow and sometimes painful. Women had been taught for centuries that their primary roles were housewife and mother. Secretarial jobs awaited single women and those whose financial situations required them to work. Young female college students often studied home economics in preparation for marriage and motherhood.

Exceptions abounded. Women had seeped into all walks of professional life before the movement, but even they understood at the time that it was a man's world.

Small steps were being taken as the first Baby Boomers were being raised. In 1963, the President's Commission on the Status of Women, which was chaired by former First Lady Eleanor Roosevelt, cited substantial discrimination against women in the workplace and recommended improved hiring practices, paid maternity leave, and affordable childcare. That year, Congress passed the Equal Pay Act, which made it illegal to pay a woman less than a man performing the same job.

The seeds of the women's movement were planted that same year when Betty Friedan published her landmark and influential bestseller *The Feminine Mystique*, which portrayed the middle-class housewife as disillusioned with her narrow role in American society.

In 1966, Friedan helped found the National Organization for Women (NOW), which addressed a myriad of issues, not the least important of which was ending sexual discrimination in the workplace.

Friedan was one of several iconic figures who played key roles early in the struggle. Another was Gloria Steinem, who launched *Ms. Magazine* at the height of the women's liberation movement in 1972. The publication became a highly popular feminist forum.

The importance of such events in laying the groundwork for the women's movement was monumental. But there was one concrete piece of legislation that has symbolized the desire for equal opportunity and compensation in the professional world for decades: the Equal Rights Amendment (ERA).

The seeds for the ERA were planted decades earlier by suffragette Alice Paul, who founded a small, militant group called the National Woman's Party that had helped win the right to vote in 1920 through marches, picketing of the White House, political boycotts, and civil disobedience. But Paul was not satisfied. In 1923, during the 75th anniversary of the first Women's Rights Convention, she introduced the ERA as a way of guaranteeing equal rights for women into the U.S. Constitution. The original amendment read: "Men and women shall have equal rights throughout the United States and every place subject to its jurisdiction." In 1943, soon after the Republican and Democratic Party added support of the ERA to their platforms, Paul rewrote it to read: "Equality of rights under the law shall not be denied or abridged by the United States or by any state on account of sex."

The ERA passed the House and Senate on March 22, 1972 but also required ratification from 38 states with a seven-year deadline imposed by Congress. It appeared to be a shoo-in when 22 states ratified it the first year, but it received just 11 more during the next four years as some states postponed votes and others defeated it. The ERA opponents such as conservative Phyllis Schlafly played huge roles in killing the early momentum. Schlafly and her supporters claimed the ERA would deny a woman's right to be supported by her husband and would lead to women being used in combat. She added that it would also lead to stronger proabortion laws and homosexual marriages. Fundamentalist religious groups also organized opposition, particularly during the Ronald Reagan presidency in the early 1980s after Congress granted a three-year extension on the deadline for state ratification. Thus, the initial attempt to pass the ERA failed.

Introduction of the ERA before Congress has since become an annual event. But in the minds and hearts of Baby Boomers, it has taken a back seat to several other issues, particularly the economy and foreign affairs. Many women of that generation have reached a comfort level in regard to equality. They regard the ERA as unimportant. They believe the fabric of American society has changed so drastically in terms of professional and personal gender relations that the ERA is unnecessary.

However, others feel inequity remains. They point to statistics indicating that women performing the same jobs still do not command the same salaries as do their male counterparts.

Although Baby Boomers did not create the fight for women's equality, they gave it a head of steam in the early 1970s. Female Baby Boomers were greatly responsible for leading the fight through giving it prolonged momentum that has continued well into the new millennium.

See also Conservatism; Reagan, Ronald; Steinem, Gloria; Women's Movement.

FURTHER READING

Boles, Janet K. *The Politics of the Equal Rights Amendment: Conflict and the Decision Process*. London: Longman Group, 1979.

Friedan, Betty. *The Feminine Mystique*. New York: Dell, 1963.

Mansbridge, Jane J. *Why We Lost the ERA*. Chicago: University of Chicago Press, 1987.

Ruthsdotter, Mary. "Women and Equal Rights." National Women's History Project. http://www.nps.gov/history/nr/travel/pwwmh/equal.htm

F

FADS Modern American society has been accused of being too serious. It has been said that it has become too technologically advanced for its own mental and emotional well-being.

It is undeniable that the fads embraced from the 1950s through the 1970s were more numerous and mindless than those that have dotted the American landscape in more recent years. It is also true that Baby Boomers enjoyed them in greater numbers than did those of any other generation.

The fads of the first two decades after World War II are recalled with great relish by many of the oldest Baby Boomers. They bring back a time of silliness, innocence, and fun associated with childhood and early friendships. They also return Baby Boomers to an era in which every neighborhood kid was playing outdoors until the last bit of precious sunlight left the sky.

Even the first Baby Boomers were too young to have participated in some of the popular fads of the 1950s. Among them was stuffing as many people as possible into telephone booths in attempts to set so-called world records. That fad not meant for the claustrophobic was practiced mainly by college students in that decade, after which it faded out. Another fad from the 1950s died via the sexual revolution. Panty raids in which male college students stormed women's dormitories or sororities and confiscated lingerie were deemed far too tame for the Swinging Sixties and simply immature and rather sexist during the height of the women's movement during the early 1970s.

But the youngest of the generation certainly created imagery still used today to describe the 1950s. Television shows from a later time such as *Happy Days* often showed kids trying to spin hula-hoops around their waists. An estimated 25 million hula-hoops were sold during a two-month span when they hit the market in 1957. Soon 100 million more were ordered internationally.

The oldest Baby Boomers also experienced another 1950s fad that grew in legend through such nostalgic movies as *American Graffiti* (1973). Drive-in diners in which patrons placed orders with roller-skating waitresses and ate their burgers and fries in the car grew in popularity during that decade. Teenagers from a previous generation would blare the early rock-and-roll sounds of such legends as Buddy Holly, Chuck Berry, and Fats Domino from the car speakers at such venues, but sometimes little sisters or brothers who qualify as the earliest of Baby Boomers tagged along.

A fad more suited for young Baby Boomers of the mid-1950s was the coonskin cap popularized by Walt Disney's television depiction of Davy Crockett. In fact, Disney earned an estimated $1 million from the selling of the furry headwear with the tail hanging from the back.

Hula-hoops and coonskin caps gave way to more mystic fads in the 1960s. Among them were lava lamps and Ouija boards. Few decorations bring the decade to mind for Baby Boomers with greater illumination than lava lamps, although in reality they were hardly illuminating. The wax-like substance inside of cylinders produced unusual shapes when heated and provided an eerie glow. Meanwhile, young Baby Boomers' increasing fascination with mysticism and spirituality jump-started the tremendous popularity of the Ouija board, a game that supposedly allowed its participants to speak with the dead and predict the future.

Not all 1960s fads reflected the times. Millions of Baby Boomers recall the thrill of bouncing their first supercharged Superball, which hit the market in 1965, by the end of which 7 million had been sold at less than $1 a piece. Baby Boomers everywhere were bouncing Superballs over their houses and schools, much to their amazement. Prolific toy manufacturer Wham-O, which also produced the first hula-hoop and highly popular Frisbee disc, came up big again with the Superball.

Female Baby Boomers might still find a bit of nostalgia in the various troll dolls sitting in boxes hidden away in the attic or on the dressers of the bedrooms that housed them when they were children. More than 1 million troll dolls were sold in the United States, mostly in the mid- to late 1960s. Troll dolls featured tiny faces and brightly colored hair and were reputed to bring their owners good luck.

Baby Boomers of both sexes could not get enough Wacky Packages in the late 1960s. The stickers mimicked everyday household products but featured silly pictures and creative takeoffs of their names such as "Crust" toothpaste, "Skimpy" peanut butter, and "Chock Full of Nuts and Bolts" coffee. The stickers were most often placed on bedroom walls and bicycles.

The societal inhibitions created greatly by teenage Baby Boomers of the late 1960s carried over to launch new fads early in the following decade. Most Baby Boomers of today recall at least one instance in which they witnessed a streaker in all his or her glory in public. The fad reached its zenith in 1973 when a streaker raced across the stage on live television during the broadcast of the Academy Awards. Singer Ray Stevens gave the fad its legendary status in 1974 with his smash hit, "The Streak."

Arguably the most nonsensical fad enjoyed by the Baby Boomer generation and beyond was the Pet Rock. Created on a lark in 1975 by California adman Gary Dahl, Pet Rocks came complete with a training manual that explained how to care for the rock and teach it to do tricks. Soon Dahl was on *The Tonight Show* with Johnny Carson and was an instant millionaire.

The desires of Baby Boomers to listen to their favorite rock music in the car helped spur the advent of the eight-track tape player during the 1970s. The first eight-tracks, produced by Motorola, were placed in Ford automobiles but soon they were everywhere. The fad died out quickly, greatly due to the inconvenience associated with the bulky tapes and the creation of easier-to-handle cassette tapes, which could include an entire album's worth of musical material.

As life produced more responsibility in the 1980s for Baby Boomers, the youngest of whom were now mostly past their teenage years, more thoughtful fads replaced the mindless ones. Among them was the Rubik's cube, a mind-bending toy that tested the patience and frustration threshold of millions. The object was to restore all six sides of the cube to their original colors. Manufacturers claimed there were 43 quintillion combinations of solving the puzzle, but many users never did solve the puzzle despite hours of trying.

Another brainteaser that hit the market with a splash turned out to be far less of a temporary success. The box game *Trivial Pursuit* launched the trivia craze in the United States and proved to be a huge hit with Baby Boomers. A wide variety of Trivial Pursuit games created thereafter ensured its success for decades to come.

By the 1980s, Baby Boomers were more interested in purchasing toys for their kids than for themselves. During that decade, several dolls exploded on to the scene that young Baby Boomer parents rushed out to buy, particularly during the holiday season. Smurfs and Teenage Mutant Ninja Turtles gained tremendous popularity, but the one that took the country by storm was Cabbage Patch Kids. American children raised them as their own. By 1983, fights even broke out in toy stores between parents seeking a particular Cabbage Patch doll for their kids.

In the 1990s, American children had been overcome by an apparent aversion to playing outdoors. The result was toys mostly enjoyed in the home that Baby Boomer parents once again felt obligated to buy. The most popular were Beanie Babies, which hit the market in 1994. More than 100 million had been sold by 1996. Each Beanie Baby was given a name of its own and kids set out to collect as many as possible. The Furby doll also found success, greatly because it was interactive and could communicate with fellow Furbys.

By the turn of the new millennium, most fads enjoyed by Baby Boomers were related to the advancing technology. One which mostly males have partaken in is fantasy sports, the most popular of which are baseball and football. At the beginning of each season, millions of participants virtually draft real-life players and create their own teams. Meanwhile, other participants do the same, thereby forming a competitive league. The performance of the drafted players in real-life competition determines the success of the team. Millions of Baby Boomers and those from younger generations play fantasy baseball, basketball, football, hockey, and even auto racing.

Some fads have come and gone quickly over the past half-century and beyond. Others still excite despite having lost much of their initial popularity. But Baby Boomers have been in the forefront of the creation and purchasing of goods that became wildly popular. Few can predict what will gain mass acceptance. But one thing is certain: The types of fads that have gained instant and surprising popularity have generally been a reflection of the times.

See also Carson, Johnny; Consumerism; Fashion; Games; Movies; Rock-and-Roll; Television.

FURTHER READING

CrazyFads.com. "The Most Popular Fads from Decades Past." http://www.crazyfads.com/
Long, Mark A. *Bad Fads*. Toronto: ECW Press, 2002.

FAMILY LIFE It seemed families were carved out of a cookie-cutter mold when Baby Boomers were being raised in the 1950s and 1960s, particularly in burgeoning suburbia. Two-parent households were presupposed. That the father worked and the mother stayed home to tend to domestic chores and the children was understood. Couples were expected to have at least two kids.

Family members often congregated around the television set, and children from throughout the neighborhood played outside until the last precious drop of sunlight disappeared from the sky. It was a time for bonding not only with friends, but also with siblings.

Meanwhile, dinnertime was an unquestioned family time. The mother had slaved over the hot stove much of the afternoon to ensure a balanced meal for all to enjoy together. The parents and their offspring discussed events of the day as they dined.

Not all, of course, was as peaceful as what was portrayed on the dozens of family shows that peppered the television schedule in those years. As the first wave of Baby Boomers became teenagers in the mid-1960s, clashes with parents grew in intensity and frequency. The serenity was often shattered by arguments over everything from clothing to hair length to rock music to the growing American presence in Vietnam. But there was always a feeling that the family would remain strong enough to withstand such disagreements. There was a comforting consistency and continuity to family life during the early years of the Baby Boomer generation.

Parents and children felt a strong familiarity with each other throughout the first quarter-century after World War II. Although family members often participated in activities away from home, they simply spent more time together during those years. They were more likely to enjoy what is perceived as wholesome activities inside of the home such as box games and ping-pong or outside of the home such as family vacations, tossing around a baseball or football in the front yard, picnics, outings at the lake, camping, and trips to visit nearby relatives. The pace of family life seemed slower in the 1950s and 1960s because kids almost exclusively lived in one home.

That changed drastically beginning in the early 1970s. Along with changing attitudes about the role of women in society that led them to join the workforce en masse, the dramatically increasing divorce rate caused at least a partial breakdown not only in the two-parent system, but also in family togetherness.

Baby Boomers experienced it as parents and children. The older Baby Boomers were part of and to some degree catalysts for the generation that no longer held sacred the bonds of marriage. Their young children often suffered from it. On the other hand, the youngest Baby Boomers experienced as teenagers the changes brought about by divorce.

The increase in the divorce rate resulted in kids bouncing back and forth from the mother's home to their father's home—if both parents remained in the picture at all. It also meant that mom and dad were generally forced to work, meaning less time children spent with one or both. The number of latchkey kids—those who returned from school to an empty house—began rising markedly in the mid-1970s and has continued to grow. According to a 2006 study by the U.S. Census Bureau, 77 percent of all American children are considered latchkey kids. The same findings revealed that 27 percent of them are living in one-parent homes.

According to U.S. Census Bureau statistics, the number of families maintained by women who never married skyrocketed from 248,000 in 1970 to 2.7 million in 1988. A significant part of that trend can be attributed to the black community, whose families went through a period of great destabilization during that time period. Black Baby Boomers who have occupied the lowest end of the socioeconomic spectrum are more likely to be involved in one-parent homes. The instability of family life in poorer black and other minority communities has resulted in problems such as drug addiction, crime, and teenage pregnancy. These problems have fed off themselves and continue today. Statistics have shown a far higher percentage of two-parent homes among middle-class or upper-class blacks. The increasing number of blacks reaching loftier economic spheres has translated into greater stability.

Many Baby Boomer parents have remarried, but economic conditions and the fact that a women's career is now deemed as essential as a man's have combined to maintain many of the same changes in family life first experienced in the 1970s. Some believe the days in which most children are greeted at the door by a parent when they return home from school are gone forever. Economic necessity has even forced many teenage children of Baby Boomers to take on jobs after school, in the evenings, and on weekends.

In addition, technological advances have further separated family members. Cell phones, computers, Blackberries, and various other forms of communication have vastly weakened the art of conversation, kept siblings apart, and resulted in less time spent between parent and child. By 2005, it was not uncommon to see every family member using a different form of communication with the outside world and uttering nary a word to one another during a typical evening or weekend afternoon.

Baby Boomers have experienced the communications revolution, which has not only featured a boom in technology and the increased popularity in various forms of communication to friends and even strangers, but also the breakdown of communication between family members. Some who cherish the latter yearn for the days when the telephone and vocal chords were the only communication devices available to loved ones.

See also Computers; Divorce; Marriage and Infidelity; Television.

FURTHER READING

Coleman, Marilyn, Lawrence H. Ganong, and Kelly Warzinik. *Family Life in 20th-Century America*. Westport, CT: Greenwood Press, 2007.

Taylor, Robert Joseph, James S. Jackson, and Linda Marie Chatters. *Family Life in Black America*. Thousand Oaks, CA: Sage, 1997.

FASHION The first conscious fashion statements made by Baby Boomers were the direct result of four moptops from Liverpool, United Kingdom, who called themselves the Beatles. When the Fab Four landed in the United States in February 1964, they not only took the music industry by storm, but they set the wheels in motion for a fashion revolution.

The first converts were teenage boys, who began growing their hair to what their parents and other adults believed to be intolerable lengths. Changes in attitude, priorities, and outlook on life, which were also greatly attributable to the Beatles as they evolved, motivated teenage boys and girls to trade in their suits and ties and dresses for attire such as tie-dye shirts, sandals, patched jeans, and love beads. Among those in the hippie generation, the differences between male and female fashions became blurred. Although such material possessions as clothing were deemed unimportant, many teenagers used such attire as a statement of nonconformity.

The late 1960s also brought about drastic changes in skirt length, which was again inspired by a Brit. A painfully thin model named Twiggy made the mini-skirt famous and set off a trend of showing off shapely legs that lasted into the next decade. By the end of the 1960s, women were also wearing ultratight short shorts marketed as "hot pants." Meanwhile, women were losing the high bouffant hairstyles that were popular early in the decade in favor of longer, straighter styles, but that change did not take hold for most until the early 1970s.

Bright colors were also in. Toward the end of the 1960s, teenagers and adults alike lost all inhibition in clothing. Men and women dressed in flowery, paisley-patterned shirts, blouses, or dresses. Nehru jackets were also in style for both sexes, but particularly for men.

Many of the late 1960s' fashions carried over into the early 1970s. Long hair and long, thick sideburns developed into the style not just for teenage boys, but for men in their thirties and even forties. The long-hair era for high-school-age boys reached a peak around the middle of that decade. Meanwhile, girls of that period tended to use little makeup, dress down in jeans and flannel shirts, and wear their hair long and straight.

Bellbottom jeans also grew in popularity in that era to the point in which teenagers and even young adults could barely find straight-leg pants. Individuality and self-expression rather than conformity still ruled the fashion scene until the disco era changed the entire landscape. Then more casual wear and dressing down gave way to white polyester leisure suits for men and brightly colored mini dresses or bellbottom slacks for women. Platform shoes also gained popularity as the ideal choice on the dance floor. The look for men was styled after that of John Travolta, who launched the disco era by starring in the 1977 smash *Saturday Night Fever*.

By that time, another music form had spawned new styles. Emerging from punk rock in London were punk fashions, which included leather jackets and torn or ripped second-hand shirts and pants. Such styles were adopted by some of the youngest of Baby Boomers who were born in the early to mid-1960s.

Popular culture and societal changes continued to be reflected in the fashions during the 1980s. Dressing to impress on a corporate level returned to the forefront after about 20 years during which it was no longer a priority. With most women now flooding the job market, the notion of looking professional grew in importance for both sexes. In the workplace, the fashion trend for women was for jackets, dresses, and blouses made to look boxy with shoulder pads to give themselves more of a masculine look whereas pinstripe suits again gained popularity among men. It was all part of "power dressing."

In social situations, some men copied actor Don Johnson, who gained fame by wearing a casual T-shirt underneath an open suit jacket in the hit series *Miami Vice*. Sandals and a 5 o'clock shadow on the face completed the picture. Others adopted the conservative "preppy" look consisting of polo shirts and argyle sweaters, such as worn on the highly popular sitcom *Family Ties* by star Michael J. Fox.

By the mid-1980s, the youngest Baby Boomers had reached their mid-twenties and some were no longer greatly influenced by trends set by the musical acts of the time, whether they were new wave acts or hair bands such as Poison and Bon Jovi. Some older Boomers of that era began wearing Birkenstock sandals and clogs while a number of men grew their hair long and wore it in a ponytail. By that time, individuality started taking over. There was no particular style or color ruling the fashion world for men or women early in the new millennium. The fascination with fashion faded as aging Baby Boomers embraced a more utilitarian attitude about clothing and accessories. The less superficial outlook on fashion allowed people to express themselves in most ways within reason without being judged.

See also Aging; Diana, Princess of Wales; Rock-and-Roll; Television; Women's Movement.

FURTHER READING

Peterson, Amy T., and Ann T. Kellogg, eds. *The Greenwood Encyclopedia of Clothing through American History, 1900 to the Present*. Westport, CT: Greenwood Press, 2008.

Thomas, Pauline Weston. "1960–1980 Fashion History." http://www.fashion-era.com/1960-1980.htm

FREE SPEECH MOVEMENT The Free Speech Movement created a firestorm of protest and controversy on the campus of the University of California (UC)—Berkeley from September 1964 to the following January. It coincided with the first Baby Boomers reaching college age.

The event provided the first major spark for the political activism that would sweep through American college campuses throughout the rest of the decade and into the early 1970s. The students at UC-Berkeley would prove to be perhaps the most radical of any in the country.

The seeds for the Free Speech Movement were planted before World War II, when the fear of Communism prompted the UC school administration to create several rules that banned student groups from partaking in political activities on campus. However, in the late 1950s, school officials authorized the use of a small strip of the campus from which these groups could operate.

In late 1963 and early 1964, protests in the Bay Area against employers practicing racial discrimination drew tremendous attention and the sympathy of Berkeley

Mario Savio, leader of the University of California demonstration protesting the university's disciplinary action against four self-styled free speech leaders, stands among demonstrators in Sproul Hall to give instruction on passive resistance as the building was locked up for the night, December 3, 1964, in Berkeley. (AP Photo/Robert Houston)

students. In fact, several of them were arrested in off-campus demonstrations. When school administrators caught wind of a plan for students to participate in demonstrations at the 1964 Republican National Convention in San Francisco, they informed them that they could no longer use the designated area on campus for political activities.

The ban was defied. A group of politically oriented students that called themselves the United Front set up tables not only in that spot, but also in front of the administration building, where they had always been disallowed. They also launched a rally and march without seeking permission. When Dean of Students Katherine Towle ordered five students to her office, about 400 showed up, clogging the hallways of the administration building and demanding that they too be disciplined. In all, eight students were suspended from school.

The students were not to be deterred. They again set up tables in front of the administration building the following day. Tension increased when campus police arrested civil rights activist Jack Weinberg. They brought in a squad car to haul him away, but students surrounded it and then deflated its tires. Soon thousands of students had migrated into the area. The car could not be moved for more than a day. Among the speakers that climbed atop the cop car to voice his opinions was a charismatic and passionate junior transfer from New York City named Mario Savio, who quickly became the unquestioned leader of the Free Speech Movement.

The United Front played their strategy by ear. They again occupied the administration building and clashed with police before leaving the building and again surrounding the squad car. About 100 fraternity boys responded by tossing lit cigarettes and eggs at the demonstrators. Kerr called in several hundred police. Savio jumped atop the car again and convinced the students to disperse. An agreement was eventually reached that resulted in the disbandment of the United Front.

However, the crisis was far from over. The Free Speech Movement soon began in earnest with Savio as the chief spokesperson. An executive committee of approximately 50 students was formed. The group negotiated with the Campus Committee on Political Activity. The primary disagreement was whether students could advocate partaking in illegal off-campus activities, such as getting purposely arrested at demonstrations. The administration wanted to reserve the right to punish the students outside of the law. The Free Speech Movement would not agree, which led to the disintegration of talks.

The confrontation escalated between the students and administration and within the Free Speech Movement. Its most conservative members left as the radicals took over. Meanwhile, the school's Board of Regents reinforced the administration's stand that students who participated in illegal off-campus political activities could be punished. That is when the Free Speech Movement voted to again occupy the administration building. But the occupation did not last and it appeared that the group was falling apart. Savio and other Free Speech Movement leaders then announced a bold move: They would organize a rally on December 2. The message to students: Bring your sleeping bags.

Approximately 2,000 students, including noted folk singer Joan Baez, occupied the administration building that day. The police were called in to clear them off. The arrests began at 3:00 A.M. It took 12 hours for nearly 800 students to be taken into custody. A general student strike was launched. Sympathetic faculty members raised bail money and drove to detention centers to rescue the arrested students. But the Board of Regents refused to change the rules on off-campus political activities.

A confrontation followed. On December 7, Savio attempted to walk to the podium to speak in front of 15,000 people assembled on campus, but several police officers emerged from behind a curtain and dragged him away. Students rushed the stage and were tackled by police. Savio eventually was allowed to speak, but he could only invite everyone to a rally at the administration building in which most of those who addressed the crowd were faculty members.

The Free Speech Movement was rewarded for its persistence the following day when the Academic Senate voted overwhelmingly against restrictions in speech or advocacy, after which the students cheered and applauded. But the Board of Regents, which set policy, soon placed great restrictions on what would be allowed. The Free Speech Movement then lost support when leader Art Goldberg was arrested for displaying and shouting a curse word at the spot designated for student group activity. Goldberg and several others were arrested and received little support from the Free Speech Movement or fellow students

Meanwhile, Free Speech Movement leaders who had been part of the occupation of the administration building were sentenced to 30–120 days in jail. Appeals were denied. The blow destroyed the Free Speech Movement, but its successes and persistence reverberated around college campuses throughout the country. Soon students would have a far more divisive issue around which to rally. By 1966, U.S. involvement in Vietnam would prompt intense and sometimes violent student protests. The war would be the cause of the greatest college campus unrest in American history.

See also Radicalism; Vietnam War.

FURTHER READING

Burner, David. "Berkeley Free Speech Movement, 1963–64: A Narrative Summary by David Burner." http://www.writing.upenn.edu/~afilreis/50s/berkeley.html
Cohen, Robert, and Reginald E. Zelnick, eds. *The Free Speech Movement: Reflections on Berkeley in the 1960s*. Berkeley: University of California Press, 2002.

G

GAMES The vast differences in the games played both indoors and outdoors by Baby Boomers in their youth in comparison to those enjoyed by their children and grandchildren are a reflection of society and technological advancement.

Although Boomers participated in organized sports such as Little League baseball and Pop Warner football, most of their time outdoors was spent playing dozens of games that kids had embraced for generations, including baseball and football with no adult supervision. Most Baby Boomers can recall laughing their way through such games as Red Rover, Kick the Can, Tag, Hop Scotch, Chicken Fighting, or 1-2-3 Red Light with several or many of the neighborhood kids who, in those days, played outside until the sun disappeared from the sky.

The favorite outdoor game often varied from summer to summer or neighborhood to neighborhood and depended on the number of participants. Chicken Fights featured battles between kids riding piggyback on teammates and attempting to knock the opposing rider to the ground by any means possible. If enough children were available, Red Rover generally provided quite a bit of entertainment. Participants on two teams would lock hands tightly and form horizontal lines across from each other. A person from one team would then call out the name of a player on the opposite team with the familiar rhyme: "Red Rover, Red Rover, let Linda come over!" Linda would then race forward and try to break through what she believed to be the weakest link in the chain of the other team.

Chicken Fights, Red Rover, and all outdoor games without adult supervision faded from popularity in the 1980s. Several developments marked the demise of what can be described as the neighborhood free-for-all. One was that the end of the Baby Boomer era resulted in fewer families with three or more children, which meant fewer kids available to play. Another was the growing protectiveness and fear among parents. Whether their perception that playing outside endangered their children was justified has been debated for the last two decades. There is certainly gray area based on the age of the children and the neighborhoods themselves. Whereas from the 1950s though the 1970s kids as young as five years old played outdoors by themselves or with friends, in many cases parents in more recent years will not allow their children twice that age to play outside alone.

Yet another factor in the move from outdoors to indoors has been the increasing popularity and sophistication of the video game and, in more recent years, computer games. As teenagers, the youngest Baby Boomers played the crudest and simplest games such as Pong, Pac-Man, Donkey Kong, Centipede, Space Invaders, and Asteroids. But although the games were addicting, they did not generally prevent kids from joining their friends outside. However, as various game systems were produced, the children of Baby Boomers began spending an inordinate amount of time sitting in front of their televisions and wielding their controllers and far less time in more physically beneficial outdoor pursuits.

Just as the children and grandchildren of Baby Boomers eschew the outdoor games embraced in the past, they also greatly reject many of the indoor games kids enjoyed from the 1950s through the 1970s. They have been deemed too slow or boring by the youngest generations. Baby Boomers spent hours a day on their living room and den floors or kitchen tables playing games such as Monopoly, Scrabble, Clue, Risk, Life, Battleship, Stratego, Mouse Trap, Hands Down, Operation, and Sorry. Most of those games still exist but are simply not as popular today. Even games that have been a fixture in American homes for a century or more such as chess and checkers, which were played often by Baby Boomers, no longer hold a fascination for children, most of whom prefer the faster paced and more visually stimulating games played on televisions or computers.

By the early 1980s, the advent of adult board games gave grown Baby Boomers an opportunity to keep playing in their spare time. The first to make a splash and certainly the most popular in that decade was Trivial Pursuit, which launched a trivia craze. Trivial Pursuit tested knowledge in various subjects and spawned many trivia game competitors. Other adult games that have since gained popularity include Pictionary, which tests players' drawing skill and speed, as well as Cranium and Boggle. Boggle challenges the ability of players to create words quickly from a linking series of letters.

The manufacturers of many games first created for adults (e.g., Trivial Pursuit and Boggle) have released versions of those same board games for children with varying degrees of success. The onus to lure kids and grandkids into playing such games, as well as such old-fashioned board games as Monopoly and Scrabble, has often fallen onto Baby Boomer parents and grandparents who must pry them away from their video and computer games. The box game industry has attempted to promote family "game nights" in which a different game is played on one night every week. But to many Baby Boomers, convincing today's children to stray from their game consoles or computers is a challenging task, although perhaps not as Herculean as luring them and many other neighborhood kids outside for a game of pickup baseball.

See also Computers; Fads; Family Life.

FURTHER READING

Aasen, Adam. "Some Ask, 'Why don't kids play outside anymore?'" Jacksonville
.com, August 24, 2009. http://jacksonville.com/lifestyles/2009-08-24/story/some_ask_
why_dont_kids_play_outside_anymore.

Parlett, David. *The Oxford History of Board Games*. New York: Oxford University Press,
1999.

GUN CONTROL The issue of gun control has been debated in the United States for generations, but it was heightened early in the Baby Boomer era and argued passionately by those from that generation.

Three trends have motivated campaigns in favor of gun control. The first was a series of political assassinations in the 1960s, resulting in the deaths of President John F. Kennedy, civil rights leader Martin Luther King Jr., and presidential candidate Robert F. Kennedy. The attempted murders of George Wallace, who was running for president in 1972, and President Ronald Reagan in 1981 later provided ammunition for gun control advocates.

The second was the increased number of handgun murders in the United States, particularly in the inner cities. However, gun-related deaths have decreased markedly since peaking in 1993, and the lack of political activism among many Baby Boomers has resulted in less of an outcry about the issue. In addition, millions of white Baby Boomers, a high percentage of which are from rural and lower middle-class backgrounds, have consistently expressed support of the right to own guns with few restrictions.

The third trend has been the increase in random multiple shootings, including the tragic and well-publicized murders in schools around the country. The Columbine High School massacre in 1999, which was made possible by the easy access to guns for the two students who perpetrated the killings before taking their own lives, increased the outcry for more stringent gun control. Baby Boomer parents were in the forefront of the push at that time because it was an event that certainly preyed upon their emotions. After all, many of their children were attending schools quite like Columbine and the threat seemed frighteningly real.

The debate over gun control stems at least partially from the interpretation of the Second Amendment to the U.S. Constitution, which states: "A well-regulated militia being necessary to the security of the free state, the right of the people to keep and bear arms shall not be infringed." Those who support unrestrictive gun laws cite that amendment as one that protects that perceived freedom. However, gun control advocates claim that the need for a well-regulated militia to maintain a free state has long since passed.

Gun control advocates also reject the argument that the right to bear arms lowers the homicide rate. They point to the United Kingdom, which boasts one of the most restrictive gun laws in the world. In 2006, that country recorded just 55 gun-related killings. That same year, there were 137 in Washington, D.C. alone. Gun control advocates contend that only very few people are saved by those wielding guns.

Those in opposition claim that people, not guns, kill people, and that without guns murderers would find other means of eliminating their prey. But the paltry number of gun-related killings in the United Kingdom provides a strong case against that argument. So do other statistics. For example, in 1993 a total of 14,000 handgun murders were recorded in the United States with other types of guns adding 3,000 more. That accounted for approximately 75 percent of all murders in the nation.

Many Baby Boomers have advocated the elimination of handguns and other weapons from American society and tragic events have served to prompt more restrictive gun laws over the years. The Gun Control Act of 1968, which virtually ended interstate transport of guns by unlicensed dealers, came on the heels of the King and Kennedy assassinations. The Brady Bill (1993), which mandated that anyone buying particular types of guns must undergo a background check and wait seven days before the purchase can be approved, was the result of the attempted murder of Reagan. Laws that require manufacturers to strengthen gun safety standards have followed.

The most powerful organization supporting the rights of Americans to bear arms has been the National Rifle Association (NRA), whose lobbying efforts have consistently served to protect the Second Amendment. The NRA has argued that if owning guns were a criminal act, only criminals would own guns. It also states that most gun owners are law-abiding citizens who are merely trying to protect themselves.

Gun control advocates do not necessarily disagree, but they claim that the elimination or strong restriction on ownership would keep guns out of the hands of most criminals and strengthen the hands of law enforcement officials. They also argue that the number of people who have prevented such crimes as homicide through gun ownership is a drop in the bucket in comparison to the number of people who have been killed by handguns and other such weapons.

See also Assassinations; Conservatism; Kennedy, John F.; Kennedy, Robert F.; King, Martin Luther, Jr.; Malcolm X; Reagan, Ronald; War.

FURTHER READING

Melzer, Scott. *Gun Crusaders: The NRA's Culture War*. New York: New York University Press, 2009.

Nisbet, Lee. *The Gun Control Debate: You Decide*. Amherst, NY: Prometheus Books, 2001.

Spitzer, Robert J. *The Politics of Gun Control*. London: Chatham House Publishers, 1999.

H

HEALTH AND HEALTH CARE Many parents of Baby Boomers enjoyed financial stability and a comparatively high standard of living in the 1950s and 1960s. One result was that their children were not concerned with their health and certainly gave no thought to health care or health insurance. Barring an unforeseen injury or illness, they simply assumed good health and that all their needs would be met.

The situation changed dramatically after millions of Baby Boomers became parents decades later. A greater awareness of health issues, an epidemic of obesity among children and adults, and a raging debate over universal health care and socialized medicine all became national headlines.

The first widespread health scare during the Baby Boomer era was a polio epidemic in the early 1950s. While researchers at four laboratories were awarded grants to discover a vaccine for the disease, the number of children afflicted with polio grew to 58,000 in 1952. By that year, early versions of a vaccine developed by Jonas Salk were deemed successful in curing a small sample of patients, but the panic continued into the second half of the decade. The Salk vaccine proved effective, resulting in a mass immunization program that decreased the number of cases to approximately 5,600 in 1957. By 1964, there were only 121 cases of polio reported nationally.

By that time, a revolution had been completed in the health insurance industry. Labor shortages and wage controls during World War II motivated employers to offer health insurance in an attempt to attract workers. The trend continued after the war when the government provided businesses income tax exemptions for expenses involved in supplying health insurance. Most Americans have received their health care insurance through their employers ever since.

Eventually more nonprofit health maintenance organizations (HMOs) were created, which controlled costs and emphasized preventive care. But the moneymaking potential pushed private insurers into the HMO realm, which in turn motivated established HMOs to become for-profit businesses.

The most important development in the world of health care in the 1960s was the enactment of Medicare and Medicaid legislation in 1965. The sweeping reform extended care to millions of uninsured Americans, including the poor and elderly, who received a stronger boost with the 1973 HMO Act, which gave start-up HMO businesses financial advantages and made health care more affordable for employers and the previously uninsured.

Millions of Baby Boomers and other Americans displayed a greater awareness of the importance of exercise and healthy nutrition in the early 1970s. Jogging became particularly popular among older Baby Boomers, who also took a strong stand against feeding their young children foods with little nutritional value, especially sugary breakfast cereals. Dozens of healthful cereals hit the market during the first half of the 1970s. The trend toward better nutrition continued well into the new millennium, although many Americans, particularly in the South and among the poor in the inner cities, continued to gorge themselves on fatty fast foods.

The most significant health scare since the polio epidemic of the 1950s occurred in the early 1980s with the discovery of AIDS, which had already claimed more than 2,300 victims by 1983. The disease could be spread through sexual contact and unsterilized needles among drug users and was particularly deadly within the homosexual community and among drug addicts. By the end of the decade, approximately 40,000 Americans had been killed by the disease. The numbers continued to rise dramatically in the 1990s; AIDS claimed nearly 50,000 American victims in 1995 alone.

Baby Boomer parents became increasingly aware of another problem by the 1990s. A lack of physical activity among the youth in many areas of the country created a generation of out-of-shape and even obese children. Millions of children of Baby Boomer parents and grandparents spent their time away from school playing video games, watching television, and sitting in front of a computer, causing Boomers to recall that they were constantly exercising and playing outdoors when they were kids. Obesity among children grew into epidemic proportions by the turn of the century, leading First Lady Michelle Obama to launch a campaign against it in early 2010. According to National Survey data, the percentage of obese children in the United States has more than tripled since 1980 and thirty percent of children are obese in 20 American states. The percentage of dramatically overweight adults also increased markedly during those years.

By the turn of the century, the health care insurance debate had reached a fever pitch. In 2007, filmmaker Michael Moore produced a documentary titled *Sicko* that compared what was claimed to be the highly successful nonprofit universal health care systems of other such countries as the United Kingdom, Canada, France, and Cuba with the for-profit U.S. system to which not all Americans have access. According to the movie, approximately 50 million Americans were uninsured and even many of those who were covered were victimized by bureaucratic red tape and policies that worked against those with pre-existing conditions. The film also criticized the American pharmaceutical industry for allegedly caring more about profits than providing affordable medicine to those who need it.

President Barack Obama launched one of the most heated debates in American history upon taking office in 2009 by directing a campaign for virtually universal health care. The debate formed on party lines with Democrats claiming that passing a bill was a humanitarian act that would give access to health care to millions of Americans who could previously not afford it and Republicans answering that the cost of such a program would increase an already substantial federal deficit and pass down that deficit to future generations.

Among the controversial issues that reached the forefront in the 1990s and remained a much-discussed topic after the turn of the century was the use of medical marijuana. Fourteen states, including California, New Jersey, Oregon, and Colorado, had legalized medical marijuana by 2010 for its benefits in combating the pain associated with glaucoma and other diseases and ailments.

Health and health care are likely to remain hot topics as Baby Boomers begin and continue to reach retirement age. Although there is a great deal of gray area in those issues, there is no debate that Baby Boomers were generally far more active and healthy during their youth than the children of the post-millennium era.

See also Drinking; Marijuana; Sex; Smoking.

FURTHER READING
Peck, Brian. *The Baby Boomer Body Book: The Complete Health Reference for Our Generation.* Naperville, IL: Sourcebooks, 2001.

HIPPIE MOVEMENT The hippie movement was born out of the 1950s Beat Generation, whose philosophies and alternative lifestyles were espoused by artists such as poet Allen Ginsberg and writer Jack Kerouac.

By the mid-1960s, many of the youngest Baby Boomers, particularly from the white middle class and upper middle class, began rejecting the deep-rooted American values of materialism and conformity. They embraced a perceived idealism and counterculture, eschewing violence and, for the most part, even the political activism in which other college-age Boomers were becoming heavily involved. As did the Beatniks of the previous generation, hippies deemed themselves to be on a spiritual quest. They explored philosophical literature and Eastern religions and used marijuana and supposed mind-expanding drugs such as LSD in an attempt to "find themselves."

The epicenter of the hippie movement was San Francisco. Like-minded Baby Boomer teenagers flocked to the Haight district of that city to form a burgeoning hippie culture. They were influenced by LSD advocates such as writer Ken Kesey and ousted Harvard University professor Timothy Leary, who implored the first Baby Boomer generation to "Tune in, turn on, and drop out." Kesey and a group of hippies called the Merry Pranksters set the tone for the psychedelic slant of the movement by traveling around the country on a bus and turning people on to LSD in what writer Tom Wolfe later dubbed in his book as the "Electric Kool-Aid Acid Test." The hippies were also attracted to early rock-and-roll psychedelic bands such as the Grateful Dead, Country Joe and the Fish, Quicksilver Messenger

Timothy Leary at the Human Be-In in San Francisco, California in January 1967. (Karl Sterne)

Service, and Jefferson Airplane. The movement was strengthened by the Beatles' foray into psychedelia.

The hippie community in San Francisco celebrated a decidedly alternative life-style. A group that called itself the "Diggers" provided as much free food and clothing as could be scrounged up for hippies who did not hold down jobs. Hippies smoked marijuana, took LSD trips, listened to rock music, painted their faces and bodies in bright colors, wore flowers in their hair, and danced about during free-flowing events such as "Be-Ins" at Golden Gate Park. Hippies rarely limited themselves to one sexual partner; in fact they sometimes attended orgies known as "Love-Ins" in which they congregated to express their sexual freedom. A free clinic helped hippies who could not afford medical treatment for sexual diseases, bad LSD trips, drug addiction, or other physical problems.

The San Francisco hippies generally rejected American society and preferred to remain separate from it. But several factors played into an explosion of publicity in 1967 that even motivated them to stage a theatrical "Death of Hippie" parade that October. Perhaps the most significant happening that called attention to the Haight hippies was the popularity of a pop song sung by Scott McKenzie called "San Francisco," which called for young people everywhere to put flowers in their hair and travel to that city. Thousands did, leading to tremendous national attention. Another event that placed a spotlight on the San Francisco hippie scene in 1967 was the Monterey Pop Festival, a rock concert that drew a heretofore unheard-of crowd of 50,000 people and featured fading bands such as the Byrds and the Mamas and the Papas, and emerging acts such as the Who, Jimi Hendrix, and Janis Joplin.

The hippie movement had already spread into other areas of the country. In New York's Central Park, 10,000 hippies converged for a Be-In in May. But by the end of 1967, the San Francisco hippie scene was beginning to die out. Some hippies returned home or entered college. Others opted to move to the hills and the countryside and form communes, which allowed them to live out the true hippie creed of antimaterialism. Still others remained in the Haight district, but many of them began experimenting with stronger and more dangerous drugs and became addicts.

By that time, the hippie culture had seeped deeply into the American culture. Even American television and print advertisers were using psychedelia to sell products, particularly to young Baby Boomers.

The height of the national movement was encapsulated in one legendary three-day event in August 1969 when a half-million hippies and other young Baby Boomers congregated in upstate New York for the Woodstock Festival. Woodstock was not only marked by the performances of some of the premier rock bands in the world, but arguably more so by the spirit of peaceful co-existence displayed by those who were proud to proclaim themselves hippies. They smoked pot, took LSD, swam naked, slid around in the mud, danced to the music, and captured the imagination of the nation through their camaraderie.

Two events soon thereafter served to destroy the hippie movement. One was the revelation that the murders of actress Sharon Tate and others just a week before the Woodstock Festival were perpetrated by a group of hippie women under the spell of satanic leader Charles Manson, who had befriended them in San Francisco. The second was the violence at the Altamont Rock Festival in Northern California as the Rolling Stones tried to perform in front of a crowd of 300,000. It was intended to be "Woodstock West," but it turned tragic when a member of the violent Hell's Angels motorcycle gang, which was inexplicably hired to control the crowd, stabbed a black patron to death.

The two tragedies spelled an end to the peaceful and heady days of the hippie movement. Millions of Baby Boomers remained hippies in spirit and conscience, but few remained so in practice. By the early 1970s, most had conformed because of the pressures of financial and social reality and had taken their places in the same business world they had rejected just a few years earlier.

Since the death of the hippie movement in the early 1970s, many Baby Boomers and younger "neo-hippies" have continued to practice the lifestyle through communal living and other alternative lifestyles. But most believe the hippies of the 1960s were naive to believe they could transform something as deeply rooted as American culture and society to one that that was antimaterialistic and strictly nonviolent.

See also Alternative Lifestyles; Consumerism; Idealism; Kerouac, Jack; Kesey, Ken; LSD; Marijuana; Religion and Spirituality; Rock-and-Roll; The Rolling Stones; The Who; Woodstock.

FURTHER READING

Stone, Skip. *Hippies from A to Z: Their Sex, Drugs, Music and Impact from the Sixties to the Present.* Buffalo, NY: High Interest Publishing, 1999.

Wolfe, Tom. *The Electric Kool-Aid Acid Test*. New York: Farrar, Straus and Giroux, 1968.

Yulish, Sam. *Where Have All the Hippies Gone?* Indianapolis: Dog Ear Publishing, 2007.

HOFFMAN, DUSTIN (1937–) The first Baby Boomers were ready for a new type of Hollywood star when they began reaching adulthood, and they received one in Dustin Hoffman. Diminutive, reserved, and boasting only modest looks, he was quickly adopted by those of the young generation as someone with whom they could identify.

The producers of Hoffman's 1967 breakout film, *The Graduate*, understood that appeal. They had originally cast sex symbol Robert Redford for the part of confused college student Benjamin Braddock but decided he was too attractive. They turned to the 30-year-old Hoffman, who not only earned an Academy Award nomination for his performance, but also played the most important role in making the film a smash hit and one of the all-time iconic movies for the oldest Boomers. Many in the young generation, particularly in the counterculture, embraced the film for spotlighting a perceived phony materialism of suburban adults and deemed Braddock a hero.

If not for a fateful decision, Hoffman would never have entertained movie audiences. Born in Los Angeles in 1937, he planned to study medicine, but his passion for the theater convinced him to take a different path. He struggled for a short time before earning a Best Actor Obie award in 1966 for his work in the off-Broadway play *The Journey of the Fifth Horse*.

After his work on *The Graduate*, Hoffman further attracted the attention and fandom of Baby Boomers by taking a chance in his career by portraying a character quite the opposite of Braddock—an unsavory, sickly New Yorker named Enrico Salvatore Rizzo—in the Oscar-winning hit *Midnight Cowboy* (1969). Hoffman again earned an Academy Award nomination for that performance.

Hoffman continued to blaze new trails in his career. He aged decades and received critical acclaim, but no nomination, for his humorous portrayal of an Indian fighter in the 1970 film *Little Big Man*; performed alongside matinee idol Steve McQueen in the prison drama *Papillon* (1973); and then portrayed troubled, crude, and brilliant comedian Lenny Bruce in *Lenny* (1974). Hoffman garnered yet another Best Actor nomination for the latter but did not win. He took on a wholly different role in every movie, including that in 1976 of *Washington Post* reporter Carl Bernstein, who helped break the Watergate cover-up, in *All the President's Men* (1976).

Divorced Baby Boomers with kids certainly identified with Hoffman's performance in the highly acclaimed 1979 film *Kramer v. Kramer*. He played Ted Kramer, a divorced father fighting for custody of his son against his unstable ex-wife. In his first role focusing on parenthood, Hoffman finally earned a Best Actor Oscar. Three years later, he again displayed his versatility in the comedy *Tootsie*, in which he played an out-of-work actor who cross-dresses to successfully win a role as a woman in a soap opera. His work in *Tootsie*, which earned him his fifth Academy Award nomination, secured his reputation as a more than capable comedic actor.

Tootsie also marked a temporary respite from film for Hoffman. His brief foray back to the stage and on to the television screen proved as successful as his movie work to date. He portrayed Willy Loman in a Broadway revival of the classic *Death of a Salesman* in 1984 and then took on the same role in a CBS television special a year later to earn an Emmy and Golden Globe.

Still unafraid to challenge himself, Hoffman in 1988 took on perhaps his toughest role, that of autistic Raymond Babbitt in the highly successful *Rain Man*. Playing alongside heartthrob Tom Cruise, Hoffman stole the show and won his second Best Actor Oscar along the way.

A new cast of characters in Hollywood diminished Hoffman's star power in the 1990s. Perhaps his most disappointing movie was the highly anticipated *Hook* (1991). He played Captain Hook in the film opposite Robin Williams, who portrayed an adult Peter Pan. Despite the fact that Steven Spielberg directed it, *Hook* failed at the box office. So did several other Hoffman movies in the 1990s, including *Wag the Dog*, which received little attention although he drew his seventh Best Actor nomination for his characterization of neurotic producer Stanley Motss.

The American Film Institute recognized Hoffman's impact when it presented him with its Lifetime Achievement Award in 1999 in a nationally televised ceremony. The event shined a spotlight on Hoffman, who had been tremendously reclusive throughout his film career. Whereas other noted entertainers embraced the talk show circuit and sought publicity, Hoffman purposely remained out of the public eye. Baby Boomers who value those who shun the often-superficial aspects of fame have appreciated his rejection of self-promotion.

Well into his sixties, Hoffman continued to take on unusual roles, including an eccentric father in the comedy *Meet the Fockers* (2004) and the owner of a magical toy store in *Mr. Magorium's Wonder Emporium* (2007), which brought little box office or critical success.

Although Hoffman's artistic peak and greatest influence on the film industry had passed before the turn of the century, he remains a Baby Boomer icon for his courage to explore new territory as an actor and the versatility he displayed in achieving critical acclaim.

See also Movies; Watergate.

FURTHER READING

Brode, Jeff. *The Films of Dustin Hoffman*. New York: Citadel Press, 1988.

Lenburg, Jeff. *Dustin Hoffman: Hollywood's Antihero*. Bloomington, IN: IUniverse, 2001.

HOMOSEXUALITY The Baby Boomer spirit of rebellion and protest that played a role in the civil rights activism of the early and mid-1960s and spearheaded the antiwar movement and women's liberation also launched the gay revolution.

Gays and lesbians emerged from the closet only at their own risk through most of American history. Those who did proclaim their homosexuality were subject not only to emotional and even physical abuse, but also widespread professional discrimination. Thousands were dishonorably discharged from the armed services after World War II, and in 1953 homosexuality became a dismissible offense for all federal employees.

Although discrimination against homosexuals still exists a decade into the 21st century, the protest movement against it that started in earnest more than four decades ago has chipped away at its various forms. The open-mindedness of the early Baby Boomers paved the way.

The seeds for the homosexual movement were planted on June 29, 1969, at a New York Greenwich Village gay and lesbian bar called the Stonewall Inn, which was also frequented by cross-dressers. Raids were commonplace at the establishment, but the one on that night turned violent. The police entered, but the patrons barricaded them inside of the building. Gays and lesbians then began rioting that lasted three days and spread throughout eight blocks of the city.

The Stonewall riots placed a spotlight upon the plight of homosexuals for perceived and real equality. Not only did many homosexuals "come out of the closet" by proclaiming their sexual orientation, but gays and lesbians from throughout the country, as well as those who sympathized with their struggle, also began working within the system to create change.

Millions have declared their homosexuality since then, and others have remained secretive in fear of the social ramifications in terms of relationships with family, friends, and strangers as well as the professional implications in regard to job discrimination.

Among the first victories to be achieved occurred in December 1973, when the American Psychiatric Association conceded to remove homosexuality from its list of mental illnesses. Acceptance of homosexuality has been accomplished with far greater ease in areas of the country considered more open-minded, such as the Bay Area in California. In 1977, San Francisco voters even elected the nation's first openly gay official when Harvey Milk was chosen as City Supervisor.

However, the backlash against homosexuality played a role in the overall shift toward conservatism in the United States in the late 1970s. Among those leading the push was singer Anita Bryant, who worked to repeal Florida laws that gave legal protection to gays and lesbians. Her anti-gay beliefs, as well as those of many others, were based on Christian fundamentalism that perceives homosexuality as sinful.

A backlash against homosexuality coincided with the beginning of the AIDS epidemic in the early 1980s. The disease was linked to a great degree to gay populations in major American cities. In 1986, the U.S. Supreme Court ruled in *Bowers v. Hardwick* that individual states had the right to criminalize even consensual homosexual activity behind closed doors. That motivated the homosexual community to react strongly. In 1987, a march on Washington attracted more than 500,000 gay rights advocates.

Until the Supreme Court struck down anti-homosexual (or sodomy) laws in the landmark *Lawrence v. Texas* ruling in 2003, it had been up to individual states to decide the legality or illegality of discriminating based on sexual preference. About half of the states had already repealed such laws from 1970 to 1989, and many others followed suit before the Supreme Court ruling, which wiped out discrimination against homosexuals in the 14 holdover states.

Despite the progress, open homosexuality has often been frowned upon in the United States. The American military instituted a "don't ask, don't tell" policy that allowed homosexuals into the armed forces only if their sexual orientation was not revealed. However, the same policy, unspoken, remains a part of everyday employment practices throughout the country. The fear of coming out of the closet is strong for private individuals and those in the public spotlight. No active athlete in a major sport such as baseball, basketball, football, or hockey has emerged from the closet.

Violence against homosexuals has also been on the rise. According to statistics from American law enforcement agencies, approximately 16 percent of all hate crimes in the United States in 2007 were perpetrated on the basis of sexual orientation. The most heated debate regarding homosexuality in the 21st century in the United States has revolved around same-sex marriage, which through October 2009 remained banned on the national level. Iowa, New Hampshire, Vermont, Massachusetts, and Connecticut have legalized gay marriage, although such unions were at the time still not recognized by the federal government. Most states still defined marriage as a union between a man and a woman.

See also Health and Health Care.

FURTHER READING
Duberman, Martin Bauml. *Stonewall.* New York: Plume, 1994.
Uniform Crime Report. Hate Crime Statistics, 2007. http://www.fbi.gov/ucr/hc2007/downloadablepdfs/victims.pdf

I

IDEALISM Middle-class Baby Boomers who reached their teenage years in the 1960s embraced and pursued idealism with more fervor and purpose than those of any generations that preceded them in the 20th century.

Idealism is the cherishing or chasing of noble principles and aspirations, as well as a belief in trying to create a world enjoying peace and harmony. It is also considered a rejection of realism, which claims that the impossibility of attaining such goals makes its pursuit a waste of time and energy.

Baby Boomer interest in idealism was piqued in the early 1960s by the expressed philosophies and actions of such Americans as President John F. Kennedy and civil rights leader Martin Luther King Jr. Kennedy urged Americans to help those less fortunate by joining the newly created Peace Corps, and young Baby Boomers did so in droves. King's call for racial equality, particularly in the segregated South, motivated some in that generation to join the movement and risk life and limb by traveling to such hotbeds of discrimination and terror as Mississippi to fight for integration and black voting rights.

More universal idealism was espoused by the first wave of Baby Boomers as the 1960s progressed. The hippie movement was based squarely on idealism. The hippies eschewed technological progress and materialism, which they thought was the cause of conflict between people and nations. In fact, many believed in the creation of a world government, which they deemed would end wars forever. They gathered en masse in San Francisco in the summer of 1967 to enjoy what they deemed an idealistic lifestyle while other like-thinking youth did the same in other areas of the country, particularly in major cities.

The hippie movement embraced a simplification of human relationships, which they thought could be achieved by going "back to nature" and experiencing a stress-free life. Those who indeed moved to or created communes generally shared everything. Hippies dreamed of a day in which all humankind would adopt an idealistic view of the world in which they lived by rejecting materialism and aggressive thoughts and actions.

The hippie utopia came together in August 1969 at the legendary Woodstock Music Festival, where young Baby Boomers proved that, at least for three days, the spirit of the generation could result in 500,000 people living peacefully.

The publicity received by that generation gives the impression that most American Baby Boomers of the era embraced idealism, but this was not the case. Millions of youth in rural areas and small towns who came from more conservative backgrounds followed the same paths as their parents and took what they believed was the natural step into the working world without giving an alternative and idealistic lifestyle a second thought. And urban, mostly black Baby Boomers were too concerned with ending racial discrimination and merely getting by economically to give a great deal of thought to idealism and other philosophies of life.

The dream of an idealistic revolution in the United States embraced by many Baby Boomers in the late 1960s was quickly destroyed by two events—the murders perpetrated by hippie cult followers of Charles Manson in 1969 and the stabbing of a concert patron by Hell's Angels motorcycle gang members inexplicably hired to maintain order during a 1969 performance by the Rolling Stones at the Altamont Rock Festival near San Francisco.

The idealism of the 1960s faded as the new decade arrived. Older Baby Boomers, who could not realistically continue to survive in American society without work, began careers, which in turn fostered a thirst and need for material possessions. Meanwhile, younger Baby Boomers who reached their teenager years in the late 1970s did not adopt the idealistic philosophies that had been cherished by their older siblings.

The events of more recent times such as the Iranian hostage crisis, murder of former Beatle John Lennon, and the terrorist attacks on the United States in 2001 caused many Baby Boomers to shed their idealism. Although the Baby Boomers who once considered it possible in the 1960s would still prefer to live within a humanity that rejects materialism and patriotism, they have come to believe it to be unrealistic. They are quick to admit that they enjoy such trappings of financial success as expensive electronic gadgets, expansive homes, luxury cars, and exotic vacations.

Some Baby Boomers who believed in idealism had the courage in the 1960s to live the lifestyle required of everyone to create a world of idealism. A few have since adopted such a lifestyle by dropping out of society and embracing communal living, but the times in which many people believe an idealistic world can be created have past.

Most have come to agree today that striving for idealism in one's personal life and relationships is a far more realistic goal that hoping to achieve idealism throughout the world. They have also come to hope that idealism and materialism can indeed co-exist.

See also Alternative Lifestyles; The Beatles; Consumerism; Hippie Movement; Kennedy, John F.; King, Martin Luther Jr.; The Rolling Stones; Woodstock.

INTERNET Baby Boomers were generally too old to be the first generation to use the Internet when the new technology exploded in popularity in the 1990s.

Younger folks more savvy in modern technology often beat them to the punch. But Boomers were too young to feel overwhelmed by the Internet and shy away from using it, as did many from the previous generation. And studies have shown that although Baby Boomers are less likely to be online than those 18–29 years old, they were utilizing the Internet more than any other age group in the United States by the end of the first decade of the new millennium.

Most Baby Boomers of all eras were raised to do research in libraries, communicate only through telephones and letter writing, and shop outside of the home. But in more recent years, they have embraced the ease of finding information online; e-mailing friends, family members, and working associates; and ordering or purchasing goods and services through Internet sites.

Several factors have entered into the popularity of the Internet among Baby Boomers. Among them is that they are more likely than those of younger generations to spend a great deal of time at home with families, thereby providing greater opportunity to surf the Internet. Another is that they have a wider array of needs that can be satisfied online than those of younger generations, such as bill-paying, gathering information about health issues, dealing with work-related research, and even planning vacations.

Most Baby Boomers appreciate the convenience of completing several tasks online because they are able to compare it through experience to the inconvenience of performing those same chores in the far more tedious ways of the past. Many in the younger generations have spent their entire adult lives working with the Internet and never grew accustomed to dealing with everyday tasks any other way.

However, the sometimes addictive nature of surfing the Internet has tended to take a negative physical toll on some Baby Boomers. The ease and enjoyment of working on the computer and even playing online games can prevent those of all generations from exercising. Spending too much time online often takes away from time that could be used engaging in sports, other recreational activities, or simply walking around the block.

Studies in 2002 and 2008 conducted by the Pew Internet and American Life Project comparing online use of Baby Boomers with those in their late teens and twenties showed that the former used Internet sites with greater frequency for several tasks, including sending e-mails, looking up health facts, gathering financial data, and finding religious or spiritual information.

The same studies indicated that Baby Boomers trailed the younger generation in Internet searches regarding sports, jobs, housing, and creating Web content. The two were fairly even in getting news reports, buying products, participating in online auctions, and checking the weather online.

Another Pew study comparing the frequency of Internet usage by Baby Boomers in 2000 and 2008 showed a marked increase. According to the research, 40 percent of Baby Boomers used the Internet in 2000 compared with 74 percent in 2008. The percentage of total Internet users from the Baby Boomer generation increased from 28 to 36 percent during that time, and Boomers reporting that they used the Internet several times a day rose from 5 to 35 percent from 2000 to 2008.

The same study revealed that 70 percent of all Baby Boomers used the Internet to research jobs, 74 percent to get news, 78 percent to gather health information, 90 percent to use such search engines as Google and Yahoo, 91 percent to e-mail, 81 percent to research products, 70 percent to buy goods, 68 percent to make travel reservations, and 55 percent to do their banking.

Another highly popular Internet activity for single Baby Boomers has been online dating sites, which have become tremendously specialized and varied in recent years and have allowed singles to find mates on the basis of many personal preferences, including lifestyle, income, professional considerations, and physical characteristics.

Although the Internet and other technological advances have made life easier for Baby Boomers, they have also been blamed for the deterioration of the art of conversation, a distinct lack of one-on-one time with family and friends, and fewer opportunities to exercise. Some Boomers who are aware of and concerned about such negative influences on their lives have worked to strike a balance between stepping into the future and maintaining the healthy aspects of life before computers and the Internet.

FURTHER READING

Cosgrove-Mather, Bootie. "Baby Boomers Take To Internet." CBS News. November 13, 2002. http://www.cbsnews.com/stories/2002/11/113/tech/main529232.shtml

J

JACKSON, MICHAEL (1958–2009) The attraction to Michael Jackson as a music icon transcended the Baby Boomer generation, not simply because he entertained the oldest from that era in the late 1960s as a child star as well as in the late 1980s and beyond as arguably the most popular pop artist in the world. Jackson's music was embraced by Baby Boomers of all ages and demographics throughout his career.

But the enigmatic superstar became known as much for his eccentricities later in life as for his musical talents. Jackson's penchant for what was perceived as grotesque facial plastic surgeries, accusations of molesting children, and unusual singular incidents tarnished his reputation before his untimely death in 2009.

Jackson was born into what would arguably become the most famous musical family in American history on August 29, 1958, in Gary, Indiana. Older brothers Jackie, Tito, Jermaine, and Marlon formed a band in 1962 that eventually morphed into the Jackson Five, which Michael joined in 1968 and was signed that year by Motown Records. Although Michael was the youngest, he emerged as the lead vocal and gained a reputation as the most talented of the Jackson brothers. Younger sister Janet also eventually blossomed into a singing superstar.

With Michael's soaring vocals and dance steps overshadowing the talents of the other band members, the Jackson Five exploded onto the pop scene in 1969 with the number one hit, "I Want You Back," which was followed to the top of the charts a year later by "ABC" and "I'll Be There."

The Jackson Five went their separate ways, which allowed Michael to embark on a solo career in 1971. He remained hot by releasing such singles as "Rockin' Robin" and "Got to Be There" but faded from the spotlight until resurfacing in 1979 with his first solo album, *Off the Wall*. Singles "Don't Stop 'Til You Get Enough'" and "Rock with You" soared to number one and soon Jackson was the most popular pop artist in the country.

The second wave of Baby Boomers, who were reaching their high school years, was particularly enamored with Jackson, although the older members of that

Pop artist Michael Jackson performs at opening night of his Victory Tour at Dodger Stadium in Los Angeles, California, December 1, 1984. (AP Photo/Lennox McLendon)

generation who enjoyed the Jackson Five a decade earlier continued to appreciate his talents.

Jackson earned his first Grammy Award for Best R&B Vocal Performance in 1980 and then reached the pinnacle of his stardom in 1982 when his album *Thriller* reached number one and remained there for an amazing 37 weeks. One of the most successful records in American pop history, *Thriller* featured such hit singles as "Billie Jean," "Beat It," "Thriller," and "Wanna Be Startin' Somethin'." The videos to that album, particularly that of the song "Thriller," in which Jackson morphs into a werewolf, have been credited for helping popularize Music Television (MTV). Jackson thrilled American television audiences in March 1983 during a quarter-century celebration of Motown when he performed his signature dance, the Moonwalk, while belting out "Billie Jean." By 1990, the album *Thriller* had gone platinum for a record 21st time and was the best-selling record in history according to the *Guinness Book of World Records*, with 65 million albums sold.

In 1984, many began wondering whether Jackson had undergone plastic surgery. His face seemed distorted and his complexion appeared lighter. Meanwhile, he had a 2,700-acre home built featuring amusement park rides in Central California that he called Neverland, which he named after the fictional world in *Peter Pan*.

Jackson continued to display his versatility and talent in 1985 by teaming up with Lionel Richie to co-write "We Are the World," with the proceeds earmarked for hunger relief in Africa. Jackson and dozens of such stars as Ray Charles, Stevie Wonder, Billy Joel, Bob Dylan, Bette Midler, Willie Nelson, Paul Simon, Diana Ross, and Bruce Springsteen recorded the song, which sold 7 million copies.

Now approaching 30, Jackson released the album *Bad* in 1987. Although it did not receive the critical or commercial success of *Thriller*, it featured several top-selling singles, including "Bad," "Man in the Mirror," and "The Way You Make Me Feel."

However, by the late 1980s and early 1990s, his popularity as a performer began to wane while his reputation as an eccentric was given more credence and he was even accused of being a child molester. In 1992, Jackson asserted on talk show *Oprah Winfrey* that he suffered from vitiligo, a skin disorder that can result in a lack of skin color. He also claimed that his father emotionally abused him as a child. A year later, he was accused in civil court of molesting an 11-year-old boy on his Neverland ranch and was forced to undergo a body search by police—an experience he later stated was the most humiliating ordeal of his life. Under an out-of-court settlement Jackson paid the boy's family more than $15 million.

As speculation about Jackson's sexual orientation mounted, he wed Lisa-Marie Presley, the daughter of late rock star Elvis Presley, in late May 1994, but the marriage lasted less than two years. Three years later, he married Debbie Rowe, a nurse, who gave birth to his son, Michael Joseph Jr., and daughter Paris Michael Katherine. But the couple split up in 1998, a year after Jackson was inducted into the Rock-and-Roll Hall of Fame.

Among the strangest and most controversial moments of Jackson's life occurred in 2002 after the birth of a second son, Prince Michael II. While in Berlin, Jackson dangled Prince over the metal ledge of a hotel balcony to show his fans and was lambasted for endangering the infant's life. A year later, Jackson's problems continued when he was charged with seven counts of child sexual abuse and two counts of administering an intoxicating agent to Gavin Arvizo, who was 14 years old at the time of the alleged incidents. Jackson was cleared of the charges in 2005.

Jackson's strange lifestyle and self-defeating life decisions culminated in his death at age 50 after going into cardiac arrest on June 25, 2009 while rehearsing for a celebratory tour. The autopsy results unveiled the following February claimed that Jackson had actually been killed by personal physician Conrad Murray, who had given him a powerful sedative called propofol to help him sleep, but the drug is not intended to relieve insomnia.

Murray was charged with manslaughter, and it was also revealed that Jackson had been taking a myriad of prescription drugs and had 13 puncture wounds on his neck, arms, and ankles.

Baby Boomers and others will remember Jackson for his musical genius and his eccentricities. But he was arguably the most significant example of an artist that transcended the generation, not merely because his career spanned several decades, but because younger and older Baby Boomers recognized his talents and embraced the music he created throughout those years.

FURTHER READING

Halperin, Ian. *Unmasked: The Final Years of Michael Jackson*. New York: Simon Spotlight
    Entertainment Publishing, 2009.
Jones, Bob, and Stacy Brown. *Michael Jackson: The Man Behind the Mask*. New York:
    Select Books, 2009.
Taraborrelli, Randy J. *Michael Jackson: The Magic, The Madness, The Whole Story, 1958–
    2009*. Boston: Hatchette Book Group, 2009.

JORDAN, MICHAEL (1963–) Millions of the oldest Baby Boomers could
regale the youngest of the generation about watching the greats of the basketball
players from the 1960s perform. Such stars as centers Wilt Chamberlain and Bill
Russell and guards Jerry West and Oscar Robertson were among the greatest who
ever played the game.

But even the staunchest Baby Boomer defenders of the talents of Hall of Famers from that decade through the 1970s have admitted that Michael Jordan, who
joined the league in 1984 after a stellar career at the University of North Carolina,
is the premier player to ever grace a National Basketball Association court. His
greatness extended far beyond his vast talent to the fact that he was arguably the
finest pressure performer in the history of American sport.

Jordan, the son of Delores and James Jordan, was born in Brooklyn, New York,
on February 17, 1963, but was raised in Wilmington, North Carolina. Remark-
ably, considering his future career, he was cut from the varsity basketball team as
a 5-foot-11-inch sophomore. But he grew four inches before his junior year, after
which he embarked on the path to superstardom.

Jordan landed a scholarship to basketball powerhouse North Carolina, and as
a freshman he waited in the shadows of Tar Heels standouts James Worthy and
Sam Perkins, although he earned the spotlight with his performance in the NCAA
Championship game by hitting a jump shot with 18 seconds remaining to give his
team the victory. Jordan earned College Player of the Year honors from *The Sporting News* as a mere sophomore and again after his junior season, after which he was
selected by the Chicago Bulls with the third overall pick in the 1984 NBA draft.

Jordan justified the choice immediately, scoring 28.2 points a game and helping
the Bulls into the playoffs in earning Rookie of the Year honors after leading the
United States team to a gold medal in the 1984 Summer Olympic Games. Baby
Boomers young and old flocked to arenas throughout the United States to watch
the phenomenon. Attendance in Chicago also rose dramatically. Jordan not only
earned several endorsements, including shoe manufacturer Nike, but he attracted
fans through his contagious smile, humility, and engaging personality.

After losing most of his second regular season to a broken foot, Jordan returned
to average an astounding 43.7 points in a playoff loss to Larry Bird and the powerful Boston Celtics, and then scored 37.1 points a game the following year. He
led the NBA in scoring at more than 30 points a game in each of the next seven
seasons. By the end of that run, the Bulls had overtaken Detroit, Boston, and Los
Angeles to become perennial league champions.

By the late 1980s, the Bulls had successfully assembled a cast including head coach Phil Jackson and small forward Scottie Pippen who could join with Jordan to create a contending team. They won their first title in 1991 by sweeping their archrival, the Detroit Pistons, in the Eastern Conference finals and storming from behind to win four in a row against Magic Johnson and the Los Angeles Lakers in the title round. Jordan averaged 31.4 points and 8.4 assists per game in earning the first of his six NBA Finals most valuable player awards.

By that time, Jordan was known all over the world for his athleticism and growing number of endorsements. He was seen leaping with his head ascending over the rim as he threw down thunderous dunks. Fans, teammates, and opponents marveled at his natural talents, but also his will to win and uncanny ability to hit clutch shot after clutch shot in the most pressure-packed situations. He scored 35 points in the first half alone in game 1 of the 1992 NBA Finals and led a game 7 comeback over Phoenix to give his team its second consecutive championship. He scored 41 points a game, including a game-winning shot with less than four seconds remaining to clinch a win over Portland and the league title in 1993.

Emotionally drained by allegations that he was gambling and, more painful, the murder of his father during an armed robbery, Jordan left the sport in 1994 in an ill-fated attempt to forge a career as a baseball player. He played one season for the Chicago White Sox minor league affiliate in Birmingham, Alabama, and batted a paltry .202 before returning to the Bulls late in the 1994–1995 season.

Jordan and the Bulls were stronger than ever by the next year. They set an NBA record by winning 72 regular-season games and blitzed past the competition in the playoffs to cruise to another championship behind Jordan, who shook off the rust from his baseball experience to lead the league at 30.4 points a game. Jordan then guided the Bulls to two more titles in a row, giving them three straight for the second time. It was the greatest run of championships since the Celtics were earning them annually in the 1960s.

Basketball burnout motivated Jordan to retire temporarily in 1999, but he returned at age 38 in 2001 by signing a two-year contract to play for the Washington Wizards. Although he played well, averaging more than 20 points a game, and increased attendance in Washington and around the league, the team did not have enough talent surrounding him and they failed to make the playoffs either year.

At the turn of the century, cable sports network ESPN extensively surveyed those in sports media, athletes, and others in the sports world to rank the greatest athletes of the 20th century. Jordan topped the list ahead of baseball superstar Babe Ruth and boxing legend Muhammad Ali.

Jordan has remained linked to basketball. He became the first African American majority owner of a major sports franchise in 2010 when he purchased the NBA Charlotte Bobcats.

See also Ali, Muhammad; Team Sports.

FURTHER READING

Halberstam, David: *Playing for Keeps: Michael Jordan and the World He Made*. New York: Broadway Books, 2000.

Jordan, Michael, and Mike Vancil. *Driven from Within*. New York: Atria Books, 2005.

K

KENNEDY, JOHN F. (1917–1963) To the youngest and least politically interested Baby Boomers, the name John Fitzgerald Kennedy triggers little more than references to the conspiracy theories surrounding his assassination on November 22, 1963. The last of the Baby Boomer generation was either not yet born when he assumed the presidency nearly three years earlier or were far too young to remember anything about it.

Kennedy was born into tremendous wealth on May 29, 1917, the second of nine children. His father, Joseph P. Kennedy, had earned millions of dollars in banking, bootlegging, shipbuilding, and stock investing. Mother Rose was the daughter of former Boston mayor John F. Fitzgerald. Joseph and Rose encouraged fierce intellectual and physical competition among the siblings in an attempt to toughen them.

Kennedy joined the U.S. Navy at the outset of American involvement in World War II and suffered great heartache when older brother Joe was killed in action. He too nearly lost his life when a Japanese destroyer sank the torpedo boat he was captaining, but he led his men back to safety, thereby earning the U.S. Navy and Marine Corps Medal for Heroism. Despite a back injury that would cause him great pain for the rest of his life and require three operations, he requested to return to duty.

Upon discharge from the military, Kennedy planned on embarking on a career in academia or journalism, but he gave in to the wishes of his family, who expected him to run for public office. Kennedy never lost an election. His first triumph was in his 1946 campaign for a Massachusetts congressional seat, which he won easily. He served three terms as a Democrat in the House of Representatives from 1947 to 1953, where he earned a reputation as a liberal on domestic issues, but a staunch anti-Communist in foreign relations.

The ambitious Kennedy could have remained in Congress but opted to run for the Senate in 1952 against popular incumbent Republican Henry Cabot Lodge. Brother Robert F. Kennedy managed his successful campaign, which resulted in a lopsided victory by 70,000 votes. Less than a year later, Kennedy married Jacqueline Lee Bouvier, who was 12 years younger. The handsome senator and beautiful socialite made a glamorous couple.

Senator Kennedy received criticism from his liberal base for refusing to fight against the excesses of Wisconsin Senator Joseph McCarthy, who in the early 1950s conducted witch-hunts to find and punish Communists in all walks of life, including those in the U.S. government. Although Kennedy disapproved of McCarthy, he claimed that half of his Massachusetts constituents considered the head of the anti-Communist campaign a hero.

Kennedy drifted to the left politically as his career in the Senate moved forward. He favored civil rights legislation as the seeds for the civil rights movement were being planted in the South in the mid-1950s. He advocated providing foreign aid to developing nations in Asia and Africa and called for France to grant Algeria its independence. He grew increasingly idealistic in his thinking and his actions.

Thrust into the limelight by his speech at the 1956 Democratic National Convention that was heard by 40 million viewers, Kennedy nearly earned the vice presidential nomination under presidential candidate Adlai Stevenson, who then lost his second consecutive election to popular Republican Dwight D. Eisenhower.

Kennedy decided to run for president against current vice president Richard M. Nixon in 1960 after Eisenhower had served out his two terms. The highlight of the campaign occurred in the first televised presidential debate. The debate on the issues was considered a draw, but the handsome, calm, and confident Kennedy gained an edge in public opinion over Nixon, who appeared uncomfortable in front of the cameras and national television audience.

Kennedy had to overcome the stigma of attempting to become the first Roman Catholic president, which he achieved by expressing his belief in the separation of church and state. He also gained support from the younger generations of the United States for his own youth and vision, which he labeled "The New Frontier." He needed every vote he could muster, and when they were all tabulated, he had defeated Nixon by less than 120,000 votes. He gave a new generation of Americans a feeling of purpose during his inauguration speech by uttering his most famous line: "Ask not what your country can do for you—ask what you can do for your country."

Kennedy's presidency was marked by two momentous events—one an unmitigated disaster and the other a historic and critical triumph. He followed the lead of Eisenhower, who ordered that the CIA equip and train Cuban exiles to invade their homeland and overthrow the new Communist government led by Fidel Castro. Advised by the Joint Chiefs of Staff that the invaders could indeed complete their task successfully, Kennedy approved of the invasion at the Bay of Pigs. But it was misplayed from the start, and invaders on the beach were killed or captured. Kennedy accepted full responsibility for the fiasco, which did not get his presidency off to a promising start, but he also vowed to investigate further any recommendations made by staff members.

The failed Bay of Pigs invasion played a role in a decision by Soviet premier Nikita Khrushchev to place short- and intermediate-range nuclear missiles in

Cuba that were capable of reaching major American cities. When the weapons were discovered, Kennedy demanded that they be dismantled, but Khrushchev refused, setting off a tense situation that had the two nations on the brink of the world's first nuclear conflict. Kennedy ordered a blockade of Soviet ships entering Cuba, but the stalemate was finally broken when he removed American missiles in Turkey as a trade-off for the dismantling of those in Cuba. Americans, including the first wave of Baby Boomers, who were now old enough to understand the gravity of the event, breathed a sigh of relief.

Kennedy sought to launch the United States into a new era, stating his desire to see the nation send an astronaut to the moon by the end of the decade. The Kennedy White House, which included his wife and children Caroline and John Jr., became known as Camelot, although the times in which they lived precluded intense media scrutiny and honesty that would have publicized Kennedy's infidelities that have since become public knowledge.

One unfinished chapter in Kennedy's presidency revolved around his policy regarding Vietnam. He sent military advisors to the troubled nation, which was torn by civil war, but whether he would have expanded the war by sending hundreds of thousands of combat troops as did Lyndon B. Johnson can only be speculated. It has been suggested that by the end of his presidency, Kennedy had decided against greater American involvement in Vietnam.

As Kennedy prepared to launch a campaign against expected Republican presidential nominee Barry Goldwater, which would have resulted in an easy victory based on the knowledge of Johnson's landslide triumph in 1964, he stopped in Dallas on November 22, 1963. Riding next to Jackie in an open limousine in a motorcade, Kennedy was shot at the base of the neck and in the head. He was pronounced dead soon thereafter upon his arrival at Parkland Memorial Hospital.

After the grieving period and the murder of Lee Harvey Oswald, whom the Warren Commission ruled was the lone gunman, several conspiracy theories were expressed. One theory was that Oswald was paid by CIA agents angered by Kennedy's handling of the Bay of Pigs invasion or by mobsters seeking revenge for Robert Kennedy's relentless fight against organized crime. It has also been offered that a second gunman was involved in the shooting. In 1979, a special House of Representatives committee ruled that a second assailant could indeed have fired at Kennedy, but missed, leaving Oswald as the lone gunman.

The truth behind the Kennedy assassination has fascinated Americans ever since. But the most asked question of Baby Boomers regarding his presidency remains, "Where were you when you heard Kennedy had been shot?" The oldest Baby Boomers at the time were still teenagers.

See also Assassinations; Idealism; Kennedy, Robert F.

FURTHER READING

Avedon, Richard, and Shannon Thomas Perich. *The Kennedys: Portrait of a Family*. New York: Collins Design, 2007.

Bugliosi, Vincent. *Four Days in November: The Assassination of President John F. Kennedy*. New York: W.W. Norton and Company, 2008.

Dallek, Robert. *An Unfinished Life: John F. Kennedy, 1917–1963*. New York: Little, Brown and Company, 2003.
Posner, Gerald. *Case Closed*. Harpswell, ME: Anchor Publishing, 2003.

KENNEDY, ROBERT F. (1925–1968) Many in the first wave of Baby Boomers were too young to feel the full emotional and political impact of the assassination of President John F. Kennedy in November 1963, but the assassination of his younger brother Robert Francis Kennedy in 1968 hit many hard.

Young, liberal Baby Boomers swept up in the political turmoil of the late 1960s embraced Kennedy as a politician who railed against Democratic and Republican policies resulting in the escalation of American involvement in Vietnam. But his assassination on June 6, 1968, after he had won the California primary and appeared to be destined for the Democratic presidential nomination, greatly

Attorney General Robert F. Kennedy uses a megaphone to address a group of civil rights demonstrators at the Justice Department on June 14, 1963. (Library of Congress)

disenchanted the Baby Boomers who supported him, although most of them were too young to vote.

Kennedy was born into great wealth on November 20, 1925, in Brookline, Massachusetts, the seventh child of Joseph and Rose Kennedy. His exclusive education included stints at Harvard University and the University of Virginia School of Law, from which he earned his degree in 1951. After managing the successful senate campaign of his brother, John, the younger Kennedy was rewarded with the post of U.S. Attorney General. Young, idealistic Baby Boomers looked favorably upon his support of the growing civil rights movement of the early 1960s. He also came into direct conflict against organized crime and Teamsters Union chief Jimmy Hoffa.

Although Kennedy remained Attorney General after his brother's assassination in 1963, he grew apart politically from Lyndon B. Johnson, who took over the presidency in 1963 and was re-elected the following November. Kennedy resigned from the Cabinet post to run victoriously for a U.S. Senate seat representing New York. During his time in the Senate, he worked to end racial discrimination and poverty. He also became disenchanted with the burgeoning American involvement in the Vietnam War, for which Johnson continued to build troop strength throughout his only full term as president.

Kennedy was undecided about running for president in 1968. But when antiwar candidate Eugene McCarthy almost defeated Johnson in the New Hampshire primary that March, a near-upset that played a huge role in the president's momentous decision not to run for re-election, Kennedy entered the fray.

As a candidate, one of Kennedy's early speeches was perhaps his most difficult. Kennedy was forced to address a crowd of mostly African Americans in Indianapolis on April 4 and inform them that civil rights leader Martin Luther King Jr. had been assassinated. His impassioned and soothing plea to keep the peace was credited for the fact that Indiana's largest city was one of the few in the United States to be free of violent race riots that night and in the days that followed.

Although many Baby Boomer college students ran a "Be Clean for Gene" campaign in an attempt to elect McCarthy, others backed Kennedy. They not only favored Kennedy's political views, but also considered him a more realistic and viable presidential hopeful. That opinion gained credence when Kennedy pulled away from McCarthy in the later primaries and defeated him on June 4 in California. Although Vice President Hubert H. Humphrey was still thought of as a threat, he was not actively campaigning and Kennedy was certainly the front-runner for the nomination.

Minutes before midnight on June 4, 1968, at the Ambassador Hotel in Los Angeles, Kennedy gave a short speech to his supporters, whom he thanked for the most important primary triumph of the campaign. He then began walking with his entourage through a narrow corridor of the hotel and was ushered by a single guard from a private security firm. (At the time, Secret Service agent protection extended only to the president, a policy that was altered because of the tragic events of that evening.) A young, diminutive Palestinian named Sirhan Sirhan, who had been angered by Kennedy's views on what at that time was a secondary issue of Middle East policy, stepped through and fired repeated shots at Kennedy. Kennedy, who was hit once in the back of the head and twice in the body, was rushed by ambulance to the hospital, where he was pronounced dead at 1:44 A.M. on the morning of June 6.

The assassination of Kennedy, which ensured Humphrey's nomination and the continuation of the pro-war plank maintained by the Democrats, radicalized and angered the politically active antiwar Baby Boomers, many of whom were college students. In August, thousands of them descended upon the Democratic National Convention and engaged in pitched battles with police in the Chicago streets, although the climax of the days of confrontation has been described as a police riot.

Kennedy was 42 years old when he was killed. Had he been elected to the White House, he would have begun his first term as the youngest president ever voted into office in American history.

The most stirring tribute to Kennedy was uttered during his memorial service on June 8, 1968, by his brother Ted, who stated the following:

> "My brother need not be idealized, or enlarged in death beyond what he was in life, to be remembered simply as a good decent man, who saw wrong and tried to right it, saw suffering and tried to heal it, saw war and tried to stop it. Those of us, who loved him and who take him to his rest today pray that what he was to us and what he wished for others will someday come to pass for all the world.
>
> "As he said many times, in many parts of this nation, to those he touched and who sought to touch him: 'Some men see things as they are and say why. I dream things that never were and say why not.'"

Millions of Baby Boomers who agreed with that assessment considered the assassination of Kennedy as a lost opportunity for the United States to return to the path of peace and prosperity.

See also Assassinations; Idealism; Kennedy, John F.; Vietnam War.

FURTHER READING

Clarke, Thurston. The *Last Campaign: Robert F. Kennedy and 82 Days That Inspired America*. New York: Holt Paperbacks, 2009.
Schlesinger, Arthur M. *Robert Kennedy and His Times*. New York: Mariner Books, 2002.
Thomas, Evan. *Robert Kennedy: His Life*. New York: Simon and Schuster, 2000.

KEROUAC, JACK (1922–1969) Jack Kerouac was a tortured soul and a drunk who turned against the hippie movement he helped spawn among young Baby Boomers, but his influence as a writer and philosopher remained unquestioned throughout his short life.

Kerouac was born Jean-Louis Kerouac in the working-class section of Lowell, Massachusetts, on March 12, 1922, and was raised during the heart of the Great Depression. The youngest of three children, he received a terrible emotional blow upon the death of older brother Gerard from rheumatic fever.

An intense and serious child, the young Kerouac fostered many friendships, as he would continue to do through most of his life. He was inspired by the suspenseful radio show "The Shadow" and by the passionate novels of Tom Wolfe, the writer who most influenced his own work.

Kerouac was raised in a family hit hard by the Depression. His father, a printer, began gambling in hopes of a financial quick fix. Kerouac was a fine athlete and yearned to save his family money by landing a football scholarship. The star running back on his high school team, he indeed earned a free ride to Columbia University in New York City. His parents followed him to the area and settled in Queens.

But Kerouac's volatility caused him to squabble with the football coach, who refused to let him play. Meanwhile, his father lost his business and became a hopeless alcoholic. Kerouac became bitter and disillusioned and dropped out of school, which further disappointed his parents. After the bombing of Pearl Harbor drew the United States into World War II, the young Kerouac joined the Merchant Marines. When on leave, Kerouac spent time in New York with a crowd of people his parents were wary of, including a number of those who would make up the heartbeat of the 1950s Beatnik movement such as Columbia student Allen Ginsberg, writer William S. Burroughs, and Neal Cassady from Denver.

By that time, Kerouac had begun to put his tormented thoughts on paper. He penned a novel about his sufferings and his attempt to balance his wild life in the city with his moralistic upbringing. His friends praised his manuscript. Ginsberg even asked his Columbia professors to search for a publisher for it. The novel, *The Town and the City* (1950), was his first and most conventional. It brought him respect as a writer but failed to gain him fame.

While working on the book, Kerouac embarked on a series of cross-country trips with Cassady, during which time he became inspired by the spontaneous prose he found in his friend's writing. Kerouac began to experiment in more of a free-form style. He expressed his emotions and feeling about his experiences on the trips without bothering to edit, fictionalize, or even give them much thought. He then gave the manuscript to his editor on a long role of paper, but his presentation was met without enthusiasm, which led to a breaking of professional ties with his editor. Kerouac waited through seven years of rejections from various editors before the iconic *On the Road* was published in 1957.

Kerouac began living a nomadic lifestyle in the early 1950s. He wrote a series of unpublished novels and carried his work around in a sack as he roamed around the country. He followed Ginsberg and Cassady to the liberal California hotbeds of Berkeley and San Francisco, where he befriended poet and Buddhist Gary Snyder, who turned his new acquaintance on to the religion. Kerouac began communing with nature and wrote a novel titled *The Dharma Bums* (1958), which described a joyous mountain climbing trip he experienced with Snyder in Yosemite in 1955. Kerouac believed himself to be on the brink of spiritual realization.

Several years earlier, Kerouac had coined the term "Beat Generation" to describe those embracing the new Bohemian lifestyle and philosophy. He and Snyder became underground celebrities after having participated in a poetry reading in San Francisco in 1955. But after *On the Road* was published and achieved tremendous sales, particularly among young people, he found it difficult to play the part of a Beatnik icon. He was hurt by the criticism hurled at him by the older generation of critics. He understood that the Beat Generation was little more than fad, but he did not want his writing to become one as well.

Kerouac nevertheless attempted to live up to the wild image he portrayed for himself in the book, which resulted in alcoholism. He lost his connection with Buddhism and embarked on long and harmful drinking binges. His friends began to view him as unstable, although the success of *On the Road* motivated publishers to place on the market his novels that were once rejected. By the 1960s, young Baby Boomers were devouring his work and embracing the philosophies of life he espoused. The hippie movement that took root around 1965 in San Francisco was a natural progression of the Beatnik movement Kerouac, Ginsberg, Cassady, and others spawned a decade earlier.

Kerouac kept busy by making television appearances, writing magazine articles, and even recording three spoken-word albums but lost his momentum as a book writer and philosopher. He became miserable. An attempt to regain his writing talent and kick the alcohol habit through a retreat to Big Sur in 1961 failed, and he returned to San Francisco for another drinking binge. He felt he was losing his mind, a fear he expressed in his last great novel, *Big Sur* (1962).

A defeated and lonely Kerouac retreated to Long Island to live with his mother, with whom he would remain until his death. While the well-publicized hippies espoused the philosophies in his writings, he became a political conservative while living with his Catholic mother. He railed against the hippies, supported American involvement in Vietnam, and even befriended iconic conservative writer and thinker William F. Buckley.

Kerouac spent the rest of his life drinking cheap wine, developing a Buddhist-influenced brand of Catholicism, and playing a strange baseball game he created with a deck of cards. His personal life remained tormented—his first two marriages ended within months and his third, in the mid-1960s, was to a Lowell woman and childhood acquaintance named Stella Sampas, who moved in with him and his mother.

The three relocated to Florida, but his health deteriorated because of his drinking and he died at age 47 on October 21, 1969.

See also Drinking; Hippie Movement.

Further Reading

Kerouac, Jack. *Big Sur*. New York: Penguin Books, 1992 (reprint).
Kerouac, Jack. *On the Road: The Original Scroll*. Penguin Books, 2008 (reprint).
Leland, John. *Why Kerouac Matters: The Lessons of On the Road (They're Not What You Think)*. New York: Viking, 2007.

KESEY, KEN (1935–2001) Some early Baby Boomers experimented with psychedelic drugs, and the writer most identified with this practice was Ken Kesey. His cross-country bus trip with a band of followers known as the Merry Pranksters helped plant the seeds of widespread use of LSD and even the hippie movement itself.

However, Kesey is best known in literary circles for his 1962 classic novel *One Flew Over the Cuckoo's Nest*, which gained even greater acclaim when it was transformed into an Academy Award–winning movie in the mid-1970s.

Kesey, son of Fred and Geneve, was born on September 17, 1935, in LaJunta, Colorado, but moved often with his family until they settled in Eugene, Oregon, in 1946. His father founded a farmer's cooperative and brought his son up as a hard-core Baptist and strong believer in the teachings of the Bible. The younger Kesey enjoyed outdoor activities like fishing and hunting and such sports as wrestling and football, both of which he excelled in during his years at Springfield High School. He also exhibited skills as an actor, winning an award for best thespian and displaying such offshoot entertainment talents as ventriloquism and hypnotism. His all-around talents motivated his classmates to vote him as the student most likely to succeed.

Acting intrigued Kesey, and he spent the summer after his senior year in Hollywood seeking bit parts in vain before starting his stint as a speech and communications major at the University of Oregon. He remained active in college, participating in the theater, wrestling, and fraternities. He worked energetically as an actor and writer for radio and television, winning another thespian award along the way. At the age of 20, he married childhood sweetheart Faye Haxby.

After earning his bachelor of arts degree, Kesey spent a year in the dairy business before accepting a Woodrow Wilson Fellowship that landed him in the writing program at Stanford University, a move that changed his life. He was not only affected by his teachers at that prestigious California school, but also his classmates and the Beatnik community at nearby North Beach. He began poring over the works of such Beat Generation writers as Jack Kerouac and William S. Burroughs. Soon Kesey was shedding his strict religious teachings and wearing a beard, drinking wine, swapping wives, smoking marijuana, and working on a novel that went unpublished titled *Zoo* about the North Beach Bohemian lifestyle.

The seeds of his notoriety as an advocate of psychedelic drugs and as a renowned writer were planted after he agreed to participate in experiments at the Veterans' Hospital in Menlo Park. Kesey was enlisted to take several psychedelic substances, including LSD, which motivated him to experiment on his own with hallucinogenics in an attempt to raise his consciousness.

Kesey was soon hired as a third-shift aide at that hospital, where his observations and his continued use of psychedelic drugs resulted in his creation of several characters for *One Flew Over the Cuckoo's Nest*. The story takes place at a mental hospital and centers on the relationship between misfit Randall Patrick McMurphy and ruthless head nurse Ratched, all of which is narrated by half-breed Native American Chief Bromden. The book raised social questions about authority figures and those they oppress and was used as a metaphor for the larger issue of government control of its citizens and big business treatment of its workers. The book was published in 1962 and earned a positive critical and popular response. While Kesey worked on another book titled *Sometimes a Great Notion, One Flew Over the Cuckoo's Nest* was adapted as a Broadway play starring Kirk Douglas and ran for 82 performances in 1963 and 1964. Kesey used sales from the book to buy land in the isolated Santa Cruz Mountains in La Honda, California.

With the intention of creating publicity for *Sometimes a Great Notion*, Kesey bought a 1939 school bus he named "Furthur" to take on a cross-country trip to New York City. But the excursion took an unusual figurative detour. Kesey painted the bus with psychedelic colors and stocked it with LSD, which was legal at the time. He installed tape players and loudspeakers, dubbed his mates the "Merry Pranksters," and set out to herald a new day to young Baby Boomers who would soon form the hippie generation. The Merry Pranksters visited cities and towns, promoting a hedonistic, back-to-nature, alternative lifestyle accompanied by the use of hallucinogenic drugs.

Upon their return to La Honda in August 1964, Kesey and the Merry Pranksters began conducting what became known as "acid tests," events that introduced LSD to more people and inspired the 1968 Tom Wolfe classic *The Electric Kool-Aid Acid Test*. But Kesey was arrested for marijuana possession in April 1965 and again early in 1966, which prompted him to flee for nine months to Mexico, where he and his followers continued to live a hippie lifestyle. Upon his return to the United States, he was fined $1,500 and sent to jail for nine months.

Kesey and the Pranksters moved to a farm in Pleasant Hill, Oregon, where he was to reside the rest of his life. He bypassed a trip to the legendary Woodstock Festival in August 1969, and then refused to allow the Pranksters to move back in with him. He remained detached from society until 1973 upon the publication of his book *Kesey's Garage Sale*, a collection of his commentaries and plays. He produced another collection, *Demon Box*, in 1986 and wrote a children's book titled *Little Tricker the Squirrel Meets Big Double the Bear* in 1990. Two years later, he penned *Sailor Song*, his first novel since 1964, a story set in the near future after a series of ecological disasters. The book received mixed reviews.

Although some believe Kesey did not remain relevant in the literary world after the 1960s, he earned distinction as the most significant link between the Beatnik and hippie periods in U.S. history. And although he complained about how the transformation of *One Flew Over the Cuckoo's Nest* into movie form was handled, his book remains a classic and the film is considered one of the finest ever produced in American cinema, winning Oscars for Best Picture, Best Actor (Jack Nicholson), and Best Actress (Louise Fletcher).

Kesey died of liver cancer at age 66 on November 10, 2001, four years after suffering a mild stroke.

See also Alternative Lifestyles; Hippie Movement; LSD; Marijuana; Movies; Nicholson, Jack; Woodstock.

FURTHER READING
Kesey, Ken. *One Flew Over the Cuckoo's Nest*. New York: Viking Press, 1962.
Kesey, Ken. *Sailor Song*. New York: Penguin Books, 1993 (reprint).

KING, BILLIE JEAN (1942–) Billie Jean King was arguably the greatest female tennis player to ever grace a court, yet she is revered equally for her impact on the women's movement of the early 1970s. And in one eventful night at the

Astrodome in Houston in 1973, she displayed her wizardry with a racket and struck a blow for women's equality at the same time as more than 50 million American television viewers watched her defeat Bobby Riggs in straight sets. The match was at the time and has ever since been celebrated as "The Battle of the Sexes."

Born Billie Jean Moffitt on November 22, 1942, in California, she later claimed that she knew what she wanted to do with her life the moment she first struck a tennis ball. She remained athletically active, as did her brother Randy, who blossomed into a highly successful Major League Baseball pitcher for the San Francisco Giants.

King purchased her first racket for the paltry sum of eight dollars earned from doing odd jobs around her neighborhood in Long Beach, California. She continued to play despite hearing stereotypical comments common at that time about the perceived masculine tendencies of female athletes. Her work paid off—by age eleven she was winning tournaments against far older players.

The image of tennis as a sport for only the wealthy also proved insulting to King, who used cheaper equipment and donned shorts and a shirt rather than the expensive tennis dresses worn by the well-to-do players. That emotional pain played a role in her future campaigns to increase the popularity of tennis for spectators and participants in other levels of the social and economic strata.

King belied the style of most young women of her era, charging the net aggressively and putting opponents away with sharp volleys and overheads. By the age of 17, she had improved her baseline game enough to vault into the rankings as one of the top 20 players in the world. She even teamed up with Karen Hantze to win the women's doubles title at the prestigious Wimbledon Championships in 1961. The following year she stunned defending champion Margaret Smith (later Margaret Court) in the second round of the singles tournament in that same event.

But tennis was still an amateur sport at the time, so King decided to further her education by enrolling at California State University of Los Angeles, which she attended because her parents could not afford to send her to schools such as the University of Southern California or Stanford. It was during that time she met law student and future husband Larry King.

King's passion for tennis lured her back in 1964 and within a year she was the top-ranked player in the United States. In 1966, she captured her first Wimbledon singles crown, then won that event and the U.S. Open the following year. She also fought to open up the sport to professionalism, which would bring great incentive for players to compete at the highest levels. The transition from amateur to professional sport was indeed completed within a few years, and King finally earned money by winning yet another Grand Slam event, the Australian Open, in 1968. In 1971, she became the first women's tennis player to earn $100,000 in one season.

But King meant much more to the women's game than merely performing it at a premier level. She was its top promoter, having played an integral role in establishing the women's Virginia Slims tour. But the reputation of the women's game took a hit in 1973 when 55-year-old former tennis star and self-promoter Bobby Riggs challenged Margaret Court to a match on Mother's Day and defeated her handily.

King watched the proceedings in anger and disbelief. She knew that she would have to avenge the defeat on behalf of women's tennis and the burgeoning women's movement. The publicity leading up to the King-Riggs match was enormous. Riggs was billed as a "male chauvinist pig" whereas King was the defender of her sex. More than 30,000 fans were on hand to watch King easily defeat Riggs.

King continued to work on behalf of women's sports and the popularizing of tennis among the masses. She and her husband founded a magazine titled *Women-Sports*, then also launched World Team Tennis. She became the first female to coach male athletes when she became player-coach of the Philadelphia Freedoms of the World Team Tennis. She also helped start the Women's Sports Foundation, which promoted equal opportunities and pay for female athletes. She spent much of her free time providing tennis lessons to kids on public courts and in poor neighborhoods.

By 1979, King had won twelve Grand Slam singles titles, including six Wimbledons. But her influence had spread far beyond the court. *Time* chose her as its Woman of the Year in 1976.

However, King's personal life was in turmoil. She decided in the late 1960s that she was a lesbian, and in 1971 she began a sexual relationship with her secretary, Marilyn Barnett, which she kept secret until 1981, thereby becoming the first female athlete to publicly announce her homosexuality. She complained that within 24 hours of her admission, she had lost all of her endorsements. She later added that if she had known she was a lesbian she never would have gotten married.

King faded from the spotlight upon her retirement in 1981, but she was voted into the International Tennis Hall of Fame in 1987 and is still credited for being a force on the court and in the women's movement.

See also Women's Movement.

FURTHER READING

DeFord, Frank, and Billie Jean King. *Billie Jean*. New York: Viking Press, 1982.
King, Billie Jean. *Pressure Is a Privilege*. New York: LifeTime Media, 2008.
Roberts, Selena. *A Necessary Spectacle: Billie Jean King, Bobby Riggs, and the Tennis Match That Leveled the Game*. New York: Crown Publishers, 2005.

KING, MARTIN LUTHER, JR. (1929–1968) When Baby Boomers reflect on recent American history, several figures stand out as beacons of morality. But only one rises to the top in leading the charge to ensure that the nation was living out its creed that all men are created equal. That man was Martin Luther King Jr.

Even during their childhood, most of the first wave of Baby Boomers were struck by the discrimination and often-violent racism endured by blacks, particularly in the Deep South. They watched on their black-and-white televisions as black civil rights marchers were beaten in the streets. They witnessed in horror as four young black girls were killed when a bomb blew up their church in Birmingham, Alabama, in 1963. And they sat incredulous as Alabama governor George Wallace uttered his most infamous words: "Segregation now . . . segregation tomorrow . . . segregation forever!" during a defiant speech in front of the

Martin Luther King Jr. waves to the crowd as he delivers his famous "I Have a Dream" speech during the March on Washington in Washington, D.C., on August 28, 1963. King was awarded the Nobel Peace Prize in 1964 for his work in the area of human rights. (AP/Wide World Photos)

door at Foster Auditorium on the campus of the University of Alabama in the late spring of 1963.

Certainly black Baby Boomers were most affected by the last vestiges of the Jim Crow era and needed a leader who would battle for their political and social equality. After all, they were the ones attending inferior schools, shunned from public venues, and forced to dine at segregated restaurants. Many mourned the lynching of family members.

Even the small minority of Baby Boomers who believed in segregation and even still embrace the ideology, perhaps having been taught so-called black inferiority in their homes, must acknowledge the overwhelming impact King had on the South and on American society as a whole.

Little was known about King until a brave black woman activist named Rosa Parks refused to yield her bus seat to a white man on December 1, 1955 in Montgomery, Alabama. The incident set off the successful Montgomery Bus Boycott, which lasted 382 days and in turn launched the civil rights movement in earnest. It also thrust King, who proved to be the emotional and spiritual leader of the boycott, into the national spotlight.

King, who served as pastor of the Dexter Street Baptist Church, immediately began tugging at the conscience of the United States and its leaders through a philosophy of nonviolence that he learned from the teachings of Mohandas Gandhi. King steadfastly refused to budge from the philosophy despite the horrific violence perpetrated against blacks and white civil rights workers, mostly by members of the Ku Klux Klan, in the late 1950s and early 1960s. But he stepped up the pressure on the federal government to enact laws ensuring equality for all people through speeches and the organizing of marches and boycotts. His influence motivated thousands to take action, whether it was participating in sit-ins at segregated restaurants, protests against bogus laws that prevented blacks from gaining their rightful place in voting booths, or marches to bring attention to a litany of injustices.

King was elected president in 1957 of the Southern Christian Leadership Conference, a fledgling organization created for the purpose of developing new leaders for the civil rights movement. He understood that although institutional racism and segregation were prevalent in the Deep South, discrimination against blacks existed everywhere in the United States. As the civil rights movement marched on, he began taking his message to other parts of the country. From 1957 to 1968 he traveled more than 6 million miles and made more than 2,500 speeches. The most celebrated was his "I Have a Dream" speech that he delivered before 250,000 people in Washington, D.C., in 1963. He also showed tremendous courage; he became well acquainted with death threats and jail cells. King was arrested about 20 times. During one stint in a prison he wrote the inspiring "Letter from a Birmingham Jail," in which he wrote of his optimism that freedom would come to Birmingham because freedom is the goal of the United States.

The following year King became the youngest man ever to earn a Nobel Peace Prize. He gained greater respect when he turned over the prize money of $54,123 to the civil rights movement.

In 1965, King and his work were recognized at the highest levels. President Lyndon B. Johnson, for whom he had campaigned in 1964, signed the Voting Rights Act and Civil Rights Act, which ensured equality for southern blacks through the letter of the law. Race relations had begun to change in the South by that time, and King was certainly more responsible for that than any other American.

Yet millions of young Baby Boomer and older blacks felt frustrated and angry at the slow pace of progress. They eschewed King's continued call for nonviolence and took to the streets in dozens of American cities. Riots broke out in Los Angeles in 1965 and continued for several years in every major city. The deadliest occurred in Detroit and Newark in 1967. King could not stem the tide of black militancy.

By that time, King had branched out into speaking his mind about other issues. He came out against the deepening American involvement in Vietnam. He deplored the fact that American youths, including a disproportionate number of blacks, were being shot and killed halfway around the world.

Wherever there was a perceived injustice, King would be there. That led him in April 1968 to Memphis, where he was to lead a march in support of striking garbage workers. Young blacks had rioted that week in Memphis and he hoped to bring calm to the city. But on April 4, he was killed by an assassin's bullet. Ironically, the death of King, who so eloquently and passionately preached nonviolence, sparked an explosion of rioting in inner cities throughout the United States. But the summer of 1968 ended the five-year spate of black rioting in the United States.

Conspiracy theories abound in regard to the King assassination. Some believe James Earl Ray was paid to murder him. But to most people, particularly Baby Boomers who admired King and were influenced by his convictions and moral leadership, being true to his legacy is far more important. He praised the American ideals of freedom and equality in life. Many Americans believe it is their duty to support his stand of nonviolence long after his violent death.

See also Civil Rights Movement; Idealism; Racism; Vietnam War.

FURTHER READING

King, Martin Luther, Jr. *A Testament of Hope: The Essential Writings and Teachings of Martin Luther King, Jr.* New York: HarperOne, 1990.

King, Martin Luther, Jr. *The Autobiography of Martin Luther King, Jr.* Lebanon, IN: Grand Central Publishing, 1998.

L

LED ZEPPELIN The Beatles had broken up by the time the second wave of Baby Boomers, born in the mid-to-late 1950s, began developing their taste for rock-and-roll music. It did not take long for some of them to adopt and even idolize another British import, Led Zeppelin, as their favorite band.

Led Zeppelin has been greatly acknowledged as the premier rock group of the 1970s. They were the quintessential stadium and large arena concert act, combining Robert Plant's soaring vocals, Jimmy Page's powerful guitar riffs, John Bonham's furious drumming, and John Paul Jones's bass and keyboard work into legendary status.

Page, who followed guitar legends Eric Clapton and Jeff Beck into the highly acclaimed 1960s band the Yardbirds, morphed that group into Led Zeppelin in 1968. Before joining the Yardbirds in 1966, Page had earned a reputation for brilliance by lending his talents to such hits of the era as the Kinks' "You Really Got Me," Them's memorable "Gloria," and the Who's teenage angst classic, "I Can't Explain." He lured Bonham and Plant away from British blues quartet the Band of Joy and added Jones, who had made an impression by working with the Rolling Stones, to complete the mix.

Many have argued that Led Zeppelin gave birth to heavy metal music, although the same has been claimed on behalf of Jimi Hendrix and others. Zeppelin has certainly been credited for inspiring the hard rock groups of the 1970s and 1980s, although they never allowed their instrumentation to drown out their melodies.

Although some hard-core Zeppelin fans contend that their first album was their best, the group did not break through commercially until the 1969 release of *Led Zeppelin II*, which featured revolutionary fuzz tone feedback in the hit "Whole Lotta Love" as well as complementary classics "Heartbreaker," "Livin', Lovin' Maid (She's Just a Woman)," and "Ramble On." They had firmly established themselves as a group aiming for the more sophisticated FM radio market rather than Top 40 AM listeners.

The band continued to pride itself on constantly evolving and experimenting, going mostly acoustic in creating *Led Zeppelin III*, which was highlighted by a wide array of musical styles, including folk in "Gallows Pole," hard rock in "Immigrant Song," and electric blues in "Since I've Been Loving You."

Led Zeppelin IV, their most commercially and arguably artistically successful album, followed in late 1971. Headlined by the epic "Stairway to Heaven," it soared to the top of the charts. That song was augmented by quintessential rockers "Rock and Roll" and "Black Dog," as well as the complex instrumentation of "When the Levee Breaks" and "The Battle of Evermore."

Exploring new territory in the eclectic *Houses of the Holy* in 1973, Zeppelin remained true to their blues roots, but most successful commercially were "D'yer Mak'er," "The Song Remains the Same," and "Dancing Days." A tremendously popular documentary film following Zeppelin on a tour titled *The Song Remains the Same* was soon released.

Now firmly established as the premier rock group in the world, Zeppelin was shattering attendance records. Their draw of 56,800 in Tampa, Florida, in 1973 broke the mark for a rock-and-roll concert set by the Beatles at Shea Stadium in New York in 1965. A year later, Zeppelin established their own record label called Swan Song, which expanded its stable of acts to include the popular Bad Company and other bands and artists.

Perhaps Led Zeppelin's most accomplished work was the double album *Physical Graffiti*, which was released in 1975 and incorporated Indian music influences in the hit "Kashmir" while maintaining their rock and blues foundation with "Trampled Under Foot," "The Wanton Song," and "Custard Pie." Many think that Page peaked with his guitar work on that album.

But personal problems, including drug and alcohol abuse and a 1975 car accident that almost cost Plant his leg, took a heavy toll on the band. Plant was sidelined for two years, during which time the group released the album *Presence*, its first to be poorly received. Just as he was recovering from his injury, Plant's six-year-old son Karac died of a viral infection. And on September 25, 1980, Bonham died from asphyxiation due to excessive alcohol consumption. The group then disbanded.

However, Led Zeppelin lived on in more than just name. In 1982, they released an album titled *Coda*, a collection of outtakes from various recording sessions. The three remaining band members teamed with drummer Tony Thompson and Phil Collins to perform a set at the legendary Live Aid concert in 1985. Page and Plant reunited in 1994 for a Music Television (MTV) show, and a year later Led Zeppelin was inducted into the Rock-and-Roll Hall of Fame in Cleveland. Since then, various compilations and box sets of Zeppelin recordings have helped maintain their immense popularity.

Their image as one of the best rock bands in history has not been tarnished although even the youngest Baby Boomers are closing in on 50 years of age. The children of Boomers have also become fans of Led Zeppelin, which continues to be particularly popular among college students. The band has sold more than 200 million albums.

See also Rock-and-Roll; The Rolling Stones; The Who.

FURTHER READING

Prochnicky, Jerry. *Led Zeppelin: Good Times, Bad Times*. New York: Abrams, 2009.

Thomas, Gareth. *Led Zeppelin: An Illustrated Biography*. New York: Welcome Rain Publishers, 2009.

Wall, Mick. *When Giants Walked the Earth: A Biography of Led Zeppelin*. New York: St. Martin's Press, 2009.

LSD Although the initial wave of Baby Boomers were the first Americans to experience widespread recreational drug use, those from future generations also experimented with drugs, including many such drugs as cocaine and ecstasy that were not in the mainstream in the 1960s. But the one drug that is most commonly associated with only the 1960s is lysergic acid diethylamide (LSD).

LSD, which later became known as "acid," was synthesized for the first time in 1938 by Sandoz Pharmaceutical chemist Albert Hoffmann, who was working in Switzerland and seeking a blood stimulant. He consumed it for the first time accidentally in 1943 and reported seeing a continuous stream of pictures, extraordinary shapes, and an intense kaleidoscopes of colors. Hoffmann then took LSD intentionally three days later.

In 1949, the drug was brought to the United States and studied in such cities as Boston and Los Angeles. In the 1950s, hundreds of papers were published discussing the effects of LSD, including experiments in which it was used to treat depression and alcoholism. Future advocates of LSD use including Beatnik icon Allen Ginsberg and Harvard University clinical psychology professor Timothy Leary experimented with it in the late 1950s and 1960s.

The American government grew wary of the increasing experimentation involving LSD in the early 1960s. Congress restricted research into the effects of the drug in 1962, but it remained legal. By the next year, it was appearing in the streets for the first time in the form of liquid on sugar cubes as such mainstream periodicals as *Look* and *Saturday Evening Post* published articles about it.

The epicenter of experimentation and its first widespread use was in California in 1965 after Owsley (Bear) Stanley succeeded in synthesizing crystalline LSD in February and began distributing it in March. Later that year, Ken Kesey, who had gained fame in 1962 by authoring the novel *One Flew Over the Cuckoo's Nest*, spearheaded a series of acid tests in Los Angeles, San Francisco, and other areas of the state. Kesey's group, the Merry Pranksters, traveled on a bus they nicknamed "Furthur" from one site to another and hosted parties in which LSD was distributed mostly to young Baby Boomers. The period of widespread experimentation was turned into a book authored by Tom Wolfe titled *The Electric Kool-Aid Acid Test*.

In 1966, Leary founded the League of Spiritual Development with LSD as both the initials and the sacrament and *Life* magazine took note, placing a story about the explosion of the drug's use on its cover. Young Baby Boomers, particularly the hippies of California but increasingly in other areas of the country, espoused LSD as a means of mind expansion and gaining self-awareness. By October it became illegal in California and was banned on a federal level in 1967, when despite its illegality it was used extensively during the Summer of Love in San Francisco. An estimated 1–2 million Americans had tried the drug by the end of the decade.

By that time, acid was being used and was associated with the rock music scene of that era and generation. Groups such as Jefferson Airplane, Quicksilver Messenger Service, the Grateful Dead, and Country Joe and the Fish performed at concerts in which they and their audiences were high on acid. By 1967, band members from the Beatles and other major acts including the Rolling Stones had admitted to taking acid and it had become apparent that their music had been influenced by their experimentation.

But by the early 1970s, the wonderment associated with trying LSD had worn off. Most Boomers who had used the drug as part of their lifestyles were negatively affected by it or simply quit and moved on to another stage of their lives. Many younger Boomers now in college took LSD on occasion, but with the hippie era over, there would never again be mass usage of the drug in a concentrated geographical area to make it a national phenomenon.

New forms of LSD began to hit the market in the late 1960s, including orange sunshine in 1969 and windowpane acid in 1971. By the middle of the decade, "blotter" acid with the drug impregnated on paper displaying colorful art forms had become popular.

Acid regained its popularity for a short time in the late 1990s among those in the "rave" subculture and actually peaked in its overall use in the United States around the turn of the century according to some estimates. By that time, Baby Boomers, some of whom had taken acid during their youths, were speaking with their own teenage and college-age kids about the drug. But its usage dropped dramatically immediately thereafter to its lowest ebb in four decades before a slight upsurge from 2004 to 2008.

Although many of the younger Baby Boomers and those from subsequent generations have experimented with LSD during their lifetimes, the drug will always be associated with the first wave of Boomers, the hippie generation, and the rock music scene of that era.

See also Hippie Movement; Kesey, Ken; Rock-and-Roll; The Rolling Stones.

FURTHER READING

Lee, Martin A., and Brian Shlain. *Acid Dreams: The Complete Social History of LSD, the CIA, the Sixties, and Beyond.* New York: Grove Press, 1994.

Stevens, Jay. *Storming Heaven: LSD and the American Dream.* New York: Grove Press, 1998.

Wolfe, Tom. *The Electric Kool-Aid Acid Test.* New York: Farrar, Straus and Giroux, 1968.

M

MADONNA (1958–) Few entertainers drew more comparisons between the artists embraced by the first wave of Baby Boomers in the 1960s and those cherished by the youngest from that generation in the 1980s than pop singer Madonna.

The distinctions made by the older Baby Boomers were not generally flattering. They asserted that although many of their musical heroes eschewed materialism and attempted to be politically relevant, Madonna bragged about being a "material girl" and was not a positive influence on her generation as a pop singer, model, or actor.

Whether such contentions were warranted in the 1980s, Madonna did invite controversy by exploring social issues throughout her career and delving into political protest after the turn of the century. Her popularity in the 1980s and 1990s was undeniable. Madonna was arguably the biggest musical star of both decades. In addition, she influenced the fashions and attitudes of the youngest Baby Boomers.

Madonna was born on August 16, 1958 in Bay City, Michigan, and was only five when her namesake mother died of breast cancer. She later admitted that she lacked respect for her stepmother, whom she treated poorly.

Madonna's talent became apparent at an early age and she earned a dance scholarship to the University of Michigan in 1978. But she dropped out after two years to move to New York City, where she lived in several rundown apartments while studying dance before helping launch a band called Breakfast Club. Her co-founder was Steve Bray, who had been her boyfriend in Michigan and who eventually helped her compose and produce dance club tracks that led her to sign a contract with Sire Records.

Madonna struggled in the late 1970s and early 1980s to make ends meet as a model, singer, and dancer. But in October 1982, her song "Holiday" made a splash and resulted in an invitation to appear on the legendary Dick Clark television show *American Bandstand*. Eight months later, she released her self-titled debut album, which featured megahits "Lucky Star," "Holiday," and "Borderline," the last of which became the first in a string of 13 consecutive Top Five songs. The following year she recorded "Like a Virgin," which was released as part of an album of the same name that also featured "Material Girl" and reached number one in the United States for three weeks, selling 7 million copies worldwide by the spring of 1985. During the production of the "Material Girl" video, Madonna caused a stir by being photographed with budding acting star Sean Penn. Several months later the couple was wed in Malibu.

By mid-1985, millions of Baby Boomers and teenagers were following the fashion trends popularized by Madonna, complete with leggings, lace gloves, and scanty dress shirts that showed off cleavage and belly buttons. She began her forays into acting by playing the role of a free-spirited New York drifter in the film *Desperately Seeking Susan* (1985).

Madonna did create controversy in 1986 with her lyrics and video for the hit "Papa Don't Preach," which featured a young unmarried pregnant woman. The video, which evoked Catholic images, and the fact that she dedicated the song to Pope John Paul II in a protest against dominant male authority figures, motivated the Pope to ask Italians to boycott her tour appearance in that country.

Madonna's popularity continued to soar and she received critical acclaim in 1989 with her *Like a Prayer* album that featured a namesake megahit song, as well as the highly popular "Express Yourself." The video of "Like a Prayer" caused tremendous backlash when Madonna was shown kissing a black saint and dancing in front of burning crosses. The controversy surrounding that performance caused the Pepsi Corporation to kill an advertising campaign that featured Madonna, but "Like a Prayer" soared to number one in the charts. That same year, she divorced Penn, stating that one does not necessarily spend one's entire life with one's soul mate.

Madonna continued to churn out the hits in the 1990s. Chart-topper "Vogue" was a staple of the Blind Ambition tour launched in April 1990. A documentary of the tour titled *Truth or Dare* received strong reviews and ticket sales. And in the summer of 1992, the song "This Used to Be My Playground" reached number one. The tune was used in *A League of Their Own* (1992), a movie about a women's professional baseball team during World War II in which Madonna played a small role.

Negative publicity resulted in the summer of 1992 when Madonna released *Sex*, a soft-core pornographic book that displayed her and several celebrities in erotic poses. The book was released to accompany her album *Erotica*, which sold 2 million copies. Although her 1994 album *Bedtime Stories* spawned the number one hit "Take a Bow," it was clear by that time that she had declined from her peak in popularity as a singer, at least temporarily.

But in 1995 Madonna displayed her versatility and a knack for keeping herself in the spotlight by landing the role of Evita Peron in the film adaptation of Andrew Lloyd Webber's *Evita*. At about the same time Madonna announced that she was pregnant with daughter Lourdes, she won the Golden Globe for Best Actress (Musical or Comedy), although her campaign to snag an Academy Award nomination proved to be in vain. She contributed to the soundtrack to the film, which included a hit dance remix of "Don't Cry for Me Argentina."

Madonna modernized musically in 1998 with the album *Ray of Light*, which was heavily influenced by studio electronics and soared to the top of the charts. She continued to branch out, working in modeling, acting, and singing. In 2003 she released the album *American Life*, which featured a song of the same name that called out the American dream as selfish and materialistic and even questioned her own role in it. The song also called for peace in Iraq.

Madonna continued to invite controversy later that year by kissing young pop music stars Britney Spears and Christina Aguilera on stage during the Music Television (MTV) Video Music Awards and in 2006 when she adopted a 13-month-old Malawi boy. The adoption, which was completed in 2008, was criticized because it supposedly broke a Malawi law that requires an individual to live in that country for one year before adopting one of its children, although Madonna claimed that no such law existed.

Inducted into the Rock-and-Roll Hall of Fame in 2008, Madonna released another highly successful album that year. The record, which debuted at number one and featured single "4 Minutes," gave Madonna her 37th Billboard Hot 10 hit, thereby pushing her ahead of Elvis Presley into first place all-time in producing Top 10 songs. By that time she was making her home in England while living with film director Guy Ritchie. In 2010, she performed at a benefit concert to raise money for earthquake victims in Haiti.

Although younger Baby Boomers have generally embraced Madonna as a musical artist with far greater passion than have older ones, all have recognized her influence in American pop culture. Many of those who have complained that Madonna contributed to what they perceived as the superficiality and materialism of her time might admit that she embarked on quite a different and more meaningful course in more recent years.

FURTHER READING
Ciccone, Christopher, and Wendy Leigh. *Life with My Sister Madonna*. New York: Simon Spotlight Entertainment, 2008.

MAILER, NORMAN (1923–2007) Norman Mailer entered the world nearly a quarter-century before the birth of the first Baby Boomer, but there was no greater literary link to the political world and left-wing philosophies for young activists in the 1960s.

Mailer was born on January 31, 1923, in Long Branch, New Jersey, and was raised in nearby Brooklyn, New York, in a middle-class Jewish family. His father was an accountant and his mother aided his uncle in the running of a small trucking company.

The young Mailer loved to read, particularly romantic adventure, and showed his ambitious nature by writing a 250-page science fiction story titled *Invasion from Mars* at the tender age of nine. A child prodigy, he graduated from Brooklyn's Boys High School in 1939 and was accepted into Harvard University at 16. During his time there, he won a student fiction-writing contest sponsored by *Story* magazine. Mailer majored in aeronautical engineering, but he had committed himself to a writing career.

Author Norman Mailer in 1948. Mailer wrote fiction and nonfiction that explored the individual's struggle for freedoms against oppressive social institutions in 20th-century America. (Library of Congress)

Mailer's writing career would have to wait. He was thrust into military service during World War II as an Army sergeant in the Pacific. But upon the conclusion of the conflict, he was a graduate student at the Sorbonne in Paris and wrote the classic novel *The Naked and the Dead* (1948) in just 15 months. The book was inspired by his experiences in the Philippines during the war and was so successful that it gave Mailer celebrity status at age 25.

Mailer moved to Hollywood to become involved in the film industry in 1949, but disillusionment quickly set in. He became fascinated by radical, left-wing politics and returned to New York to immerse himself in the artistic hotbed of Greenwich Village. He wrote two poorly received novels that reflected the fear and political tensions revolving around Senator Joseph McCarthy's witch-hunt for Communists—*Barbary Shore* (1951) and *Deer Park* (1955). By the end of the decade, he had penned several enlightening and even startling magazine articles on such topics as sex, drugs, race, and violence. His 1957 essay titled "The White Negro" compared the United States' growing racial tensions with the alienation experienced by young Beatniks embracing a new Bohemian lifestyle. Some of his most passionate and controversial work appeared in a book titled *Advertisements for Myself* (1959).

At this time, Mailer founded *The Village Voice* newspaper, the first alternative weekly in the United States. While he increased his left-wing rhetoric, his personal life became more turbulent. He became involved in drinking, drugs, and violence. In 1960, he stabbed wife Adele Morales with a penknife after a long night of partying. However, she declined to press charges, and Mailer received a suspended sentence. The couple later divorced.

Mailer proved to be in his element during the political and social upheaval of the 1960s. The first wave of Baby Boomers, who were now old enough to understand his writing and political views, embraced his work, which contributed to the rise of the counterculture and even the sexual revolution. He covered the 1960 Democratic and Republican conventions as a journalist; reported on the administration of President John F. Kennedy in a collection of writings titled *Presidential Papers* (1963); and wrote about sex, politics, and violence in his novel *An American Dream* (1965). The prolific Mailer continued with his social commentary with *Cannibals and Christians* (1966).

Growing increasingly and ardently against American involvement in Vietnam, Mailer linked himself inextricably with the growing number of politically active Baby Boomers in 1967 by joining 50,000 protesters in a march to the Pentagon. He wrote about the motley and diverse crew of hippies and antiwar advocates in his book *Armies of the Night* (1968), earning a Pulitzer Prize for Nonfiction in the process. His follow-up, *Miami and the Siege of Chicago* (1968), recounted his coverage of the 1968 Republican and Democratic National Conventions, the second of which was wrought with violent confrontations between antiwar protesters and Chicago police. Mailer ran unsuccessfully for mayor of New York in 1969 and then drew the ire of the growing feminist movement with his 1971 work *The Prisoner of Sex*.

By the mid-1970s, Mailer was receiving criticism for his slowdown in production, but he returned to the spotlight in 1979 by earning his second Pulitzer Prize with what was described as a nonfiction novel, titled *The Executioner's Song* (1979). The book was about the life of "spree killer" Gary Gilmore, who was in a Utah prison. Gilmore was sentenced to die, and he chose death by firing squad. His was the first American execution since the 1960s.

Mailer continued to explore new territory with his novel *Ancient Evenings* (1983), which took place in ancient Egypt. He then embarked on writing a screenplay for director Sergio Leone's *Once Upon a Time in America* (1984) before penning a detective story titled *Tough Guys Don't Dance* (1984) that was transformed into a film he directed himself.

Mailer then traveled to the Soviet Union, where he reported prophetically in 1984 that the Communist empire that many Americans still feared was on the verge of collapse. He revisited the history of the Cold War in a fictional account of life in the Central Intelligence Agency titled *Harlot's Ghost* (1992) and used unpublished documents from Soviet intelligence to craft an account of the life of Kennedy assassin Lee Harvey Oswald in *Oswald's Tale* (1995). Two years later his career took another twist when he wrote about the life of Jesus in *The Gospel According to the Son* (1997).

Mailer continued to be among the most prolific writers in the United States despite his advancing years and turbulent private life that now included six marriages. His last works were *The Castle in the Forest* (2007), a novel about the childhood of Nazi dictator Adolf Hitler as described by a demon, and *On God: An Uncommon Conversation*, published just weeks before his death in 2007.

Some Baby Boomers might have lost touch with Mailer by the early 1970s, but he focused on socially and politically relevant issues to the end.

See also Antiwar Movement; Hippie Movement; Kennedy, John F.; Vietnam War.

FURTHER READING

Mailer, Norman. *The Prisoner of Sex*. New York: Little, Brown and Company, 1971.
Mailer, Norman. *Armies of the Night: History as a Novel; the Novel as History*. New York: Plume Books, 1995 (reprint).
Mailer, Norman. *The Executioner's Song*. New York: Vintage, 1998 (reprint).

MALCOLM X (1925–1965) Among those in the first wave of black Baby Boomers, Malcolm X rivaled Martin Luther King Jr. as the most influential political figure.

Whereas King continued to preach patience and nonviolence, Malcolm X fueled and spoke to the anger and frustration felt by young Boomers over the slow pace of progress in the civil rights arena during the early-to-mid 1960s.

Malcolm X was born Malcolm Little in Omaha, Nebraska, on May 19, 1925, and was one of eight children. His father Earl was a politically active and outspoken Baptist minister greatly influenced by black separatist Marcus Garvey, who raised many an eyebrow during that era by proposing that American blacks return to Africa. Earl Little's civil rights activities so angered a white supremacist organization called the Black Legion that they sent death threats, forcing him to move to Lansing, Michigan. But the group traced the family to their new home and burned it to the ground. Two years later, Little was found dead near the town's trolley tracks. Although police ruled the house burning and Little's deaths as accidents, family members were certain that the Black Legion was to blame.

The incidents had a profound effect on Malcolm and the family. Mother Louise suffered from a breakdown and landed in a mental hospital. Malcolm and his siblings were separated and put into various foster homes and orphanages. The tragedies in his life had made him distrustful of white people. But despite the setbacks, he performed brilliantly in school, soaring to the top of his junior high class, until he confided to one of his favorite teachers that he yearned to be a lawyer, only to hear the reply that such was not a realistic goal for a young black man.

Disenchanted and poor, Malcolm dropped out of school and spent time in Boston and New York, where he survived through petty crime. As an older teenager, he was heavily involved in pedaling prostitution and drugs. He returned to Boston and was soon sent to jail for 10 years for burglary. He earned parole and was released after seven. He used that time in jail for self-reflection and education. His

Malcolm X (1925–1965) during a press conference for Dr. Martin Luther King Jr. in 1964. (Library of Congress)

brother Reginald, who had recently joined the Nation of Islam, visited him often in prison and discussed the conversion to Islam.

Malcolm began gravitating toward the teachings of Elijah Muhammad, founder of the Nation of Islam, who believed that white society purposely kept blacks from achieving success politically, professionally, and socially. Muhammad agreed with Garvey that blacks needed to establish their own state, although not through migration to Africa. Malcolm concurred, became a devoted follower of the Nation of Islam, and traded in his last name, which he considered a slave name. By 1952, he was calling himself Malcolm X.

Malcolm quickly ascended to become an influential member of the movement through his intelligence and eloquence. He gained enough trust and confidence from Muhammad to be placed in charge of establishing new mosques in various major cities, as well as earn the title of national spokesperson for the group. Malcolm X spread the message through print and electronic media sources. His magnetic personality helped increase Nation of Islam membership from 500 in 1952 to 30,000 in 1963. Although black Baby Boomers were still too young to grasp that message, many of them were certainly open to any black leader who would challenge King for their hearts and minds. The white power structure was giving ground to King and the civil rights movement only grudgingly in the early 1960s, leaving the door wide open for Malcolm X, who offered his view that if whites were not going to willingly give them equality, they should take it by force.

Malcolm X drew tremendous media attention. National newscaster Mike Wallace featured him in a weeklong television special in 1959 titled "The Hate That Hate Produced," which delved deep into the emergence of Malcolm X, as well as Nation of Islam philosophies and actions. His popularity had outgrown that of Muhammad, which motivated the FBI to spy on him and the Nation of Islam.

Malcolm X was now a bigger name in the Nation of Islam than Muhammad, but he continued to look up to his mentor until 1963, when it was revealed that the married Muhammad was having affairs with six different women who were involved with the group, a few of whom had given birth to his children. Among the teachings of Muhammad held sacred by Malcolm X had been celibacy in marriage. Malcolm X not only felt betrayed, but he believed he had betrayed the thousands of members he had lured into the Nation of Islam into following a false prophet. He quit the organization in 1964 and founded a new religious group called Muslim Mosque, Inc.

Malcolm X was growing as a man and as a religious leader. He experienced an awakening during a pilgrimage to Mecca, Saudi Arabia, during which time he developed positive relationships with people from different cultures for the first time. He exclaimed that it was there that he discovered blond-haired, blue-eyed men he could call his brothers. It imbued him with a rosier outlook on the future and changed his views about integration. He hoped to deliver a message of unity to all races.

However, Malcolm would not live to spread that message. After repeated attempts on his life, on February 21, 1965, three assassins rushed up on a stage in which he was speaking and shot him 15 times. The murderers were discovered to be members of the Nation of Islam.

The legacy of Malcolm X has arguably been stronger and more influential than his impact when he was alive. His original communication of anger, frustration, and resentment of the white power structure played a role in the upheaval in the black community during the mid-1960s. Led by young Baby Boomers, black rioting occurred in the ghettoes of every major American city. The two deadliest were just days apart in the summer of 1967 in Detroit and Newark.

The most publicized work on the life of Malcolm X was a movie directed by famed black director Spike Lee in 1992 simply titled *Malcolm X*.

See also Assassinations; King, Martin Luther, Jr.; Racism; Radicalism; Religion and Spirituality.

FURTHER READING

Malcolm X Official Website. http://www.malcolmx.com/.

Tyner, James. *The Geography of Malcolm X: Black Radicalism and the Remaking of American Space*. New York: Routledge, 2005.

X, Malcolm. *The Autobiography of Malcolm X (as told to Alex Haley)*. New York: Ballantine Books, 1992.

MARIJUANA No activity defined the generation gap between Baby Boomer teenagers and their parents with greater clarity in the late 1960s and early 1970s than the smoking of marijuana.

Ironically, few issues in recent years have challenged Baby Boomer parents, particularly those who smoked pot in their youth, more than their stand on marijuana when dealing with their own children.

Marijuana was known before the mid-1960s. The 1936 film *Reefer Madness* exaggerated its perceived negative effects to what today most consider a comical extent. Beatniks and others were known to partake in the drug in the late 1950s and early 1960s, but Americans did not take notice and become fearful until millions in the Baby Boomer generation began to embrace it as part of their lifestyles. The use of marijuana exploded on college campuses and in other areas in which youth congregated in the second half of the 1960s. The use became so widespread that marijuana became slang as "pot," "grass," and "weed."

The primary reason for the rapid increase in use of marijuana was social. Unlike cigarettes and to a great extent alcohol, marijuana is shared. Marijuana pipes, bongs, and cigarettes, commonly known as "joints," are passed around from one user to another.

There were also political and even spiritual aspects to the widespread use of marijuana during that era. The statement college students and older teenagers attempted to make was that they were different from their parents and others of the older generations, whose mind-altering drug of choice was alcohol. The young Baby Boomers considered marijuana a mellowing, peaceful, and thought-provoking drug rather than one that tends to bring out the aggressive side of human nature, such as beer or liquor do.

Many Baby Boomers argued that marijuana was physically and emotionally safe despite a lack of medical evidence. Critics and even those who stopped using marijuana claimed that it is emotionally addicting, possible physically addicting, and causes mild paranoia and slows or even kills motivation.

The growing casual use and popularity of marijuana near the end of the 1960s and into the 1970s and even early 1980s gave legitimacy to those charges. Teenagers, college students, and older Baby Boomers now in their twenties tended to smoke pot more extensively, often on a daily basis. A high percentage managed to go about their daily routines at school and work without negative influence, but the performance of many others was hindered greatly by the daily use of the drug. Those who managed to limit their marijuana smoking to occasional parties or weekends tended to be far less affected by it.

By the 1970s the debate over legalization of marijuana intensified. Many argued that pot is no more and perhaps even less dangerous than alcohol; others retorted that its use still results in negative consequences and should therefore remain illegal.

That debate continued through the new millennium with complete legalization still a pipe dream for those in the forefront of the fight in favor of it. More pertinent to the lives of Baby Boomers in more recent times has been confronting the possible and real use of marijuana by their own teenagers. Baby Boomers who never smoked pot or merely experimented with it and remained morally against it have found it quite easy to warn their offspring and threaten them with punishment. But Boomers who used marijuana in their own youth or smoked it later in life or even today have found it far more difficult to strongly dissuade them. Many adults have kept their past or present use of pot a secret from their kids. Others have acknowledged their use and claim that it is because of that experience that they are admonishing them to keep off the grass. Still others have given their kids the green light to experiment with marijuana but advise them to use it in moderation. Most Baby Boomers who smoked pot regularly or even still partake in the drug recognize its negative effects and are eager to pass on their knowledge and fears to their children.

A small percentage of Baby Boomers have remained pot smokers. According to surveys taken from 2002 to 2008 by the Substance Abuse and Mental Health Services Administration, the number of users age 50 and older in the prior year skyrocketed from 1.9 to 2.9 percent during that time period. The increase was most dramatic among those between 55 and 59 years of age. Their use jumped from 1.6 percent in 2002 to 5.1 percent in 2008.

Advocacy groups such as the National Organization to Reform Marijuana Laws (NORML) have fought for the legalization of the drug, and although Americans and their government are more likely to accept marijuana than they were before the widespread use in the 1960s, other more pressing issues have kept the pot debate out of the mainstream. The poor economy in more recent years has provided ammunition for NORML and others who state that legalizing marijuana would take profits away from street dealers and taxing it would provide badly needed revenue for the United States that could help the lives of its citizens.

The research findings of the medical benefits of marijuana have also changed the course of the debate and even resulted in the legalization of pot for medical use in more than a dozen states. It has been established that those suffering from the pain of other age-related physical issues have received relief through marijuana. Pot has been credited for relieving problems of aging such as glaucoma and macular degeneration. But it has also been warned that marijuana increases the risk of heart disease and can cause dizziness and cognitive impairment.

The subject of marijuana is far less controversial today than it was in the 1960s and early 1970s. That millions of Americans use it is greatly accepted by society, although it is likely that a stronger threat of legalization that is experienced today would heighten the debate and emotions on both sides of the argument.

See also Health and Health Care.

FURTHER READING

Associated Press. "Pot Use among Seniors Goes Up as Boomers Age." Msnbc.com. February 22, 2010. http://www.msnbc.msn.com/id/35519187/

Earleywine, Mitch. *Understanding Marijuana: A New Look at the Scientific Evidence.* New York: Oxford University Press, 2002.

Fox, Steve, Paul Armentano, and Mason Tvert. *Marijuana Is Safer So Why Are We Driving People to Drink?* White River Junction, VT: Chelsea Green, 2009.

Rosenthal, Ed, and Steve Kubby. *Why Marijuana Should be Legal*. Philadelphia: Running
    Press, 2003.

MARRIAGE AND INFIDELITY The difference between Baby Boomers and
their parents since the end of World War II has not been a willingness to marry; it
has been the commitment to remain wed.

Statistics have shown that the number of marriages has increased and that the
percentage of men and women tying the knot has remained steady over the years.
However, there is no doubt that young couples from previous generations accepted
the sanctity of the phrase "till death do you part" with greater fervor.

Several reasons have been cited for the failures of Baby Boomer marriages,
which have resulted in a skyrocketing divorce rate in the 1970s and 1980s that has
remained comparatively high ever since. Among them was that the commitment
to stay wed until death indeed separated husband and wife became far less of a
priority in more modern society. Another was the sexual revolution, which played
a role in making infidelity a more accepted and even desirous practice. In addition, the changing female roles in society, which included the mass integration of
women into the work force, resulted in some couples spending less time with one
another and drifting apart physically and emotionally.

Most Baby Boomers, even in urban black areas where single parenthood
reached epidemic proportions in later years, recall tremendous marital stability
growing up. Their parents argued and struggled more than what was portrayed
in the media, particularly on the antiseptic television programs of the 1950s and
early 1960s, but most Baby Boomer children recall their parents being part of
unthreatened marriages. Mothers and fathers generally believed in working out
their differences and infidelity was comparatively rare. Statistics showed that
more than 90 percent of all Baby Boomers of the first two decades after World
War II were raised in two-parent homes.

However, in the late 1960s, the first wave of Baby Boomers helped create a more
open society. The notion of one man for one woman before and after weddings was
placed into question. Millions of Boomers developed sexual relationships with
more than one partner because the birth control pill allowed women to consent to
men's advances without worrying about pregnancy, and changing morals made
sex before marriage a far more common practice. Such was not generally the case
among Baby Boomers in rural areas and small towns throughout the country, but
those from suburban and urban parts of the country had changed the landscape of
American sexuality.

The result was a dramatic shift in marital commitment by the early 1970s.
Many Boomers decided to live with their partners rather than marry them and
others who did exchange vows no longer considered infidelity or divorce indefen-
sible. The shedding of religious beliefs also played a role in the changing mindset
among Baby Boomers in comparison to their parents. Those of previous generations often believed that an allegiance to marital vows was a commitment to God.
But Boomers who were far less religious than their parents or no longer believed
in a higher power felt no moral or religious constraints to remain faithful.

The breakdown of so many marriages in American society caused many to search for answers. Studies showed that men often lost interest in their wives sexually over time and cheated on them for that reason. Studies also claimed that women more often partook in extramarital affairs to make an emotional connection elsewhere that they felt was lacking in their lives at home.

Another result of the increasing number of divorces was the growing number of marriage counselors and psychologists working with couples attempting to revive their relationships, although, ironically, studies showed that men and women working in those very vocations were more likely to get divorced than those from other medical fields. However, many husbands and wives took their suggestions such as trying new sexual approaches, taking vacations with and away from children, and working to get back in touch with each other's feelings. Those who were willing to put forth great effort to keep their marriages alive were far more likely to succeed.

Increased research into failing marriages and infidelity uncovered several flash points. Infidelity is most likely to occur after the first year of marriage, when the "honeymoon period" ends and the daily grind and routine of maintaining a strong, loving relationship begins. The birth of the first child can also damage a marriage. A baby not only takes away a mother's and sometimes a father's attention from the spouse, but giving birth also tends in some marriages to make a wife less attractive in the eyes of her husband.

However, most marriages survive those two obstacles. But the tedium and lack of spontaneity that often results once couples have remained together for five years or longer can prove harmful. Men and women are also susceptible to mid-life crises that can motivate them to seek love and companionship elsewhere.

Baby Boomer marriages in which the couples reached the age of 50 and had been wed for 25 years or longer were far more likely to survive. Many felt just as strongly about their spouses as they did on their wedding days. But even if the love and affection disappeared from those relationships, husbands and wives felt too entrenched in their marriages to seek the motivation to end it or have an affair. In other cases, unhappy life partners believed they would be lost emotionally and financially without their spouses.

The Baby Boomer generation has been greatly responsible for the increase in the number of failed marriages, but millions of Boomers have experienced happy wedded lives. A passionate, physical attraction and relationship with one's partner might dissipate with time, yet a love based on respect, admiration, and soulful connection can grow. The notion embraced by their parents that marriage is a sacred bond has not been lost on most from that generation, but the belief that divorce must be avoided at all costs, including the happiness of the couples involved, seems to no longer be valid in the hearts and minds of arguably most Baby Boomers.

See also Divorce; Family Life; Women's Movement.

Further Reading

Infidelity Statistics. http://www.infidelityfacts.com/index.htm

Weiss, Jessica. *To Have and to Hold: Marriage, the Baby Boom, and Social Change.* Chicago: University of Chicago Press, 2000.

M*A*S*H The television revolution launched by sitcom *All in the Family* in 1971 opened the door for social and political issues to be interspersed and even spotlighted within the comedy.

No show featured a stronger combination of ratings and critical success embracing the new wave of sitcom programming than *M*A*S*H* (1972–1983). The CBS hit was set in South Korea during that nation's war against North Korea and China in the early 1950s and revolved around the daily lives and challenges of an American medical unit.

The show was an extension of the highly successful and critically acclaimed 1970 film of the same name. And although it was indeed set during the Korean War, the program itself debuted during the late stages of the Vietnam War and its antiwar theme was pronounced.

The connection between *M*A*S*H* the movie and the television program and the controversial Vietnam War was undeniable. Baby Boomers who gave impetus to the antiwar movement about five years earlier and played a role in the fact that most had established a negative view of American involvement in Vietnam by that time embraced *M*A*S*H* for its humor and its message, which included biting antiwar commentary.

M*A*S*H was placed within what many consider to be the greatest sitcom lineup in television history, the Saturday night block that included *All in the Family*, *The Mary Tyler Moore Show*, and *The Bob Newhart Show*. The time slot and surrounding programming proved beneficial, and the combination of humor and taut drama set *M*A*S*H* apart from other shows of that or any other era.

Scene still from *M*A*S*H*. Shown: Mike Farrell (as Captain BJ Hunnicut), Jamie Farr (as Corporal/Sergeant Maxwell Q. Klinger), and Alan Alda (as Capt. Benjamin Franklin "Hawkeye" Pierce). (Photofest)

Several central characters were featured on the program, but the spotlight was often on chief surgeon Benjamin "Hawkeye" Pierce, played by Alan Alda. Pierce was fiercely against the war and greatly angered and disturbed by what he perceived as the senseless violence and killing. He was overcome by boredom during the long stretches of inactivity and overwhelmed by the tedious sessions of patching up young soldiers whose primary concerns just weeks or months earlier, he stated, was how to best cover up a hickey.

The only other featured characters to last the duration of the show were Max Klinger (Jamie Farr), who wore women's clothing in a vain attempt to be kicked out of the Army before eventually giving up the ruse, chaplain John Patrick Francis Mulcahy (William Christopher), and head nurse Margaret "Hot Lips" Houlihan (Loretta Swit), whose character evolved greatly during the course of the show. Houlihan was first characterized as dependent on others emotionally but grew into a strong, independent, and proud woman.

Her love interest in the first several years of the show was comedic foil Frank Burns (Larry Linville), an unskilled and undedicated doctor whose gung-ho militarism, blatant stupidity, and questionable morality were the target of humor. When Linville left the show after the fifth season, he was replaced by David Ogden Stiers, who portrayed wealthy, haughty surgeon Charles Emerson Winchester III. Stiers too evolved during the last six years of the program from an uncaring and egotistical socialite to a more sensitive and sympathetic character.

Pierce gained close friendships with two roommates, the first of which was the lighthearted, fun-loving John "Trapper" McIntyre (Wayne Rogers), who was followed after the third season by the more thoughtful B.J. Hunnicut (Mike Farrell).

The most shocking moment of the show's 12-year run revolved around commanding officer and surgeon Henry Blake (McLean Stevenson). The bumbling, disorganized Blake, an ardent civilian forced into the military, was beloved by everyone in camp aside from Houlihan and Burns. He was especially adored by his corporal, Walter O'Reilly (Gary Burghoff), whose psychic abilities earned him the nickname of "Radar." On the final episode of season three, Blake was given a fond farewell because Stevenson wanted to leave the show. Blake left for his Indiana home, but millions of television viewers were shocked at the end of the episode when a choked-up O'Reilly entered the operating room and announced that Blake's helicopter had been shot down over the Sea of Japan and that there were no survivors.

Stevenson was replaced by veteran actor Harry Morgan, who entered to play Colonel Sherman Potter. Potter provided a more serious characterization. Levelheaded and scrupulous, Potter became a mainstay on the program for the last nine seasons.

One criticism of *M*A*S*H* in its later years was that it became a bit too preachy in its antiwar stand, as well as other social and political issues, which some believed caused it to lose its humor. The laugh track that accompanied funny moments was removed a few years into the show's run, after which the program became even more innovative. One particular episode featured a clock remaining on the screen from beginning to end as the doctors frantically, yet skillfully, attempted to save the life of a soldier under that exact time constraint.

The program's popularity continued unabated. The two-hour series finale in 1983, which featured Hawkeye fighting an emotional and mental breakdown, remains the highest-rated show in American television history. It attracted more than 100 million viewers. *M*A*S*H* stayed in the Top 10 of the Nielsen Ratings every year but its debut in 1972 and in 1975. It peaked at number three in 1982.

M*A*S*H remains arguably the most critically acclaimed sitcom of all time. It received an Emmy Award for Outstanding Comedy Series in 1974 and might have received more had tremendous competition not been received from such stalwarts as *All in the Family* and *The Mary Tyler Moore Show*. Alda, Burghoff, Swit, and Morgan also won Emmys for their performances.

Ironically, the spinoff *AfterMASH*, which featured Morgan, Farr, and Christopher working in a hospital in the United States after the war, flopped miserably. It lasted three seasons with plummeting ratings before being dropped by CBS.

Unlike most shows of its era, the popularity of *M*A*S*H* did not die when it died. Syndication has allowed it to be embraced by new generations of viewers.

See also All in the Family; Television; Vietnam War.

FURTHER READING
Alda, Alan. *Things I Overheard While Talking to Myself*. New York: Random House, 2008.
Kalter, Suzy. *The Complete Book of M*A*S*H*. New York: Harry N. Abrams, 1988.

MEDIA PORTRAYAL OF The American mass media has always been far more intrigued with the sensational than with the ordinary. In a capitalistic society, such coverage of people and events sells more papers and commercial air time on television. Freedom of the press allows the media to portray any person or group any way it wishes short of slander.

One noteworthy example of sensationalism was the media portrayal of Baby Boomers in the late 1960s. Although comparatively few from that generation shed traditional lifestyles and the professional and financial goals usually associated with the "American Dream," the print and electronic media spotlighted the hippie movement, particularly in San Francisco, but also in other areas of the country. Boomer hippies were certainly colorful and they did create a counterculture that altered traditional outlooks on life, but most young people born in the half-decade after World War II and raised in small towns, rural areas, and even suburbia and urban centers followed the same path as did their parents with virtually no media attention.

The difference was that those who represented most of the Baby Boomer generation were not vocal in their desire for social change or were in favor of the status quo. The media gave tremendous attention not only to Boomers who flaunted society's social conventions and embraced nontraditional lifestyles, but also those who were outspoken in their criticism or actively involved in protest against government policies, such as those in regard to American military involvement in Vietnam and domestic race relations.

In the 1960s, the American media represented older generations. Many of its members did not understand or agree with the stands or reactions of Baby Boomers to controversial issues. Although the media generally reported objectively and even sympathetically on war protests and early civil rights demonstrations in which young Boomers were greatly involved, they began lambasting those from that generation when frustration over lack of progress in ending the war and wiping out racism and discrimination resulted in violence.

The first wave of black Baby Boomers was particularly chastised by the media in the mid-1960s and beyond. Boomers who responded to the call for nonviolent change by civil rights leader Martin Luther King Jr. through sit-ins and peaceful demonstrations were lauded at least by the northern media, but when frustration boiled over into mass rioting, which started in the Watts section of Los Angeles in 1965 and continued in major cities throughout the country for four years, young Boomers were for the most part greatly criticized by the media. Media reaction to the more violent approach taken by radical Baby Boomers in protesting the war, race relations, and even the capitalist system served to frighten the mainstream American citizenry.

However, times changed in the late 1960s and early 1970s. Journalists such as Hunter S. Thompson brought their own unique style to the field and sympathetically portrayed active left-wing and counterculture Boomers. The shift in overall opinion against American involvement in Vietnam also brought media understanding to causes embraced by antiwar Baby Boomers.

By the mid-1970s, when the war had ended, issues became far less divisive, and more of the youngest Baby Boomers had begun to join and influence the media. The spotlight dimmed on causes with which the most active in the generation had been involved, which in turn took the focus off them. But when many of the same Baby Boomers who had embraced pacifism and criticized the military in the 1960s called for swift and harsh retaliatory action upon the taking of American hostages by radical Iranian students in 1979, some in the media questioned whether they had grown conservative.

The embracing of conservatism and materialism in the 1980s also motivated media members, including Baby Boomers, to further scrutinize the generation. Boomers who had eschewed the pursuit of financial wealth and material goods two decades earlier were now playing a role in the "yuppie" (young, upwardly mobile professional) movement, although the trend toward conservatism and materialism among those of that generation was generally spearheaded by those born in the late 1950s and early 1960s.

However, by the 1990s, the media had greatly accepted that Baby Boomers were bound to have changed over the past two or three decades. Retrospective pieces were written or broadcast by media members, most of whom by that time were Baby Boomers, about the changing attitudes and priorities of those from that generation. They compared the lifestyles and outlooks of teenage Boomers of the 1960s and early 1970s with those of their offspring who were now of similar ages.

The growing unpopularity of the war in Iraq by 2005 gave the media another opportunity to compare Baby Boomers of the 1960s with those of that time. Despite the fact that about the same percentage of Boomers were against the

American handling of the war in Iraq as they were the country's involvement in Vietnam forty years earlier, Boomers were distinctly less actively critical. The media questioned why Baby Boomers who had grown weary and even angry over President George W. Bush's policies in regard to the Iraq War were not organizing or becoming involved in protests whereas demonstrations against Vietnam War policy numbering a half-million people, most of them Baby Boomers, were not uncommon from 1967 to 1971.

In more recent years, the media began to focus on the oldest of Baby Boomers reaching retirement age and how the huge number of Boomers in their sixties and seventies and beyond will affect the Social Security system and businesses such as nursing homes and assisted living facilities.

See also Alternative Lifestyles; Civil Rights Movement; Conservatism; Consumerism; Hippie Movement; Racism; Radicalism; Thompson, Hunter S.; Vietnam War.

FURTHER READING

Cravit, David. *The New Old: How the Boomers Are Changing Everything . . . Again.* Toronto: ECW Press, 2008.

Lipschultz, Jeremy Harris, and Michael L. Hilt. *Mass Media, an Aging Population and the Baby Boomers.* Mahwah, NJ: Lawrence Erlbaum Associates, 2005.

MOORE, MARY TYLER (1936–) The television personality who best characterized the evolving role and goals of women in society in the early 1970s was actress Mary Tyler Moore. Her portrayal of Mary Richards in the *Mary Tyler Moore Show* (1970–1977) was among the first and easily the most noteworthy in television history of a working woman not defined by her relationship with a man.

Moore was born on December 29, 1936, in Brooklyn, New York, but moved with her family to California at the age of eight. Although her childhood was troubled—partly because of her mother's alcoholism—her attractiveness, talent, and bubbly personality landed her roles as a dancer and actor as a young adult. She was just 18 when she secured work in commercials as a dancing elf for Hotpoint appliances. She earned a recurring role as a service girl for detective Richard (Sam) Diamond on *Richard Diamond, Private Detective* in the late 1950s.

Moore received her first major break in entertainment in 1961 when she won the role of Laura Petrie, wife of comedy writer Rob Petrie, in *The Dick Van Dyke Show.* Moore and the highly acclaimed ensemble cast, which included Dick Van Dyke, earned several Emmys for their work on the show, which was considered more sophisticated than other sitcoms of its time. Moore caused an uproar when she wore slacks on the show. Until that time, married women on television were always seen in dresses. Moore won an Emmy for Outstanding Continued Performance by a Lead Actor in a Comedy Series in 1964 and 1966.

Moore embarked on a career as a movie actress after *The Dick Van Dyke Show* went off the air in 1966. Her most significant movie role between her two television series was as a simple-minded aspiring actress in the movie *Thoroughly Modern Millie*, which starred Julie Andrews (1967). Moore dabbled in dramatic acting as well during the late 1960s before accepting the role of Mary Richards.

The Mary Tyler Moore Show was produced by MTM Productions, a company she had formed with second husband Grant Tinker, who later gained more success as a producer of other successful programs. Set in Minneapolis, the sitcom featured Richards as a producer for the lowest-rated television news show in town. Although she displayed aptitude as a comedic actress, Moore greatly served as the straight woman surrounded by a cast of such funny and eccentric characters as best friend Rhoda Morgenstern and anchorman Ted Baxter. The humor on the show revolved around the relationship between the characters with Richards often solving problems for and between them. *The Mary Tyler Moore Show* earned seven Emmy nominations for Outstanding Comedy Series, winning the award in 1975, 1976, and 1977. Moore won Emmys for Best Lead Actor in a Comedy Series in 1973, 1974, and 1976.

Typecast as Mary Richards, Moore struggled after the run of *The Mary Tyler Moore Show* ended in 1977, but she rebounded by earning an Academy Award nomination for her portrayal of a cold mother who resents her younger son after her favorite son dies in a boating accident in the critically acclaimed film *Ordinary People* (1980). Moore continued to garner critical acclaim in television movies such as *Lincoln* (1988), in which she played troubled Mary Todd Lincoln, and as a baby smuggler in *Stolen Babies* (1993), for which she won her sixth Emmy.

Moore suffered through great tragedy in her personal life, including the accidental shooting death of son Richie. Sister Elizabeth died of a drug overdose in 1978, and brother John died of cancer after a failed assisted suicide attempt. Moore herself overcame a bout with alcoholism in the 1970s and was later diagnosed with diabetes. An active spokesperson for animal rights and the battle against diabetes, Moore divorced Tinker in 1981 and married Robert Levine.

See also Movies; Television.

FURTHER READING

Alley, Robert S., and Brown, Irby B. *Love Is All Around: The Making of the Mary Tyler Moore Show*. Brooklyn, NY: Delta, 1989.
Moore, Mary Tyler. *After All*. New York: Dell, 1996.
Moore, Mary Tyler: *Growing Up Again: Life, Loves, and Oh Yeah, Diabetes*. New York: St. Martin's Press, 2009.

MOVIES Most Baby Boomers recall with fondness that as children the iconic film *The Wizard of Oz* (1939) was shown annually on television around Thanksgiving or Christmas. Boomers younger and older waited with great anticipation for its broadcast every year.

The movie has been cherished by Baby Boomers for more than a half-century. Although it was produced in 1939, they embraced it as one of their own. For Boomers, its viewing was an event. Once the home video era began, kids and adults could watch *The Wizard of Oz* any time they wanted, which made it less special.

Much of the dialogue from the film seeped into the American lexicon as it grew in popularity in the 1960s. It received far more critical acclaim than viewership when it was first released. Nearly all Baby Boomers can such identify lines as "Follow the yellow brick road," "We're off to see the wizard," "Lions and tigers and bears, oh my!," "We're not in Kansas anymore," and "There's no place like home."

Such movies as *The Wizard of Oz* and *Gone with the Wind* (1939) gained iconic status among Baby Boomers although they were produced well before anyone from that generation was produced. One film that falls into that same category that was released around the same time the first Boomers were born was *It's a Wonderful Life* (1946).

The cherished Christmas tale starring the beloved Jimmy Stewart embraces the notion that people are generally good and that human relationships are far more important than material possessions. That would be a philosophy put into practice by millions among the first wave of Baby Boomers in the 1960s and early 1970s.

Some movies hold a special place in the hearts of Baby Boomers because they elicit fond memories of times spent with parents or siblings. Millions of families flocked to see the popular musicals of the mid-1960s such as *Mary Poppins* (1964), *The Sound of Music* (1965), and *My Fair Lady* (1964). However, the musical Baby Boomers embrace as the first statement of their generation is the movie *A Hard Day's Night* (1964). The immense popularity of the Beatles, who had taken the United States by storm just a few months earlier, warranted the production of a film starring the rock-and-roll giants. The documentary style with Beatles' musical performances interspersed within the dialogue made the movie a huge success.

The Graduate (1967) was another film Baby Boomers flocked to see. They enjoyed the soundtrack produced by folk rock duo Simon and Garfunkel and identified with the main character, Benjamin Braddock, who was played by emerging movie star Dustin Hoffman, a confused recent college graduate who is exploited unwittingly by members of the older generation and seduced by the wife of his father's business partner before falling in love with her daughter. Boomers embraced what they perceived as the message of the movie, which was the corrupt nature of the older generation and the choices many in the younger generation were making against joining the sterile corporate world.

The cult film *Easy Rider* (1969), starring Peter Fonda, Dennis Hopper, and an emerging Jack Nicholson, took eschewing of the traditional American dream a step further and was also appreciated by many Baby Boomers. The story revolves around motorcycle-riding hippies and their adventures and marijuana-induced discussions about their love for counterculture values.

By the 1970s, most Boomers were of movie-going age. Films of that decade became more disturbing. *The Godfather* (1972) and *The Godfather II* (1974) told a violent tale of a mafia family and remain two of the most critically acclaimed films of all time. Although they made no specific statement about the Baby Boomer world, they are both movies that millions from that generation will remember for the rest of their lives.

Also memorable was *The Exorcist* (1973), which centered on a young teenage girl whose body and soul had been taken over by the devil. Millions of Baby Boomers flocked to the theater to see this film, which many believe was the most frightening yet critically successful horror flick in American movie history.

The era of disturbing films continued in 1975 with *Jaws*, the story of a New England Amity Island where the summer tourism economy is threatened by a killer shark in its waters. While the beast closes on its prey to a haunting, threatening tune that has become iconic in American movie lore, and then chomps on its doomed victims, the mayor of Amity Island who is concerned only with financial considerations continues to deny there is a problem. The movie captures the belief of many Baby Boomers in the greed of the older generation and political leaders.

An even more unsettling movie from that year was *One Flew Over the Cuckoo's Nest*, an adaptation of a book written by Ken Kesey, who gained fame in the 1960s as a guru of psychedelia and LSD use. The film, which won Academy Awards for Best Picture, Best Actor (Jack Nicholson), and Best Actress (Louise Fletcher) revolves around the lives and treatment of patients in a mental institution in the fall of 1963. The main character is a misfit and prison castoff who does not belong there and leads a rebellion against the oppressive and dictatorial head nurse. The movie serves as an indictment of the state of mental health care institutions at that time.

The late 1970s also featured several movies that brought back haunting, although recent, reminders of the just-concluded Vietnam War. Many Baby Boomers thought that the antiwar themes and the depiction of the brutalities of war and emotional distress brought to veterans in films such as *Coming Home* (1978), *The Deer Hunter* (1978), *Apocalypse Now* (1979), and later *Platoon* (1986) justified their own antiwar activities in the 1960s and early 1970s.

Baby Boomers of all ages also felt engaged in movies of the 1970s and 1980s that certainly had no political or social messages. Absurd comedies became prevalent as the youngest Baby Boomers reached their teenage years and beyond. Silly flicks such as *Monty Python and the Holy Grail* (1975) and *Airplane!* (1980) quickly became classics. Meanwhile, the magical tale of an extraterrestrial that visits a typical American family titled *ET* (1982) enraptured some Baby Boomers of all ages.

One movie that provided social commentary and entertainment for the last wave of Baby Boomers was John Hughes's *The Breakfast Club* (1985), which spoke about the unhealthy nature of cliques and social stratification in American high schools.

Baby Boomers of all ages who were now parents became familiar with dozens of children's animated films in the 1990s and beyond. Among the most popular were *The Lion King* (1994), *Toy Story* (1995), *Shrek* (2001), *Monsters Inc.* (2001), *Ice Age* (2002), *Finding Nemo* (2003), *WALL-E* (2008), and *Up* (2009).

See also Hoffman, Dustin; Kesey, Ken; Nicholson, Jack; Rock-and-Roll; Vietnam War.

FURTHER READING

Friedman, Lester, ed. *American Cinema of the 1970s: Themes and Variations*. New Brunswick, NJ: Rutgers University Press, 2007.

N

NADER, RALPH (1934–) In the 1960s, Ralph Nader emerged as the leading consumer advocate, a hero who would serve as a watchdog against big business, along with those working for several public interest groups that he founded. He was a model of idealism for many Baby Boomers. But four decades later, some of those same Baby Boomers were blaming Nader for the defeat of Democratic presidential candidate Al Gore in the contested 2000 election against George W. Bush.

Nader was born on February 27, 1934, in the small town of Winsted, Connecticut. He was the son of Lebanese immigrants who ran a restaurant and bakery. The idea of becoming a lawyer who worked for the American people was instilled in him at an early age. His parents even ran lively seminars in the home about the duties of citizenship in a democracy during which the meaning of justice was often broached.

Upon the completion of his studies at the Gilbert School in 1951, Nader enrolled at the Woodrow Wilson School of International Affairs at Princeton University. He majored in government and economics and proved to be a brilliant student, graduating magna cum laude in 1955. He then attended Harvard Law School, from which he graduated with honors. Nader also worked as an editor of the *Harvard Law Review*.

Nader quickly forged a career and set up his legal practice. But he became increasingly aware and angered about what he perceived as the uncaring attitudes of American corporate leaders and the detrimental results of their actions. He began to express his dissatisfaction with what he saw as abuse of power in the world of big business. Nader thrust himself into the spotlight by authoring *Unsafe at Any Speed* (1965), which roundly criticized the automobile industry and General Motors particularly for its alleged poor safety standards and manufacturing of unsafe cars. Young Baby Boomers applauded him for the book and embraced him further when General Motors was forced to apologize to Nader before a nationally televised U.S. Senate committee hearing for hiring private detectives to harass him.

As the 1960s and 1970s progressed, some young Baby Boomers joined what was termed as "Nader's Raiders," a band of progressive and active lawyers

Consumer advocate Ralph Nader speaks during an interview on September 10, 1975. (Library of Congress)

and researchers who embarked on a campaign against the neglect of corporate America, as well as the government. The group uncovered the existence of industrial hazards, pollution, unsafe products, and alleged government disregard for consumer safety laws. Nader is widely accepted as the founder of the consumer rights movement and played a critical part in the creation of the U.S. Environmental Protection Agency, as well as other consumer advocate agencies and legislation such as the Occupational Safety and Health Administration, the Freedom of Information Act, and the Consumer Product Safety Commission.

Nader eventually became more directly involved in politics. He founded a group called Public Citizen, which pushed for the reform of the American political system. He grew increasingly disenchanted with the Democratic and Republican parties for their dependence on wealthy contributors and ties to corporate America. He embarked on a token run for president in 1996 as a candidate for the Green Party but appeared on the ballot in only some states and made a limited number of public appearances.

Many Baby Boomers who embraced Nader in the 1960s and 1970s, as well as other staunch Democrats, became angry at him in 2000. After a far more energetic campaign for president that year as a Green Party candidate, he won nearly 3 million votes nationwide. Although he did not come close to winning any states, he substantially affected the outcome of the closest race in American history. Critics who believed Nader took votes mostly away from Democratic candidate Al Gore, particularly in razor-thin defeats in New Hampshire and Florida, claimed he inadvertently gave Republican George W. Bush the presidency. Some progressives criticized so-called liberals for accepting the two-party lock on power and wanting to keep the best candidate out of the running and from even debating the major-party candidates simply because he could not win. Nader was using the campaign process, in which he spoke to enthusiastic crowds at campaign stops across the country, to move the major-party candidates to more progressive positions.

Nader faded from attention after the 2000 election, although he ran for president as an independent in 2004 and 2008. A documentary film about him, *An Unreasonable Man*, came out in 2006. Throughout his career, he has been a prolific author and co-author with publications such as *The Ralph Nader Reader* (2000) and *Crashing the Party: Taking on the Corporate Government in an Age of Surrender* (2002). His first novel, *Only the Super-Rich Can Save Us!* (2009), was about the secret collaboration of 15 wealthy people, led by industrialist Warren Buffet, who took action after visiting New Orleans in the devastating wake of Hurricane Katrina.

Now in his seventies, Nader continues his non-stop work for social and economic justice, although many of his tremendously important contributions to American society are uncelebrated.

See also Elections; Environmental Movement; Idealism; Political Participation.

FURTHER READING

Marcello, Patricia Cronin. *Ralph Nader: A Biography*. Westport, CT: Greenwood Press, 2004.
Martin, Justin. *Nader: Crusader, Spoiler, Icon*. New York: Basic Books, 2002.
Nader, Ralph. *Unsafe at Any Speed*. New York: Grossman Publishers, 1965.
Nader, Ralph. *Only the Super-Rich Can Save Us!* New York: Seven Stories Press, 2009.

NAMATH, JOE (1943–) Football legend Joe Namath typified the rebelliousness of the late 1960s and the self-indulgence of the 1970s with great flair. "Broadway" Joe was an anti-establishment hero to millions.

The New York Jets quarterback was admired by young Baby Boomers for his charisma and devil-may-care approach to life. He was best known for making good on his legendary off-the-cuff prediction in 1969 that his team would beat the powerful Baltimore Colts in Super Bowl III.

Namath was born and raised in a predominantly African American section of Beaver Falls, Pennsylvania, in a region that later became known as the "Cradle of Quarterbacks" after having produced fellow Pro Football Hall of Famers George

Blanda, Johnny Unitas, Dan Marino, and Joe Montana. Namath proved himself a tremendously versatile and talented athlete, excelling in football, baseball, and basketball at Beaver Falls High School. He turned down a baseball career for a football scholarship at the University of Alabama.

Namath's outspokenness and unwillingness to obey team rules became pronounced during his four years playing for legendary Crimson Tide coach Bear Bryant, who nevertheless proclaimed him the best athlete who ever graced the Alabama gridiron. Namath was benched late in his junior season for breaking curfew and would sometimes argue with bigoted teammates from that Deep South school about race relations during the height of the civil rights movement, several years before the team became integrated.

Namath led the Crimson Tide to a 10-1 record as a mere sophomore by throwing for 1,192 yards and 12 touchdowns, but his senior season was marred by a knee injury that would plague him for the rest of his football career. However, his physical limitations did not prevent the Jets from signing him to a three-year contract in January 1965. Namath showed his rebelliousness by signing with a team from the upstart American Football League (AFL), which had been competing with the well-established National Football League (NFL) for five years. Hiring Namath away from the NFL was considered a coup.

By 1967, Namath had blossomed into a star. He threw for a whopping 4,007 yards and 26 touchdowns that season and then passed the Jets to the AFL title the following year. But the league was considered vastly inferior to the NFL, whose Packers had easily captured the first two Super Bowls. The Colts had won all but one game in 1969 and were expected to handily dispose of the Jets. But when asked for his prediction, Namath coolly guaranteed that the Jets would win. Sure enough, in arguably the most stunning upset in football history, his poise, accuracy, and guile shone through in a 16-7 victory.

By that time, Namath was rivaling Muhammad Ali as the most famous athlete in the United States. Many young Baby Boomers were attracted to his freewheeling lifestyle. He not only grew his hair long and wore a mustache and long sideburns, but he was thought of as an antihero, a symbol of change from the conservative and staid athletes of the past. His flamboyant personality and rugged good looks thrust him into full-fledged sex symbol status.

Although his football career peaked in 1969 and his wobbly knees prevented him from maximizing his talents, Namath remained a hero to Baby Boomers and others throughout the first half of the following decade. He endorsed shaving cream and was unafraid to potentially tarnish his image by wearing panty hose in a television commercial. He dabbled in acting, furthering his image as a Renaissance man, even appearing as himself in an episode of iconic Baby Boomer sitcom *The Brady Bunch*.

Boomers were particularly impressed when he stood firm, at least temporarily, to the establishment in the early 1970s. NFL Commissioner Pete Rozelle demanded that Namath sell his New York nightclub, Bachelors III, which the former claimed was frequented by gamblers. Rozelle threatened to suspend Namath from football if he did not comply. Namath refused at first and announced his retirement, but his love for the game and commitment to his team motivated him to sell the establishment and return to the Jets.

Namath played through 1977, finishing his career with the Los Angeles Rams. Although he continued to be a prolific passer, his teams never matched the success enjoyed by the Jets of the late 1960s. He missed nearly half of the games his team played between 1970 and 1973 with knee problems.

Although Namath had a short stint as an NFL color commentator, including one year on *Monday Night Football*, he was often condemned for his overcritical style and lambasting of the current crop of players.

In December 2003, the reputation of the aging Namath took a hit when he publicly asked attractive interviewer Suzy Kolber to kiss him during coverage of a Jets game on cable network ESPN. He later apologized and soon admitted to being an alcoholic, after which he entered an outpatient treatment program.

Like many entertainers of the 1960s, particularly in the music industry, fame and admiration were fleeting for Namath. But in his heyday, no athlete was more admired for his talent, flamboyance, rebelliousness, and guts for playing a dangerous game in pain.

See also Team Sports.

FURTHER READING
Kriegel, Mark. *Namath: A Biography*. New York: Viking Press, 2004.

NICHOLSON, JACK (1937–) Although actor Jack Nicholson was born nearly a decade before the oldest Baby Boomer, the generation regards him as one of its own.

One of the most famous and accomplished film actors of the 20th century, Nicholson expressed their angst and rebelliousness in highly acclaimed roles, particularly early in his career, before mellowing to play more thoughtful characters with equal success in the 1980s and beyond.

Known for his reclusive nature and shunning of the spotlight, except when seen on national television occupying a front-row seat at Los Angeles Lakers basketball games, Nicholson was destined for an unusual upbringing from his conception. Mother June was a 17-year-old dancer when she was impregnated by a married thespian named Don Furcillo-Rose. The two wed anyway in secret, whereupon June moved in with mother Ethel in Neptune, New Jersey, and delivered the baby. June (fine) was passed off as Nicholson's sister while Ethel raised him. His real grandfather, John Joseph Nicholson, raised him as a son until his death in 1955.

Nicholson embraced acting with far greater passion than he did his studies at Manasquan High School in the New Jersey town of the same name. He starred in several school plays before a trip to California at age 17 convinced him to throw all of his energies into acting. He trained with the Players Ring Theater and landed parts on such popular television series such as *Bronco* and *Hawaiian Eye*, but his movie career was slow to develop. He appeared in more than a dozen films before his embracing of the counterculture of the 1960s led to a professional breakthrough. He wrote a movie about LSD experiences called the *The Trip* (1967) and a freak-out flick starring the pop group the Monkees titled *Head*

(1968). During that period, he befriended fellow actors Peter Fonda and Dennis Hopper, who asked him to portray a southern lawyer in their own film project, *Easy Rider* (1969). Nicholson accepted and played the role well enough to earn an Academy Award nomination. His professional fortunes began to soar.

Nicholson was nominated for his first Best Actor Oscar for his role as disaffected musical prodigy Bobby Dupea in *Five Easy Pieces* (1970), which was highlighted by an iconic diner scene in which he engages in a verbal confrontation with a waitress tied to strict ordering rules. In the climax of the scene, which served as a metaphor for the rebelliousness of the young Baby Boomer generation, Dupea tells the waitress to hold the chicken—between her knees. Informed that he and his group would have to leave, Dupea swats everything off the table and onto the floor.

Unafraid to take chances, Nicholson followed by playing a lecherous skirt chaser in the controversial *Carnal Knowledge* (1971) before earning a Best Actor Oscar nomination for his portrayal of a tough officer giving an arrested man a final fling on the way to jail in *The Last Detail* (1973). Nicholson remained hot, snagging yet another Best Actor nomination for his role as a private detective in the highly acclaimed *Chinatown* (1974).

In his next major role, Nicholson established himself as one of the finest actors in the country. He played free-spirited petty crook and brawler Randall P. McMurphy, who was placed unfairly in an insane asylum in *One Flew Over the Cuckoo's Nest* (1975). Nicholson displayed a zest and passion for the role, showing his ability as a comedic and dramatic actor that finally resulted in him receiving his first Best Actor Oscar. His performance was made even more remarkable by the fact that he had just learned the truth about his family. His real mother died of cancer in 1963 and his grandmother, whom he thought was his mother, died in 1970. The shocking truth was revealed to him through a phone call to his real father, but Nicholson would not allow that relationship to flourish.

However, Nicholson did match the free spirit in his private life that he most often displayed on the screen. He was married to actress Sandra Knight for a short time during the 1960s and spent 16 years in a relationship with actress Anjelica Houston but has also been linked romantically to several actresses, including Lara Flynn Boyle, who is 30 years his junior. Nicholson fathered children with actresses Knight, Rebecca Broussard, and Winnie Hollman.

Throughout the 1970s, Nicholson remained choosy about the jobs he would take, turning down lead actor roles in such highly successful films as *The Godfather, The Sting, Apocalypse Now*, and *Coming Home*. He finally accepted the part of haunted hotel caretaker Jack Torrance in *The Shining* (1980) before inviting controversy by taking on a role in *Reds* (1981), a film sympathetic to the Russian communist movement. That movie was released just after the presidential election of Ronald Reagan—a most conservative time in U.S. history.

Nicholson continued to further his reputation two years later, earning a Best Supporting Actor Oscar for his portrayal of a flirtatious former astronaut in *Terms of Endearment* (1983) and then earning Academy Award nominations for his roles as a hit man in *Prizzi's Honor* (1985) and drifter in *Ironweed* (1987). He received critical acclaim as a hardened military man in *A Few Good Men* (1992), but perhaps the most beloved performance of his career was as lonely obsessive-compulsive Melvin Udall in *As Good As It Gets* (1997), a Best Picture Oscar winner that gave Nicholson his third Best Actor award.

Nicholson's link to the Baby Boomer generation continued to be forged well into his sixties, particularly in his Oscar-nominated role as a shy, quiet widower in *About Schmidt* (2002) and as a terminally ill man seeking one last fling with life in *The Bucket List* (2007). Just like Boomers who have vowed to remain vibrant in retirement, Nicholson continued to portray characters with a lust for life.

See also Movies.

FURTHER READING

McDougal, Dennis. *Five Easy Decades: How Jack Nicholson Became the Biggest Movie Star in Modern Times*. Hoboken, NJ: Wiley, 2008.
McGilligan, Patrick. *Jack's Life: A Biography of Jack Nicholson*. New York: W.W. Norton and Company, 1996.

P

PARENTING The philosophies of parenting have certainly not been uniform during any era in American history. Individual parents have embraced their own methods based on personal choice. But the overall trend toward less discipline began when the first Baby Boomers were in their youths and continued when they became parents.

However, parenting has changed during that time. Although the parents of Baby Boomers and Boomer parents themselves have generally espoused greater nurturing than did parents of generations past, more recent trends have resulted in the development of a two-way communication process with children. Baby Boomer parents have tended to accept the benefits of talking with their kids rather than at them. That philosophy has come under criticism by those who believe it fails to establish parental control in the relationship.

Couples married at a younger age and had more children during the period after World War II than they had in previous generations. Millions of families moved from the cities to the suburbs. Many parents subscribed to the theories of pediatrician Benjamin Spock, who rejected the methods of the past, which included rigid feeding, bathing, and sleeping schedules and supported less discipline and greater displays of affection.

Young Baby Boomers of various backgrounds in the 1950s and 1960s were being parented differently. Studies found that middle class parents during that time were more likely to follow Spock's teachings and train their children in achievement and personal responsibility, whereas working class parents most often demanded obedience and tended to rely more on corporal punishment for discipline.

The first wave of Baby Boomers was raised almost exclusively by their mothers. The first two decades after World War II featured mostly working dads and stay-at-home moms. However, during the 1960s some believed American parents had grown too permissive and allowed too much freedom of thought and action. Some feared that parents were being taken advantage of by their children, who thought they could get away with negative behavior without consequence.

But although the generation gap of that period was well publicized, it has also been offered that there was a greater gap between Baby Boomers of different economic and social classes than there was between Baby Boomers and their parents.

By the late 1970s, parents, including young Baby Boomers, had grown far more protective of their children. Anxieties over various dangers, including crime in the streets and the threat of other potential harm that parents feared could be inflicted upon their kids, resulted in baby-proof homes and the use of car seats and bicycle helmets. The increased number of mothers in the workforce and fewer children in American families played roles in the establishment of greater structure in the lives of youngsters. Unsupervised play and outdoor activities declined significantly, particularly by the mid-1980s, because of heightened parental concern and the fact that there were simply fewer kids with whom to play.

Baby Boomer parents in more recent years have become far more likely to consult with professionals to gain a greater sense of expertise about rearing children. The decreased number of children in American families has generally resulted in more attention paid to each and a greater drive to maximize the potential of all. But parents have also been forced to sacrifice one-on-one time with their children because women have generally accepted the concept of maximizing their professional potential and economic reality has most often forced them both to work. The result is that many children of Baby Boomer parents and even grandparents in more recent years have had every event and activity planned for them throughout the course of a day, week, or even school semester. It has been claimed that the proliferation of planned activities has placed more pressure on children, many of who have also felt a greater burden to excel in school.

Baby Boomers have lamented that when they were children, the neighborhood was filled with kids playing any number of activities until sunset and that such is no longer the case. But many of those same Baby Boomers have grown hyperprotective of their children because of the heightened fears of perceived dangers in the streets. Several highly publicized incidents in more recent decades in which children were kidnapped or killed have driven parents to make certain their kids are within eyesight of them or other trusted adults.

The increased number of one-parent households over the past several decades has also altered philosophies and effectiveness of parenting. Studies have shown that approximately one half of all of today's children will have spent at least some time in a one-parent household. The divorce rate among Baby Boomer parents raised significantly over that of the previous generation. So did instances of single parenthood by choice, which has also limited the quality time that children can spend with their parents.

However, in the end, the energy, commitment, and love with which Baby Boomers and others have put into their parenting has played a much larger role in the success of their efforts than have any mitigating factors. Studies have shown that in more recent years, fathers in particular have dedicated themselves to spending more time with their kids.

See also Divorce; Dr. Spock; Family Life; Games.

PARENTS, RELATIONSHIP WITH The expression that emerged from the 1960s to describe the relationship between young Baby Boomers and their parents was "generation gap." That gap has been closed greatly since that time as Boomers and their parents gained years and perspective, but it was certainly an accurate description at the time.

The title lyrics sung by folk artist and songwriter Bob Dylan in the 1960s' song "The Times They Are a-Changing" spoke of the winds of change in many aspects of society, but particularly the relationships and worldviews of Baby Boomers coming of age and their parents, who represented what he considered to be a dying breed.

A generation gap has existed to some degree between teenagers and their parents throughout American history. Generally, the absolute authority of the parent had been unquestioned. Although there were exceptions, a teenager could generally disagree with, but not argue with, an order given by a parent.

The acceptance of questioning authority in all forms, including parents, became popularized around the mid-1960s. Some Baby Boomers were less likely to adhere to their demands simply because they were authority figures. Many Boomers decided they did not want to live their lives as had their parents, whom they considered unhappy and unfulfilled in their roles as workers inside and outside of their homes. Others perceived their parents as hypocrites. For instance, millions of parents strongly requested their teenagers not to smoke marijuana, yet they themselves drank alcohol.

Many Baby Boomers maintained a symbiotic relationship with their parents through the 1960s and early 1970s, yet others established wide gaps in several issues, including fashion, politics, and lifestyle. The first wave of Boomer boys began growing their hair long after the Beatles arrived in the United States in 1964, much to the dismay of their parents. Baby Boomers during the next decade began taking dressing down to an extreme, which also sometimes angered their parents, and listened to rock music their parents neither enjoyed nor understood.

The gap often grew in regard to political thought. More conservative parents were likely to back the growing American involvement in Vietnam, at least until the overall view of the war shifted in 1968, whereas many of their kids had grown vehemently against it well before that time. Black Baby Boomers were also in conflict with their parents on the subject of the civil rights movement. Although blacks of all generations sought equality and an end to racial discrimination, many in the younger generation grew impatient with the pace of change and espoused a militancy and penchant to riot to force change, philosophies often not shared by their parents.

Meanwhile, many Baby Boomer teens began to question the American dream that those of previous generations had chased and embraced. Some Boomers, mostly from white middle-class or upper middle-class backgrounds, pursued hippie or other alternative lifestyles that eschewed the pursuit of money and material possessions. Conflict often resulted with parents, who were sometimes forced to fund the necessities of life for teenagers who rejected the capitalist system and the notion of financial security.

The relationship between parents and Baby Boomers born in the late 1950s and early 1960s mellowed as the turbulence of the latter decade ended. Although the increased use of marijuana and other issues remained in contention, the younger Baby Boomers were more likely to accept a more traditional path in regard to personal lifestyle in the 1970s, whereas many adults had grown to accept their taste in clothing and music. Meanwhile, the first wave of Baby Boomers were reaching their mid-twenties and had grown more understanding of their parents and more protective of them as they aged.

By the late 1980s and 1990s, millions of Baby Boomers encountered the quandary of how to take care of parents who could no longer live on their own. The advent of assisted living eventually gave them a more favorable, but far more expensive option, than nursing homes. Boomers were forced to weigh the strong desire and even insistence of parents who yearned to remain in their homes with the possibility that they were no longer capable of taking care of themselves. Many Boomers moved in with their parents or invited their parents to live with them. A 2006 study from the University of Southern California revealed that Baby Boomers born in the 1950s and 1960s were more committed to caring for their aging parents than were those from the previous generation.

Although the strong disagreements over several issues between millions of Baby Boomers and their parents in the 1960s ruined some relationships forever, most patched up their differences and developed a bond of love and respect that continued as long as those of the older generation have lived.

See also Alternative Lifestyles; The Beatles; Civil Rights Movement; Dylan, Bob; Hippie Movement; Rock-and-Roll.

FURTHER READING

Moschis, George, and Anil Mathur. *Baby Boomers and Their Parents*. Ithaca, NY: Paramount Market Publishing, 2007.
Seniorjournal.com. "Baby Boomers More Caring of Aging Parents Than Earlier Generation." December 1, 2006. http://seniorjournal.com/NEWS/Boomers/6-12-01-BabyBoomers MoreCaring.htm

POLITICAL PARTICIPATION Some Baby Boomers have complained that young people were more active politically in the 1960s than they are today. They point out with pride that they even played a major role in the political process before they were eligible to vote, citing that the voting age was only lowered from 21 to 18 in time for the 1972 presidential election.

Although such claims are considered a gross generalization—older teens certainly affected Barack Obama's successful campaign in 2008—the political participation of the first wave of Baby Boomers is undeniable.

In the mid-1960s, idealistic white Boomers, sickened by the continued resistance against the civil rights movement in the South, gained attention by traveling to that volatile and dangerous area of the country to fight for integration and black voting rights. Soon the first wave of Baby Boomer college students were not only working for racial equality, but planting the seeds of the antiwar movement as the first American ground troops had been sent to Vietnam and those of the same age group were returning to the country in body bags.

The most active Baby Boomers during that time were organized left-wingers on college campuses, including the Students for a Democratic Society (SDS), which was founded in 1962 and grew increasingly radical as the events of that decade unfolded.

Although few Baby Boomers were yet of voting age in 1968, several college students who backed antiwar candidate Eugene McCarthy for president shaved their beards and dressed traditionally in waging a "Be Clean for Gene" campaign.

Meanwhile, many other Boomers who espoused a hippie lifestyle or simply grew apathetic about American politics removed themselves from the political process in a rejection of materialism and in the belief that the capitalist system was corrupt. And during that same era, millions of Baby Boomers from small towns and rural areas quietly became what eventual president Richard M. Nixon perceived as the "silent majority" and maintained the conservatism embraced by their parents.

Baby Boomers complained vehemently in the 1960s that they were old enough to be killed in a war halfway around the world, yet not old enough to vote. Political leaders eventually agreed and the voting age was lowered from 21 to 18. According to the U.S. Statistical Abstract of 2001, more than 50 percent of Baby Boomers between the ages of 18 and 24 participated in the 1972 presidential election. Their turnout dropped after the Watergate scandal in the 1970s when voter anger and apathy peaked, but between 50 and 70 percent of Baby Boomers have consistently cast their ballots in presidential elections ever since.

The large number of voting-age Baby Boomers and their comparative interest in the political process has resulted in their greatly affecting the outcome of presidential elections. Boomers played a huge role in the elections of liberal Democrats Jimmy Carter in 1976 and Bill Clinton in 1992 and 1996. A dramatic shift to the right in the late 1970s allowed conservative Republican Ronald Reagan to win over millions of Baby Boomers in 1980 and 1984.

Meanwhile, Boomers have proven justified in their contention that younger generations have become less politically aware and involved. One example was the reaction to the unpopular war waged in Iraq after the terrorist attacks on the Pentagon and the World Trade Center on September 11, 2001. By the middle of the decade, polls indicated that more than half of all Americans were against further involvement in the conflict, and later surveys showed that the Iraq war had grown more unpopular than the Vietnam War had been four decades earlier. Yet although Baby Boomers organized frequent and vehement protests against American involvement in Vietnam that sometimes numbered as many as 500,000, the struggle in Iraq motivated comparatively little protest. However, some cited the fact that Baby Boomers who had protested in the 1960s had lost their activism and were not marching against the Iraqi War either. They claimed that the primary reason for their protests against Vietnam was that the draft threatened to send them to war. There was, after all, no draft to stock the military during the Iraq War.

Baby Boomers and voters from other generations turned out in droves to vote in the landmark 2008 presidential election won by Obama, but the shift toward greater political activism and interest has not been proven. Dissatisfaction with both political parties has resulted in anger and apathy, although some conservatives of all generations banded together in 2009 to form the Tea Party movement, which has protested what they perceive as government overstepping its bounds in its involvement in the lives of Americans.

See also Antiwar Movement; Clinton, Bill; Civil Rights Movement; Conservatism; Elections; Hippie Movement; Radicalism; Vietnam War.

FURTHER READING

Brokaw, Tom. *Boom! Voices of the Sixties: Personal Reflections on the '60s and Today.* New York: Random House, 2007.

2001 U.S. Statistical Abstract. Elections. http://www.census.gov/prod/2002pubs/01statab/election.pdf

Wattenberg, Martin P. *Is Voting for Young People?* New York: Longman, 2007.

R

RACISM Racism has been defined as the assertion of a superiority of one group over another, although it has also been described as the acceptance or embracing of a belief in racial or ethnic stereotypes.

Racism in the United States in recent times has been accompanied by far less violence since the last wave of Baby Boomers were born in the mid-1960s, but the wider number of racial and ethnic groups that have been targets of overt discrimination and hatred has increased over those same years.

The oldest Baby Boomers were too young to understand the significance of racist ideology and practice when the civil rights movement began in earnest in the mid-1950s. The country had been built on the slave trade and labor of blacks from Africa. In addition to enslaved Africans, in the 1800s and 1900s Native Americans and various immigrants such as Jews, Irish, and Chinese experienced racism. By the middle of the 20th century, racism was most pronounced, and therefore well publicized, against blacks in the South and North who had been a part of the waves of the Great Black Migration.

Some Baby Boomers recall a watershed moment during their childhood when they became aware of racism, quite likely through a televised event that marked the civil rights movement such as the beating of blacks during marches, angry whites screaming at black children attempting to integrate a school, or any number of bombings of black churches.

But just as likely their first taste of racism was experienced through words spoken against one or more racial or ethnic group by a family member or young friend. Some Boomers were taught racist beliefs in their youths and adopted them. Many of those did shed them in later years, but others embraced them and accepted perceived racial or ethnic stereotypes or the superiority of one group over another.

The first wave of black Baby Boomers became accustomed to dealing with racism at early ages. Those in the South were forced to attend inferior schools and directly experienced the indignity of many other forms of segregation. Many young white Baby Boomers in that area of the country witnessed the same racism in action. Although it has been stated that some blacks and whites of all ages in that era took segregation for granted, that certainly became less the case as the civil rights movement took form and highlighted its injustices.

Both black and white Baby Boomers changed their perspective on racism as the 1960s progressed and they grew old enough to form more learned opinions about it. More politically aware and active whites became angered at the inequities of race relations in the United States, which despite the strides toward integration in the South and other areas of the nation still existed in regard to housing, employment, education, and the media. But other issues such as the Vietnam War captured their greater attention. Many black Baby Boomers for whom racism and discrimination were the primary concern grew far more militant, choosing to follow such leaders as Malcolm X and, later, the Black Panthers. The result was a break from civil rights leader Martin Luther King Jr.'s call for nonviolent change and a demand for immediate action, which often resulted in rioting in the inner cities that generally included young Baby Boomers. During the height of the civil unrest in the 1960s, the Kerner Commission report stated plainly that impacted racism and discrimination played the most significant role in the outbreak of violence.

Although most white Baby Boomers applauded the efforts made in employment and integration in regard to education and housing in the late 1960s and early 1970s, others joined some from older generations in expressing their concern or even strong distaste for such developments. Racism was particularly rampant where blacks began to integrate previously all-white suburban neighborhoods and where busing was introduced as a means of providing equal levels of education to children of both races. The latter was perceived as forced integration.

Although racism against blacks continued to some degree, events inside and outside of the United States later resulted in the targeting of other racial and ethnic groups. People of Middle Eastern descent were victimized by those who tied them unjustly to the Iranian students who took Americans hostage in Tehran in 1979. The influx of undocumented immigrants from Mexico raised the level of racism against that minority in subsequent decades.

In later years, some Baby Boomers who had called for the end of racism in the 1960s became racist, but most remained tolerant and helped initiate and further societal changes. It has been stated that racism is passed down within families through generations, and that has, for the most part, held true. Boomers who learned racism in the 1950s, 1960s, and early 1970s from their parents often remained racists thereafter.

A greater sensitivity toward and intolerance of racism in more recent years has resulted in a greater awareness of its targets. The attacks on the Pentagon and World Trade Center of September 11, 2001, markedly increased racism against those of Middle Eastern descent, or those thought to be, in the United States. Also significant has been the recognition of black racism toward whites. Blacks and some whites have claimed that the continued economic disparity between the two races precludes the existence of black racism against whites, but others have argued that it should not be considered a factor and that blacks should not blame whites for the discriminations of the past.

The work of many ordinary Americans and those in leadership roles to stem the tide of racism has certainly made more people more tolerant today than they were a half-century ago. Perhaps more than those from any other generation in the history of the nation, Baby Boomers have spearheaded the drive to weaken the forces of racism.

See also Civil Rights Movement; King, Martin Luther, Jr.; Malcolm X; Terrorism.

FURTHER READING

Bonilla-Silva, Eduardo. *Racism Without Racists: Color-Blind Racism and the Persistence of Racial Inequality in America*. Lanham, MD: Rowman & Littlefield, 2006.
D'Souza, Dinesh. *The End of Racism*. New York: Free Press, 1995.
Feagin, Joe R., and Melvin P. Sikes. *Living with Racism: The Black Middle-Class Experience*. Boston: Beacon Press, 1995.

RADICALISM At any point in American history, at least a small group of people was tied in action or philosophy to a politically radical group. But no generation embraced left-wing radicalism with greater fervor than the young Baby Boomers born in the five years after the end of World War II in 1945.

The number of Boomers who actively participated in radical politics was comparatively small, but many were unafraid to make bold statements, particularly in the late 1960s, when their hatred for American involvement in the Vietnam War and mistrust of the U.S. government and military grew in intensity.

From the late 1940s through the early 1960s, a small percentage of the parents of Baby Boomers were political extremists, although many of them in thought only. The most popular radical groups on the left were the Communists. Their numbers shrunk in the wake of the witch hunts against members of their political party in the early 1950s and the revelations about the brutality of the regime of Soviet leader Joseph Stalin before, during, and after the war. Among the far right-wing organizations that gained members about a decade after World War II was the Ku Klux Klan (KKK), particularly in the Deep South.

The burgeoning civil rights movement resulted in the fear of integration among some political radicals, although their numbers also shrunk through disgust with the violence perpetrated by the KKK in the late 1950s and the early 1960s, as well as a penchant for greater tolerance of blacks and other minorities during that time.

However, by the late 1960s both forms of political extremism were considered outdated. Old-school Communism had been replaced among the most radical Baby Boomers by several offshoot left-wing philosophies, many of which called for the overthrow of the U.S. government and the military-industrial complex that was perceived to have been the real catalyst for American involvement in Vietnam. Among the far left-wing groups of the era included those who espoused the philosophies of such Communist revolutionaries as Che Guevara, Ho Chi Minh, and Mao Tse-Tung, but they gained little favor, even among radical Baby Boomers.

The most publicized was the Weather Underground, a radical offshoot of the Students for a Democratic Society (SDS). The Weathermen, headed by Mark Rudd, who led a 1968 student strike and campus takeover at Columbia University, called for a second American revolution and set out on several violent rampages, but they were simply too radical to gain mass acceptance. The Youth International Party (Yippies) also earned much attention after heading a contingent of antiwar protesters at the 1968 Democratic National Convention in Chicago. The Yippies, led by Jerry Rubin and Abbie Hoffman, were far less conventional than other radical groups and even pretended to put a pig named Pigasus up for the presidential nomination. Their street theater tactics were used to garner media attention. Rubin and Hoffman were among those arrested at the convention who received tremendous publicity during what became known as the Chicago 7 trial.

Also a defendant in that legendary court case was Bobby Seale, who was a member of the Black Panthers, a radical group joined in spirit or action by thousands of young black Baby Boomers, particularly in major cities. Some Black Panther leaders, including Seale, Huey Newton, and Eldridge Cleaver, called for a violent overthrow of the government, although they also worked to instill racial pride in young blacks, particularly children.

Active left-wing political radicalism had all but flickered out by the early 1970s. Some Baby Boomers from the other side of the political spectrum embraced a new radical right-wing movement led by David Duke, who was attempting to place a more human face on the KKK while preaching segregation in response to the racial integration that was flourishing in all walks of American life, including housing, employment, and education. But Duke faded into obscurity, as did his short-lived movement. Baby Boomers and Americans in general had moved to the right by the late 1970s, but radicalism on both sides was no longer a factor in the U.S. political scene.

That has remained the case ever since. It has been argued that once-radical Baby Boomers who were now raising families and concerned about their careers had lost their zeal for the causes in which they once believed, but it has also been contended that the end of the war and the aging process combined to kill their far left-wing beliefs.

See also Antiwar Movement; Civil Rights Movement; Conservatism; Elections; Malcolm X; Political Participation; Racism; Vietnam War.

FURTHER READING

Elbaum, Max. *Revolution in the Air: Sixties Radicals Turn to Lenin, Mao and Che*. New York: Verso Books, 2002.

Jones, Charles E. *The Black Panthers*. New York: Aperture, 2006.

Rudd, Mark. *Underground: My Life with SDS and The Weathermen*. New York: William Morrow, 2009.

REAGAN, RONALD (1911–2004) The person who best symbolized the generation gap and the eventual shift toward conservatism among Baby Boomers was Ronald Reagan.

The old-time actor succeeded in his foray into politics by winning the governorship of California in 1966. Reagan ran unsuccessfully for the presidency in 1976 and then took advantage of widespread disenchantment and national political momentum to the right, which he helped create, to defeat Jimmy Carter in the 1980 presidential election. He served two terms in office.

Republican presidential candidate Ronald Reagan flashes a big grin at a campaign stop in Columbia, South Carolina, on October 10, 1980. (Ronald Reagan Library)

Most Baby Boomers knew little or nothing about Reagan's pre-politics career. Born into a poor family in tiny Tampico, Illinois, in 1911, he proved to be a well-rounded child. His teenage years were marked by an eight-summer stint as a lifeguard, during which time he rescued 77 people at a park along Rock River.

Upon graduation from small Eureka College during the height of the Great Depression, Reagan landed a job as a sports radio broadcaster in Davenport, Iowa, which launched a long career in the entertainment industry. He earned a position at WHO in Des Moines reconstructing and announcing Chicago Cubs games from reports sent via telegraph. By the late 1930s he was living his dream as a movie actor in Hollywood.

Reagan's first significant role was as college football star George Gipp in the movie *Knute Rockne—All American* (1940). His political views began to take shape after World War II. Although he served as president of the liberal Screen Actors Guild, he developed a strong anti-Communist sentiment.

A failing movie career forced Reagan to turn to the new medium of television. He began hosting a half-hour dramatic series titled *General Electric Theater* in 1954 and eventually became the spokesman for the successful western series, *Death Valley Days*. His abilities as a speechmaker were strengthened during a series of speaking engagements for GE in which he stressed his anti-Communist views.

Reagan gravitated toward politics and in 1962 became a member of the Republican Party. Although the country was moving left politically, Reagan was entrenched far enough the other way to write a speech supporting right-wing Republican presidential candidate Barry Goldwater in 1964.

Although Lyndon B. Johnson overwhelmed Goldwater in the election, several California conservatives were impressed enough with Reagan to convince him to run for governor of that state. California voters, uneasy about student strikes on college campuses, including one that had rocked the foundation at the University of California at Berkeley, as well as the burgeoning hippie movement and the overall radicalization of the young, gave Reagan a landslide victory.

The confrontation between Reagan and young California Baby Boomers was set. In one speech, Reagan said hippies were people who looked like Tarzan, walked like Jane, and smelled like Cheetah. He placed himself squarely in opposition to left-wing student activists, particularly as growing American involvement in Vietnam became an increasingly heated issue on campuses throughout the state.

That Reagan would ever be considered a presidential candidate would have been considered a joke to most Baby Boomers in the 1960s and early 1970s. That the same generation would have given him most of their votes someday would have been considered unthinkable. But as national and world events such as hyperinflation, the gas shortage, and the taking of American hostages in Iran moved Baby Boomers to the right politically, candidates such as Reagan seemed more appealing. In 1980, a disenchanted American public voted him into office in a lopsided election. Baby Boomers gave him more than 50 percent of their vote.

Among Reagan's noted achievements during his two-term presidency was re-instilling the nation with patriotism. Many Americans had lost pride in their country, which had been shaken by the deep divisions over Vietnam and the ensuing Watergate scandal. Despite his saber rattling and pronounced anti-Communism, Reagan's befriending of Soviet leader Mikhail Gorbachev brought the two countries closer together and aided in the downfall of that political and economic system throughout Eastern Europe. Soon after Reagan's plea to Gorbachev to tear down the Berlin Wall, the wall indeed came down.

Reagan did receive criticism from Boomers for vastly increasing military spending, much of which was funneled to conduct covert operations in Central American countries such as El Salvador and to prop up regimes deemed friendly to the United States in that area of the world.

But still-liberal Baby Boomers were relieved that Reagan's right-wing rhetoric belied many of his actions, including his appointment of the first female Supreme Court justice (Sandra Day O'Connor), his removal of U.S. Marines from Lebanon after an attack cost 240 of their lives, and his continued work to normalize relations between the United States and the Soviet Union.

The identification with Reagan among Baby Boomers continued after his presidency, which he ended at age 77. He eventually developed Alzheimer's disease, which was affecting many Baby Boomer parents and grandparents. Reagan's announcement in November 1994 that he was struggling with the debilitating disease brought greater awareness to the problem, especially to Baby Boomers who were approaching the age at which it could affect them. The difficulties Reagan's wife Nancy experienced dealing with the day-to-day challenges of taking care of a loved one with Alzheimer's was also felt by Baby Boomers throughout the country.

Reagan died at age 93 on June 5, 2004. Conservatives have lauded him as one of the greatest presidents in history and have even offered that his likeness should be sculpted into Mount Rushmore. And many liberals, including Baby Boomers who would have been sickened in the 1960s and early 1970s by the mere thought of Reagan occupying the White House, conceded that he brought a sense of pride back to the country and also played at least a contributing role in the downfall of European communism and the healthier relations the United States has developed with Russia.

See also Conservatism; Elections; Hippie Movement; Movies; Political Participation; Radicalism; Vietnam War.

FURTHER READING

D'Souza, Dinesh. *Ronald Reagan: How an Ordinary Man Became an Extraordinary Leader*. New York: Free Press, 1999.

Mann, James. *The Rebellion of Ronald Reagan: A History of the End of the Cold War*. New York: Viking Press, 2009.

Reagan, Ronald. *The Reagan Diaries*. New York: HarperCollins, 2007.

RELIGION AND SPIRITUALITY Baby Boomers were generally raised in the same religion as were their parents, but often not with the same fervor. Many Boomers rejected religion or embraced a different one upon reaching the age at which they could decide for themselves. Many of them reverted back to the religion of their youth in later years.

Demographics played a major role in the distinction between Baby Boomers who were likely to break away from their religious upbringings and those who maintained status quo. Those who were raised religiously in small towns, lower middle-class suburbia, and rural areas were more likely to remain tied to the same church. But, particularly in the 1960s and early 1970s, Boomers brought up in middle-class and upper-middle class neighborhoods tended to explore their spirituality or shed themselves of all religious belief.

The first generation born into mass affluence, Baby Boomers were most often provided with all necessary creature comforts. Many think that made them less likely to accept religious teachings and explore on their own for spiritual fulfillment. Others contend that higher education tended to motivate Boomers to question their religions. The college campuses of the 1960s and early 1970s were a breeding ground not only for all forms of questioning authority and things previously taught, but also for spiritual study and experimentation.

By the mid-to-late 1960s, Baby Boomers who were not content with their current religions often explored Eastern religions such as Hinduism or Buddhism, which they believed provided a greater opportunity for inner peace and tranquility. Millions of others simply stopped attending church or temple and lost their religiousness in the belief that the vast problems facing the world precluded the existence of God or because religion had simply never been important enough in their lives to continue practicing it after moving away from home.

The trend toward Eastern religions was furthered by Beatnik philosophies of the previous decade and the embracing of Transcendental Meditation taught by Maharishi Mahesh Yogi, to whom George Harrison, the most introspective of the Beatles, became a devoted follower. Although Eastern practices and thought such as meditation and yoga eventually worked their way into the American mainstream, most Baby Boomers who experimented with Hinduism or Buddhism in the 1960s eventually rejected it or simply lost touch with it. Some became part of the fanatic Christian revival among young Baby Boomers in the late 1960s, and a few embraced offshoot religious cults, but the majority either returned to their religious roots or became comparatively nonreligious.

The era of great religious experimentation ended when the first wave of Baby Boomers reached their mid-to-late twenties and the youngest of the generation became teenagers.

Studies showed that although many Boomers maintained their religious beliefs, embraced some form of spirituality, or at least claimed they believed in the existence of God, the percentage of those who practiced religion and attended church or temple regularly shrunk.

Although most Baby Boomers believe in some form of afterlife, the number of those willing to accept agnosticism has been far greater than that of previous generations. The belief that people would not be damned to a hell because they were nonbelievers has gained greater acceptance over the last several decades.

Despite the sometimes dramatic shift in beliefs among Baby Boomers, many who strayed from the religious teachings of their childhood returned to their churches and temples later in life and have raised their children in the same religion as they were raised themselves. However, Boomers are more likely to understand and accept that their children and grandchildren could stray from their teachings in a search for spiritual fulfillment in the future, just as many of them had done in their youths.

FURTHER READING

Roof, Wade Clark. *Spiritual Marketplace: Baby Boomers and the Remaking of American Religion.* Princeton, NJ: Princeton University Press, 2001.

ROCK-AND-ROLL Baby Boomers didn't create rock-and-roll music, but they did expand its boundaries and give it far greater social and political relevance as musicians and were responsible for its explosion in popularity as listeners.

The passion of Boomers for rock and roll was, along with other pursuits, cited for the creation of the generation gap of the 1960s and remained a source of friction between teenagers and their parents well beyond that time.

The initial wave of Baby Boomers feasted their ears on rock music for the first time in the 1950s, but it was most often emanating from radios and record players belonging to older siblings. Conservative parents and civic leaders became alarmed when millions of white kids began embracing the music of such black artists as Chuck Berry ("Johnny B. Goode"), Little Richard ("Good Golly Miss Molly"), and Fats Domino ("Blueberry Hill").

Critics concerned with "race mixing" expressed their fears that the beat of the rock-and-roll was "negroizing" white teenagers. White rockers such as Elvis Presley ("Hound Dog") and Jerry Lee Lewis ("Great Balls of Fire") heightened those fears by adopting similar musical traits and gaining tremendous popularity during that era. The music industry responded to those fears by convincing what they considered far less threatening artists to record toned-down versions of popular rock songs, such as when Pat Boone covered Little Richard's rollicking "Tutti Frutti."

The 1959 plane crash that killed rock-and-roll stars Buddy Holly ("Peggy Sue"), Ritchie Valens ("La Bamba"), and the Big Bopper ("Chantilly Lace"), as well as the dispatching of Presley into the military, weakened the popularity of rock-and-roll, although groups such as Dion and the Belmonts ("Runaround Sue") kept the genre alive. The emergence of the California surf music sound as personified by the Beach Boys ("I Get Around") in the early 1960s sparked interest in the United States among young Baby Boomers.

The first wave of Baby Boomers came of age chronologically and musically when the Beatles arrived in the United States in early 1964. The British quartet not only revolutionized rock-and-roll with a richer sound, but also began transforming the fashion scene immediately with their long hairstyles. Most significantly, teenagers and even some adults loved their early songs that soon became classics, including "She Loves You," "I Wanna Hold Your Hand," and "Money Can't Buy Me Love." By the spring of that year, the Beatles held each of the top five slots on the *Billboard* charts.

The Beatles' success launched what became known as the British Invasion. Some bands that were not highly respected or embraced across the Atlantic gained a tremendous following from young American Baby Boomers who lapped up anything from the United Kingdom, including Herman's Hermits ("Mrs. Brown You've Got a Lovely Daughter") and Gerry and the Pacemakers ("Ferry Cross the Mersey"). But other early British Invasion bands gained critical acclaim and commercial success, including the Kinks, who emerged with a number one hit with what today is often considered the first hard rock song in "You Really Got Me," as well as the Dave Clark Five ("Glad All Over") and the Animals ("House of the Rising Sun").

Meanwhile, young black and many white Baby Boomers were also being turned on by the Motown sound. By the mid-1960s, black groups such as the Supremes ("You Can't Hurry Love"), the Temptations ("My Girl), and Smokey Robinson and the Miracles ("The Tears of a Clown") captured a wide Baby Boomer audience and marketed themselves as "The Sound of Young America."

By that time, another British Invasion group, the Rolling Stones, was challenging the Beatles for supremacy in the United States. The Stones took longer to find an audience in the United States, but emerged in 1965 with hits such as "Get Off of My Cloud" and "Satisfaction," which is still considered by some as the greatest rock-and-roll song ever. The British Invasion continued around that time with the emergence of the Who, who found success with early hits "I Can't Explain" and "My Generation" and remained one of the premier rock bands for decades thereafter, as well as the Yardbirds ("Heart Full of Soul"), which launched the careers of guitar greats Eric Clapton, Jeff Beck, and Jimmy Page and later morphed into Led Zeppelin, arguably the greatest band of the post-Beatles era.

A year after the British Invasion began, American rock-and-roll bands finally retaliated. Folk music artist Bob Dylan adopted the genre and, in the process, created a style called "folk rock" with which bands such as the Byrds ("Mr. Tambourine Man"), the Mamas and the Papas ("California Dreaming"), and the Association ("Along Comes Mary") gained tremendous artistic acclaim.

Despite the proliferation of successful British and American bands, the Beatles continued to set the direction of rock-and-roll music. Their 1967 album *Sgt. Pepper's Lonely Hearts Club Band* launched what became known as the "psychedelic era," which was influenced by the growing use of hallucinogenic drugs and Eastern musical styles, including the inclusion of the sitar. Psychedelic Beatles songs such as "Strawberry Fields Forever" and "I Am the Walrus" played a role in changing popular culture. California hippie bands such as Jefferson Airplane ("White Rabbit," "Somebody to Love") and the Doors ("Light My Fire") were embraced by mostly white, suburban youth. The 1967 Monterey Pop Festival, which attracted 55,000 Baby Boomers, sent premier rock-and-roll performers permanently from clubs into arenas and stadiums. The first rock festival also made a major star out of Jimi Hendrix ("Purple Haze"), who is widely accepted to be the most talented guitarist in the history of the genre.

The rock-and-roll scene of the late 1960s, which culminated in the legendary Woodstock festival in August 1969, expanded its horizons. Bands such as folkie Crosby, Stills, Nash, and Young ("Ohio"), Bayou rockers Creedence Clearwater Revival ("Proud Mary"), jazz-influenced Chicago ("Make Me Smile"), and symphony rock artists the Moody Blues ("Tuesday Afternoon") continued to send rock-and-roll music into different directions.

A new generation of Baby Boomers born in the late 1950s and early 1960s began embracing a new generation of rockers in the 1970s, including Led Zeppelin ("Whole Lotta Love," "Stairway to Heaven"), piano-playing Elton John ("Rocket Man"), Lynyrd Skynyrd ("Sweet Home Alabama"), as well as Alice Cooper ("School's Out") and David Bowie ("Changes"), whose facial makeup and futuristic apparel launched an era of transgender images and crossover stage personas in the genre. Black and white Baby Boomers of that era also enjoyed the blossoming of funk, which was launched in the late 1960s by Sly and the Family Stone ("Dance to the Music") and advanced by groups such as Earth, Wind, and Fire ("Shining Star").

Many of the youngest Boomers who reached their high school years in the late 1970s and early 1980s caught on to New Wave and such new pop rock music bands as the Talking Heads ("Psycho Killer"), the Police ("Don't Stand So Close to Me"), and the Cars ("My Best Friend's Girl"). Such punk rock groups as the Clash ("London Calling") and the Sex Pistols ("God Save the Queen") provided a return of rebelliousness and anti-establishment feel to the rock scene.

By the mid-to-late 1980s, many of the oldest Baby Boomers had teenage children of their own. Although some now in their forties enjoyed the popular groups of that era such as the heavy metal band Metallica ("Seek & Destroy"), others contended that they were too loud, their lyrics were unintelligible, and that the messages of peace and protest of their era had been replaced by those of anger. More thoughtful and politically and socially outspoken bands such as R.E.M. ("It's the End of the World as We Know It") and U2 ("Sunday Bloody Sunday") gained popularity in the 1980s, but by the early 1990s, Boomers were lamenting the fact that newly created rock-and-roll could hardly be heard on the radio anymore and that the popularity of hip-hop, rap, and teenybopper soloists and bands had taken over the airwaves and the places in the hearts and tastes of the new generation.

Many Baby Boomers have tried with some success to turn their kids on to music of their generation. Millions of teenagers and young adults of Baby Boomer parents enjoy the music of such greats of the 1960s and 1970s as the Beatles, the Rolling Stones, Led Zeppelin, the Temptations, the Who, and others. Millions of Baby Boomers grow indignant when current popular music acts are compared favorably with the rock-and-roll stars of their generation, claiming that performers of the 1960s and 1970s were judged by their talent and the songs they produced and that the popularity of today's acts are earned mostly through image and marketing.

Whether or not that is accurate, there is no doubt that rock-and-roll music played a huge role in entertainment, politics, social consciousness, and fashion throughout the Baby Boomer generation.

See also The Beatles; Dylan, Bob; Hippie Movement; Racism; The Rolling Stones; U2; The Who; Woodstock.

FURTHER READING

Brackett, David. *The Pop, Rock and Soul Reader: Histories and Debates.* New York: Oxford University Press, 2008.

Rolling Stone. *The Rolling Stone Illustrated History of Rock and Roll: The Definitive History of the Most Important Artists and Their Music.* New York: Random House, 1992.

Szatmary, David P. *Rockin' in Time: A Social History of Rock-and-Roll.* Upper Saddle River, NJ: Prentice Hall, 2009.

THE ROLLING STONES To Baby Boomer parents who perceived the Beatles as wholesome purveyors of a burgeoning art form, the Rolling Stones were anti-heroes. To Baby Boomer parents who despised rock-and-roll and all it represented, the Stones were like the anti-Christ.

Image notwithstanding, their musical talents, creativity, and longevity have established them as arguably the greatest group in the history of the genre.

The seeds were planted in 1951 when Mick Jagger and Keith Richards formed a boyhood friendship in Dartwood, Kent, United Kingdom. Although they separated when their families moved several years later, they reunited by chance at a train station in October 1960. By that time, Jagger had developed a passion for rhythm and blues music as personified by the likes of Muddy Waters, whereas Richards favored such American rock-and-roll artists as Chuck Berry. Richards was soon invited into Jagger's band, Little Boy Blue and the Blue Boys.

The group was a regular attraction in London blues halls, where Jagger and Richards befriended guitarist Brian Jones, who was playing for Blues

Incorporated. Highly impressed by Jones's talents, they invited him to collaborate with them. By 1962, the Rolling Stones had been formed, having taken their name from the title of a Muddy Waters's song. The first lineup also included bassist Dick Taylor, keyboardist Ian Stewart, and drummer Mick Avory, who later landed a spot in the highly acclaimed British band the Kinks.

The Stones gained a large and enthusiastic following playing at the Crawdaddy Club in London, which rivaled the Cavern Club in Liverpool, where the Beatles had gained fame. Soon drummer Charlie Watts and bassist Bill Wyman had replaced Avory and Taylor and Stewart established himself as their road manager. While the popularity of the Beatles was already exploding through their covers of American pop songs and their own burgeoning writing talents, the Stones were exploring a darker and more sexually suggestive side of rock that would provide an antithesis to their British rivals for the rest of the decade.

As Beatlemania swept the United States, the Stones were touring the United Kingdom and releasing their first hit singles, "Not Fade Away" and "It's All Over Now," which rose to number three on the British charts and also made a dent in the United States. But the first Stones tour of the states, which began on June 1, 1964, was met with comparative apathy. It was not until their second tour late that year, which was launched by an appearance on the *Ed Sullivan Show,* that the Stones took off commercially in the United States. When they released the iconic rock-and-roll hit "Satisfaction" in 1965, they received the critical and commercial success they had been seeking. The song, which rocketed to the top of the British and American charts, is still widely considered the greatest in the history of rock-and-roll. It not only featured Richards's fuzztone guitar riff, but it also expressed teenage Baby Boomer angst and frustration, played a role in widening the generation gap, and placed them solidly into the small but growing group of counterculture heroes through its anti-establishment message.

Jagger and Richards continued to write their own material. Their 1966 album release *Aftermath* consisted solely of their own creations, including such standards as number one hit "Paint It Black," "Under My Thumb," and "Let's Spend the Night Together." During one of six appearances on the *Ed Sullivan Show*, the Stones were forced to sing the latter's lyrics as "let's spend some time together" to appease the censors.

Changing times and the Beatles' breakthrough album *Sgt. Pepper's Lonely Hearts Club Band* forced the Rolling Stones to respond with a "flower power" record of their own, which they did with *Their Satanic Majesties Request*, featuring such psychedelic classics as "She's a Rainbow" and "2000 Light Years from Home." But despite their continued success, personal problems beset the group. Jagger, Richards, and Jones were all busted for drugs in 1967, which strengthened their reputation as the bad boys of rock.

The Stones reached a creative peak while breaking away from trends set by the Beatles in 1968 with the release of the album *Beggar's Banquet*, which was highlighted by such hard-driving tunes as "Sympathy for the Devil" and "Street Fighting Man." But they also became the first of many groups to fall victim to drug or alcohol abuse when Jones began to deteriorate under the weight of his addictions. Less than a month after the Stones cited musical differences for his departure from the band and replaced him with Mick Taylor, he was found dead in his swimming pool.

The group did not miss a beat. In fact, their 1969 album *Let It Bleed* was one of their best. Filled with references to sex and violence, it placed the Stones back on their own path for good with classics such as "Gimme Shelter" and "You Can't Always Get What You Want." But it was in that fateful year that the Stones made their biggest mistake by inexplicably hiring members of the notorious Hell's Angels motorcycle gang to serve as security for the Altamont Speedway Free Festival, an event billed as "Woodstock West" and one they were to headline. As the Stones attempted to perform, one Hell's Angel stabbed a patron to death near the stage.

The Stones continued to milk their reputation as the raunchiest group and argu-ably the best in 1971 after the Beatles had broken up. That was the year the Stones released *Sticky Fingers*, a quite suggestive name on an album that featured a man's pants and a zipper down the middle on the cover and was highlighted by song such as "Brown Sugar," "Wild Horses," and "Bitch." The follow-up double album *Exile on Main Street* offered hits "Tumbling Dice" and "Happy."

Although the Rolling Stones only created a few more megahit singles, such as "Angie," "Start Me Up," "Beast of Burden," and "It's Only Rock and Roll," they made their mark in the 1970s and beyond as arguably the greatest stadium concert band in history. As the genre was elevated from the club and small arena scene, the Stones developed into huge draws that often attracted 70,000 fans or more for their tour dates. With Jagger and Richards well into their sixties, the band con-tinued to tour throughout the first decade of the 21st century, even performing at halftime of the 2006 Super Bowl.

Although the Stones created dozens of hits, they were driven more by Jagger's blues roots and remaining true to what beckoned them creatively than producing as many top-of-the-chart smashes as possible. Many believe that dozens of songs they never released as singles were their best efforts.

See also The Beatles; Rock-and-Roll.

FURTHER READING

Davis, Stephen. *Old Gods Almost Dead: The 40-Year Odyssey of the Rolling Stones*. New York: Broadway Books, 2002.

The Rolling Stones. *According to the Rolling Stones*. San Francisco: Chronicle Books, 2003.

Wyman, Bill. *Rolling with the Stones*. New York: DK Adult Books, 2003.

S

SATURDAY NIGHT LIVE Through the early 1970s, the target audience for television comedy-variety shows was the parents and even grandparents of Baby Boomers. Only the occasional appearance by a rock band would attract the younger generation.

That changed with great aplomb beginning on October 11, 1975, the debut of *Saturday Night Live (SNL)*, a revolutionary concept in programming created for and performed by Boomers. Little could anybody project that the 90-minute show would become a staple of American late-night television for the next two generations and perhaps beyond.

Developed by Dick Ebersol and produced by Lorne Michaels to give the network a Saturday night hit to supplement the highly popular weeknight *Tonight Show* that was hosted by American icon Johnny Carson, *SNL* filled the bill from its debut. The first cast members, who called themselves the "Not Ready for Prime Time Players," gained immediate stardom. Particularly popular were Chevy Chase and Dan Aykroyd, who doubled as two of the show's comedy writers, Bill Murray (who replaced the departed Chase in 1977), John Belushi and Gilda Radner, whose talents were supplemented by those of Laraine Newman, Garrett Morris, and Jane Curtin. Weekly guest hosts included such Baby Boomer favorites as comedians Steve Martin and George Carlin.

Few subjects were taboo as each cast member explored new territory and established well-loved, quirky characters. Sketches such as the Weekend Update news show brought new catch phrases to the American lexicon ("Jane, you ignorant slut!"), whereas clever commercial parodies had viewers laughing and weekly musical guests also motivated Baby Boomers to tune in.

Critical claim came immediately. *SNL* earned four Emmy awards in its first year and was nominated for more than a dozen from 1976 to 1978. The cast members, all of whom had been unknown nationally, became household names. But that fame also served to hasten their departure. Hollywood beckoned Chase in

Comedian Chevy Chase, second from left, joins cast of NBC-TV's *Saturday Night Live*, February 16, 1978 in New York, where he first got his start with the "Not Ready For Prime Time Players." Others are, from left, Jane Curtin, Bill Murray, Gilda Radner, and Laraine Newman. (AP Photo/Marty Lederhandler)

1977, as well as the immensely talented Belushi and Aykroyd, who forged fame together as the Blues Brothers. When Michaels left the show after the 1979–1980 season, the original cast disbanded.

The talent and creativity of the show suffered, particularly the next year, but the addition in 1981 of budding star Eddie Murphy breathed new life into *SNL*, as did the addition of Billy Crystal in 1984. A year later, Michaels rejoined the show as producer and spearheaded its second golden era, led by cast members Dana Carvey, Jon Lovitz, Kevin Nealon, Phil Hartman, Al Franken and Jan Hooks. Carvey gained particular popularity through his spot-on impersonations, including that of President George H. W. Bush. Franken, who later became a U.S. senator from Minnesota, also emerged as a favorite in front of the camera after spending a decade as one of the show's writers. It was that group that maintained *SNL* as an entertainment force among Baby Boomers, although the attraction had greatly been passed on to the youngest of that generation.

The first ten years of *SNL* produced a myriad of popular characters and catch phrases, including Radner's Roseanne Roseannadana ("It's always something") and Emily Litella ("Never mind"), Belushi's Samurai, Aykroyd's fast-talking product-hawker, Murray's night club singer, Murphy's Mr. Robinson, Crystal's Fernando ("You look mahvelous"), Carvey's Church Lady ("Isn't that special?"), and Lovitz's pathological liar ("Yeah . . . that's the ticket!").

During a three-year period beginning in 1989, six popular new cast members were added in Mike Myers, Chris Farley, Julia Sweeney, Chris Rock, Adam Sandler, and David Spade, which created arguably the strongest and deepest ensemble in show history. Myers combined with Carvey to create the immensely popular "Wayne's World" sketches whereas Farley, a disciple of Belushi, gained fame through his characterization of hyper motivational speaker Matt Foley.

Many believe that the departure of nearly all of those cast members by the mid-1990s marked an end to the show's creative and comedic success. None of the cast members hired since that time has captured the imagination of television viewers, although several guest stars have piqued interest. Among them was former cast member Tina Fey, whose impersonation of controversial Republican vice-presidential candidate Sarah Palin in 2008 was done so well that it was hard to tell them apart.

Several former *SNL* cast members have struck it rich as movie actors, including Chase (*Caddyshack, Seems Like Old Times, National Lampoon's Vacation*), Aykroyd (*Ghostbusters, Trading Places, Driving Miss Daisy*), Murray (*Ghostbusters, Caddyshack, What About Bob?, Groundhog Day, Lost in Translation*), Murphy (*48 Hrs., Trading Places, Beverly Hills Cop, Coming to America, The Nutty Professor, Shrek*), Crystal (*The Princess Bride, When Harry Met Sally, City Slickers*), and Myers (*Austin Powers, Shrek, Inglourious Basterds*).

Tragically, others lost their lives through misfortune or self-destruction. Belushi and Farley fell victim to substance abuse whereas Radner died of ovarian cancer and Hartman was killed by his wife in a murder-suicide.

Although many Baby Boomers lost interest in *SNL* since the cast from the early-to-mid 1990s disbanded, the show remains popular enough among their children and grandchildren to stay on the air as it heads toward its 40th year.

See also Movies; Television.

FURTHER READING

Hill, Doug, and Jeff Weingrad. *Saturday Night: A Backstage History of Saturday Night Live*. New York: William Morrow and Company, 1989.

Radner, Gilda. *It's Always Something*. New York: Harper, 2000.

Shales, Tom, and James Andrew Miller. *Live from New York: An Uncensored History of Saturday Night Live*. New York: Little, Brown and Company, 2002.

SEX More than any other generation, Baby Boomers were responsible for the shedding of the taboos that surrounded the subject of premarital sex. The oldest Boomers certainly felt a greater sense of freedom to participate in sex at an earlier age and before marriage than did their counterparts from previous generations. They were also more likely to have sex with multiple partners than were those from generations past.

Research taken in 2006 from the federal National Survey of Family Growth indicated that the parents of Baby Boomers were not as dedicated to remaining virgins until marriage as some might believe. The study showed that among all Americans who had turned 18 from 1954 to 1963, approximately one quarter had had sex.

The number more than doubled to 48 percent among those who reached their 20th birthdays and tripled among those who turned 25 during that same period.

Although Boomer parents were not as chaste in their premarital years as the media, and particularly television programming, might have indicated at the time, they were certainly less likely to engage in sex than were Baby Boomers themselves and far less likely to admit it or speak about it freely. There were two reasons for the increase in premarital sexual activity and the greater openness about the subject. One was the availability of the birth control pill in 1960 and beyond, which allowed young women to partake in sex without concern about becoming pregnant. The other was the sexual revolution of the 1960s and early 1970s, which led Boomers to openly talk about the subject; engage in sexual activity with a multiple partners; and, to some degree, legitimize the notion of having sex with partners other than one's spouse or steady mate.

The same study showed that nearly 40 percent of all Americans who turned 18 from 1964 to 1973 had lost their virginity and approximately two thirds had engaged in sex by their 20th birthdays, which indicates that Baby Boomers on college campuses were far more sexually active than were those attending universities from the previous generation. By the age of 25, nearly 90 percent of all single Americans had been sexually active. Some Boomers were waiting until they got married to have sex.

Between 1974 and 1983, when the last wave of Baby Boomers were reaching their teenage years and flooding the college campuses, the number of high school students who had already lost their virginity continued to skyrocket. The National Survey of Family Growth indicated that approximately half of those who turned 18 during that 10-year period had engaged in sexual intercourse. The number of those who had had sex by the age of 20 and 25 had also jumped dramatically. The number of sexually active, unmarried, young black Boomers, many of whom still lived in the inner cities of the United States, also rose markedly during that time. The teen pregnancy rate in that demographic reached epidemic proportions in the 1980s.

During the 1970s and 1980s, the sexual revolution permeated the media. Several articles and books were written about various sexual positions, how to best gratify one's self and one's partner during sexual activity, and how men could maximize opportunities to seduce women. Nightclubs and dance clubs, particularly during the disco era and in the early 1980s, became a breeding ground for unmarried, or, on occasion, married, Baby Boomers in their twenties, thirties, and sometimes beyond seeking and finding partners for one-night stands.

The AIDS scare of the 1980s certainly made millions of Americans—and Boomers in particular—more careful about with whom they slept; however, the National Survey of Family Growth indicated that it did not deter many from engaging in sex. Condom use, which had declined in the 1960s after the introduction of the birth control pill, increased dramatically in the 1980s, but the study showed that the number of high school students, many of whom were now children of Baby Boomers, who had engaged in sex was still rising significantly. Approximately 13 percent of Americans who turned 15 from 1984 to 1993 had already lost their virginity and nearly 60 percent had been sexually active by their 18th birthday.

A drive toward convincing teenagers to abstain from sex made a slight impact from 1994 to 2003, when the percentage of those who had had sex by the time they had turned 18 and 20 dropped slightly for the first time since at least the 1950s. The median age of first premarital sex, which was at 20.4 during the 1950s and had dropped to 17.3 from 1984 to 1993, actually rose to 17.6 from 1994 to 2003.

The changing attitudes of the 1960s and early 1970s about sex were spearheaded by Baby Boomers who scoffed at the notion that it was something to be talked about behind closed doors and engaged in with only one partner. Although their joyful and open approach to sex was tempered in the early 1980s by the introduction of AIDS into society, the sexual revolution launched by Baby Boomers was never reversed.

See also Divorce; Homosexuality; Marriage and Infidelity.

FURTHER READING

Allyn, David. *Make Love, Not War: The Sexual Revolution: An Unfettered History*. New York: Routledge, 2001.

Finer, Lawrence B. "Trends in Premarital Sex in the United States, 1954–2003." PubMed .gov. http://www.ncbi.nlm.nih.gov/pubmed/17236611.

SHOPPING The demographic and technological changes Americans have experienced over the years have altered the way Baby Boomers have shopped as children with their parents and as adults.

Although some large shopping centers dotted the landscape before World War II, the mass movement from the cities to the suburbs after the war resulted in the construction of many more. The oldest Baby Boomers might recall shopping with their parents at singular department stores for a wide variety of goods, as well as at neighborhood grocery stores for food. In small towns and rural communities, mom-and-pop shops remain commonplace, but in larger cities and surrounding areas, the vast majority of Baby Boomers have grown accustomed to shopping at huge and impersonal chain department stores and supermarkets.

In more recent years, the Internet has provided a vast marketplace for specific purchases, although most goods and services are still bought outside of the home.

The earliest Baby Boomer children often accompanied their mothers or fathers to the heart of downtown to buy any number of items or to one of dozens of small regional chains or locally owned grocery stores. Shops were small and patrons often felt a sense of kinship with their employees and even owners. Some items such as dairy products were even delivered right to the door. The cherished memory of the milkman visiting homes is growing increasingly distant with time.

The burgeoning of American suburbia brought with it large outdoor centers that allowed shoppers—including Baby Boomers now old enough to shop for their parents and themselves—to purchase a wide array of products in one area, in most cases the strong sense of identity and closeness forged between the buyers and the sellers had dissipated only slightly. In the 1950s, 1960s, and well into the 1970s, the variety of locally owned stores remained essential to the fabric of the community.

Most Baby Boomers fondly recall visiting dozens of different specialty shops, including shoe stores, butchers, bakeries, candy stores, jewelers, hardware stores, clothing stores, and drug stores. Although department stores and grocery chains sold many of the items that could be found in specialty shops of the day, many shoppers remained loyal to the locally owned stores because they and their ancestors had been patronizing them for generations.

The takeover of local grocery chains by supermarket conglomerates, the formation of huge department store complexes, and the advent of the supersized indoor malls in the 1980s changed the shopping experience for Baby Boomers and those of younger and older generations. The teenage children of older Baby Boomers and many Boomers themselves began to shop almost exclusively at the expansive indoor malls and lost the identity with locally owned specialty shops, some of which went out of business because of a lost battle in competition against mall stores.

Such was not the case in rural and small-town United States. Although indoor malls were often constructed within driving distance and Baby Boomers and others from those areas trekked out to visit them on occasion, the greatest shopping convenience remained by patronizing locally owned stores. Those living in smaller and rural communities have maintained a kinship with the owners and employees of several shops, including the local grocery store, which has often been a center of activity for generations, as well as such gathering places as barber shops.

By the early 1990s, the creation of huge retail stores that sold everything from food to clothing to electronics, as well as shopping clubs that offered food in large quantities and low prices, again changed the way many Baby Boomers and those in younger generations have shopped. Such stores as Wal-Mart, Target, and Aldi have resulted in the demise of some indoor malls that had been flourishing just a decade earlier. The indoor malls offered shopping in one trip, but the expanded retail stores truly offered one-stop shopping, including the availability of food items. In contrast, supermarkets have grown to offer products outside of their traditional realm of food and paper goods.

The popularization of the megastores and the struggling post-millennium economy have combined to send many local shops out of business. Baby Boomers seeking convenience in their shopping have flooded the huge retail stores. Furthermore, corporate takeovers have resulted in the disappearance of small grocery stores in suburban areas, which has in turn transformed huge, impersonal stores owned by regional and national chains as the lone alternative.

Urban and suburban Baby Boomers, particularly those born immediately after World War II, have gained the widest shopping experiences of all Americans because many have become fluent in online shopping whereas their parents have not. Although online shopping can certainly be considered one wave of the future, it is limited. Not only do shoppers enjoy getting out of the house to search for goods, but one rarely shops for daily groceries and items such as toiletries online.

Some Baby Boomers who have grown tired of the impersonal trends in shopping and disheartened by the failures of family-owned businesses have gone out of their way to patronize locally owned stores in their communities.

See also Consumerism.

FURTHER READING
Dicker, John. *The United States of Wal-Mart*. Portland, OR: Powell's Books, 2005.
Hine, Thomas. *I Want That: How We All Became Shoppers*. New York: Harper Perennial, 2003.
Underhill, Paco: *Call of the Mall: The Geography of Shopping*. New York: Simon and
    Schuster, 2004.

SMOKING The health of some Baby Boomers had been compromised before they were even born by the smoking habits of their parents, especially their mothers. Although researchers had begun to learn enough to warn Americans of the dangers of tobacco, the evidence against it in the late 1940s and early 1950s had yet to mount and millions of pregnant females continued to puff on cigarettes and unknowingly harm their fetuses.

The undeniable proof of the negative effects of cigarette smoking did not stop millions of Baby Boomers themselves from experimenting with it and becoming addicted during their teenage years and beyond. However, the generation became the first to lead the charge in dramatically reducing the number of smokers in the United States, to fight to keep their own children from lighting up, and to work to eliminate smoking in public places throughout the country.

Smoking was prevalent before World War II, but after the war, the parents of Baby Boomers actually smoked more. According to a 1949 poll, half of American men and one third of the women smoked at that time. A year later, a medical study claimed that 96.5 percent of lung cancer patients interviewed were moderately heavy smokers or chain smokers. By the mid-1950s, most physicians and more women had given up smoking, but the percentage of men in the United States who smoked had skyrocketed to nearly 57 percent.

It would seem that the landmark Surgeon General report in 1964 that alerted Americans to the certain link between cigarettes and lung cancer would have precluded a smoking problem among Baby Boomers, the oldest of whom were only 18. The American Medical Association then recommended that hazard labels be placed on cigarette packs, but in 1965 the overall percentage of smokers in the United States had remained virtually the same and had actually increased among women. That same year, tobacco manufacturers were indeed required to put warnings on the side of their cigarette packs.

The tobacco industry began fighting the trend against smoking by allegedly attempting to secretly fund the publication of a book written by Lloyd Mallan titled *It Is Safe to Smoke* in 1967. A congressional investigation learned of the deception, and the book was removed from the market.

Millions of Baby Boomers began smoking in the 1960s. Some were influenced by such rock stars as the Beatles and the Rolling Stones, who were seen smoking in public. Several Baby Boomer concert-goers at the legendary Woodstock music festival were also shown smoking.

The battle against smoking began in earnest in the 1970s. In 1970, consumption of cigarettes had dropped to 44 percent among males and 31.5 percent among females. That same year, Pan American Airlines established smoking sections on its jumbo jets and American Airlines did the same in 1972. Two years later, as an overall trend toward a healthy lifestyle had been adopted by many Baby Boomers and millions of other Americans, Congress enacted the Public Health Cigarette Smoking Act that banned cigarette advertising on television and radio and required a stronger warning on cigarette packages. The first Great American Smokeout in 1977 was greeted with enthusiasm, and by the end of the decade, approximately five percent fewer Americans smoked than when it began.

By the mid-1980s, Baby Boomers, some of who still smoked, were for the first time attempting to convince teenagers of their own not to do so. Surgeon General C. Everett Koop tried to help with his 1988 report that called nicotine a powerfully addicting drug, but the tobacco industry had fought back with their Joe Camel campaign that many believed targeted children in an attempt to make smoking seem cool. One study revealed that 91 percent of six-year-olds had the same recognition of Joe Camel as they did Mickey Mouse and that they were able to connect the former with cigarettes. In 1987, the number of 18-year-old smokers who used Camel had risen from 0.5 percent to 32.8 percent. Five years later, a Gallup survey discovered that 70 percent of smokers ages 12–17 would not have begun smoking if they could reverse time and 60 percent yearned to stop. However, more than half had attempted to quit and failed.

The growing number of establishments that had banned smoking, including fast-food giant McDonald's in 1994, and the general acceptance about its dangers helped to decrease the overall number of smokers, which included approximately 25 percent of adult Americans in 1993.

However, a 1997 study showed that the average age of first-time smokers was just 13. The number of cigar smokers in the United States had leaped from 3 million in 1993 to 10 million in 1999. According to a 2000 study, more than 30 percent of all high school students had smoked within the past 30 days.

After the dawning of the new millennium, the number of smokers and new smokers in the United States had leveled off. A 2004 study revealed that approximately one quarter of all adults smoked, and the number of cigar smokers had increased again to nearly 15 million. An increased number of Americans were using artificial means to kick the habit, including nicotine patches.

Many Baby Boomers who never smoked or were among the millions who have quit find it difficult to believe considering all of the evidence of its dangers and its likelihood of shortening lives that approximately one fourth of American adults smoke cigarettes. Considering the universal knowledge of its harmful effects, the number of people who continue to smoke is a testament to the addictive qualities of nicotine.

See also Health and Health Care; The Rolling Stones; Woodstock.

FURTHER READING

Brandt, Allan M. *The Cigarette Century: The Rise, Fall, and Deadly Persistence of the Product That Defined America.* New York: Basic Books, 2007.

Kluger, Richard. *Ashes to Ashes: American's Hundred-Year Cigarette War, the Public Health, and the Unabashed Triumph of Philip Morris.* New York: Knopf, 1997.

SONTAG, SUSAN (1933–2004) No intellectual expressed more insightful observations and views about the growing counterculture of the 1960s and the political radicalization of many young Baby Boomers during that era than writer Susan Sontag.

Never one to shy away from stating controversial opinions, Sontag wrote extensively and expertly not just as a novelist, but also as an essayist and film critic. She delved into a wide array of subjects, including art, music, religion, photography, suicide, sex, and war.

Born Susan Rosenblatt in New York in 1933, Sontag's mother quickly left her to join her fur trader husband in China and placed Sontag and sister Judith in the care of their grandparents. Upon the death of Sontag's father, her mother returned to the United States and moved with her two daughters to Tucson, Arizona.

Sontag was disenchanted and restless through much of her childhood as she developed an intellectualism that far surpassed that of her fellow students. She was accepted into the University of California at Berkeley at age 15 in 1948 before transferring to the University of Chicago a year later and graduating from college at 17. Just 10 days after her graduation ceremony, she married her sociology professor, Philip Rieff.

Sontag continued her education, earning degrees in English literature and philosophy at Harvard University in the mid-1950s before seeking her doctorate. She studied in the United Kingdom and then transferred to the University of Paris and fell in love with the French capital. She would eventually return and begin spending half a year there annually.

Divorced from Rieff, she and her six-year-old son moved to New York in 1959 with just $30 to her name. She accepted a position teaching at City College and Sarah Lawrence College while contributing to *Commentary*, a Jewish-centered monthly magazine. That work piqued her interest in pursuing a career as a freelance writer, but her greatest success would have to wait. She toiled in the religious studies department at Columbia University through the first half of the 1960s and had her first novel published. *The Benefactor* (1963) focused on a man tortured by his dreams who realizes that they are telling him to make changes in his life.

Sontag became attracted to the New York liberal literary scene and landed a much-desired job writing for *Partisan Review*. She broke through in 1964 with an essay titled "Notes on 'Camp,'" which claimed that one must go against the grain of his or her own sex to reap the greatest sexual pleasure and attain the highest level of sexual attractiveness. Sontag had come to the realization years earlier that she was a bisexual.

The hotly debated essay boosted Sontag's career. She followed in 1966 with one titled "Against Interpretation," an embracing of existentialism in which she offered that art should not be interpreted, but rather judged on a personal and pure sensory level. She touched upon issues of the era such as the Vietnam War and the radicalization of the young in 1969 essays "Trip to Hanoi" and "Styles of Radical Will." To produce the former, Sontag, like actress Jane Fonda, visited the North Vietnamese capital. She wrote positively about her experience there. However, Sontag was not tied to either American political party and had certainly drifted away from any support for Communism when she stated during a 1982 rally in New York City for the Polish Solidarity movement that the Polish political and economic system was akin to Fascism with a human face. Her comments about Communism were interpreted that she had been transformed into a right-winger.

Although that was not the case, Sontag, like most Baby Boomers of the era, did distance herself from left-wing radicalism in the 1970s, but she remained relevant. Her essay "Illness as Metaphor," which was written in 1978, three years after she had been diagnosed with cancer, was deemed as arguably her finest work. In 1977 she won a National Book Critics Circle award for criticism for her treatise *On Photography*. In 2003, a year before Sontag died from cancer, she penned another work on the subject, *Regarding the Pain of Others*, in which she claimed that war photos influenced the political and artistic views of those who took and viewed them.

Sontag continued throughout the 1980s to display her versatility, speaking at international writers' conferences and supporting fellow writer Salman Rushdie, whose life was being threatened by Muslim extremists after the publication of his work, *Satanic Verses*. She branched out further in 1993, publishing her first play, *Alice in Bed*.

On a personal level, Sontag, who had striking good looks, became romantically involved with such notable personalities as French actress Nicole Stephane and photographer Annie Leibovitz.

Sontag died of cancer at age 71 on December 28, 2004.

FURTHER READING

Sontag, Susan. *Against Interpretation: And Other Essays*. New York: Picador USA, 2001.
Sontag, Susan. *Illness as Metaphor and AIDS and Its Metaphors*. New York: Picador USA, 2001.

SPACE RACE AND MOON LANDING   In May 1961, President John F. Kennedy stated a commitment to land an American on the moon by the end of the decade.

The race to the moon was literally and figuratively launched on October 4, 1957, when the Soviet Union orbited Sputnik 1, the first artificial satellite. A month later, a larger and heavier satellite called Sputnik 2 carried the first living creature, a dog named Laika, into orbit.

During the height of the Cold War, those achievements stunned Americans and their leaders, who worried that they had technologically fallen behind the Russians. The first U.S. response failed when its Vanguard rocket exploded during liftoff, thereby intensifying those fears. The space race began in earnest when the United States sent Explorer 1 into orbit on January 31, 1958.

The first shot in the 1960s race to the moon was delivered by the Soviets when young fighter pilot Yuri Gagarin embarked on the first manned space mission on spacecraft Vostok on April 12, 1961. He orbited the Earth in less than two hours. Three weeks after Gagarin's mission, Alan Shepard boarded the Mercury spacecraft, which he named Freedom 7, and became the first American in space. Soon thereafter Kennedy made his historic proclamation and the U.S. space program went to work to pull ahead of the Soviets, although some at the National Aeronautics and Space Administration (NASA) questioned the ability of its program to land a man on the moon by the end of the 1960s.

The Soviets remained ahead in the space race in the early 1960s. John Glenn earned hero status in the United States when he became the first American to orbit the Earth on February 12, 1962, doing so three times, and three more astronauts followed Glenn into orbit, including Gordon Cooper, who spent more than a day in space, but those flights were overshadowed by Soviet achievements. Cosmonauts Andriyan Nikolayev and Pavel Popovich staged the first dual spaceflight in 1963, and Valentina Tereskhkova was the first woman in space, traveling for three days that same year. The Soviets remained ahead of the Americans when they launched three cosmonauts into space. The Russians even accomplished the first spacewalk in March 1965 when cosmonaut Alexei Leonov left compatriot Pavel Belyayev to pilot the Voskhod 2 and spent several minutes floating in space.

The feat seemed to leave the American space program far behind. But NASA was busy planning the Gemini missions, which would prove to be more sophisticated and far-reaching as well as a bridge to the Apollo missions that achieved the first moon landing. From 1965 to 1966, 10 Gemini crews pioneered new techniques in space exploration, including spacewalks that lasted more than two hours and one mission in which the astronauts broke the record with 14 days in space. The Gemini crews also were the first to have two spacecrafts meet, the first to dock in space, and the first to re-enter into the Earth's atmosphere. The United States had finally taken the lead in the space race.

Both countries embarked on a series of robotic testing in the mid-1960s. American craft Mariner 4 took the first close-up pictures of Mars in 1965. The Soviets made the first soft landing on the moon a year later when the Luna 9 dropped on the Ocean of Storms and sent back photos of its surface. The United States then dispatched a series of craft to the lunar surface in preparation for its historic piloted mission several years later.

The space race engendered historic and tragic failures on both sides. On January 27, 1967, the first manned American Apollo mission met disaster when fire swept through the cabin, dooming astronauts Gus Grissom, Ed White, and Roger Chaffee. The investigation revealed technical flaws in the design of the craft, which set back the Apollo program nearly two years.

Three months later, Soviet cosmonaut Vladimir Komarov, piloting the Soyuz 1, was killed when the craft slammed into the Earth's surface at a high rate of speed after malfunctions had forced officials to order its return.

The precursor to the American lunar landing occurred on November 9, 1967, when the 363-foot Saturn 5 moon rocket lifted off, powered by 7.5 million pounds of thrust. And when the Apollo program was reborn during an 11-day space test in the fall of 1968, it was decided that the crew piloting the subsequent Apollo 8 voyage would orbit the moon. It was believed that that Soviets were planning a similar mission, so on December 24 of that year American astronauts Frank Borman, Jim Lovell, and Bill Anders made history by beginning their 66-hour trek across 230,000 miles of space and achieving the first lunar orbit. The crew took photographs of the moon and sent live television images back to Earth and then returned.

By that time, several Americans, including young Baby Boomers, were questioning the cost of such missions. They believed the billions of dollars spent on exploring space could have been used to improve the lives of those on Earth. Thousands were dying daily from starvation in other parts of the world and idealistic American youth did not think that the tangible benefits of landing a man on the moon outweighed the need to feed the hungry and shelter the homeless, particularly when so much money was being spent on what they considered to be an immoral war in Vietnam.

However, the protests were like calls in the wilderness to many. The United States in the late 1960s was in turmoil. Race riots, antiwar protests, and assassinations rocked the foundation of the nation and turned American against American. It was believed that the accomplishment of landing a man on the moon would serve to help bring the country together. That view was proven right.

The success of Apollo 8 was a blow for the Soviets, who were forced to accept the inevitability of the first manned moon landing being achieved by the Americans. The successful Apollo 9 and 10 missions were for the most part dress rehearsals for the historic Apollo 11 spaceflight.

On July 16, 1969, a crowd of approximately 1 million people congregated at Cape Kennedy in Florida for the Apollo 11 launch, which climaxed at 9:32 A.M. when the Saturn 5 rocket sent astronauts Neil Armstrong, Buzz Aldrin, and Mike Collins into space. Three days later, they arrived in lunar orbit. On July 20, Armstrong and Aldrin took their places in the lunar module Eagle, and Collins piloted the command ship Columbia. The spacecrafts separated and the Eagle descended toward the moon's Sea of Tranquility. Armstrong steered the craft to a safe spot and radioed Earth with the now legendary proclamation, "The Eagle has landed." Nearly seven hours later, as he set foot on the moon, he uttered an even more famous statement: "That's one small step for man, one giant leap for mankind."

Soon Armstrong and Aldrin were collecting rocks and planting the American flag on the moon. They experienced the thrill of bouncing on a surface with one sixth of the gravitational pull of that on Earth before returning to their craft and Earth.

Several other space missions followed over the years, but only the historic Apollo 11 trip captured the imagination of most Americans. The memory of Armstrong stepping onto the moon is especially treasured by Baby Boomers, the oldest of whom were 23 at the time, and most of who were filled with wonderment and excitement over arguably the most historic achievement in the history of humankind.

See also Television; Vietnam War.

FURTHER READING

Allen, Michael. *Live From the Moon: Film, Television and the Space Race*. London: I.B. Tauris, 2009.

Cadbury, Deborah. *Space Race: The Epic Battle Between America and the Soviet Union for the Dominion of Space*. New York: HarperCollins, 2006.

Dickson, Paul. *Sputnik: The Shock of the Century*. New York: Walker & Company, 2007.

STEINEM, GLORIA (1934–) Gloria Steinem was the most effective and active leader in the women's rights movement of the late 1960s and 1970s. Her outspoken support of women's enfranchisement and her founding of *Ms.* magazine

As a feminist activist and founding editor of *Ms.* magazine, Gloria Steinem has been a symbol of the women's liberation movement in the United States for more than 30 years. (Library of Congress)

played key roles in the revolution that dramatically shifted female roles in American society.

That Steinem became a feminist and a writer might have been predicted. Grandmother Pauline was a prominent suffragette and mother Ruth toiled as a journalist. But Steinem's's childhood had more than a few rocky periods.

Born in Toledo, Ohio, on March 25, 1934, Steinem spent her summers with her family at their resort in Clark Lake, Michigan. Father Leo, an antique dealer, took the family with him on his many business trips around the country. The nomadic lifestyle prevented Gloria from attending formal school full time and forced Ruth to tutor her when they were on the road.

Tragedy struck Steinem at the age of eight when her parents divorced. She lived in poverty with mother, whose depression was so severe that she was no longer able to work. At 15, Gloria moved to Washington, D.C., to live with her sister before enrolling at Smith College. Steinem proved to be a brilliant student, earning Phi Beta Kappa and magna cum laude honors and winning a fellowship to study in India upon graduation in 1956.

Steinem's experience in India widened her scope and tugged at her heartstrings. She became acutely aware of the depth of pain and suffering felt by millions of people around the world. She grew bitter over the differences in lifestyle between most Americans and those in developing countries, many of who could not afford the basic necessities of life. She was taken aback by the starvation and disease plaguing the citizenry during her time in India. Her experiences there motivated her to forge a career as a journalist.

Steinem found immediate success in her field after moving to New York City in 1960. Several popular magazines purchased her freelance articles while she also thrived at script writing for the noted news and feature television program *That Was the Week That Was*. Her eyes were open to sexism while on assignment investigating the working conditions of Playboy bunnies. A highly attractive woman, Steinem went undercover by securing a job as a bunny and working as one for three weeks. Her resulting exposé revealed the poor conditions under which they worked, as well as their paltry income. Nearly a decade later, she published her long interview with *Playboy* founder Hugh Hefner during which they debated several issues related to the women's movement, including the sexual revolution and the philosophy with which he ran *Playboy* magazine.

The creation in 1968 of *New York* magazine, for which Steinem served as a contributing editor, gave her an opportunity to write a weekly column on a myriad of subjects, including her left-wing views. She became motivated by her political beliefs to work directly for Democratic candidates, including Eugene McCarthy, Robert F. Kennedy, and George McGovern. Her activism in the women's movement was sparked when she covered a meeting held by a New York feminist group that called itself the Redstockings. Although she attended as a journalist, she became increasingly interested in the stories they told, particularly those regarding illegal abortions.

The seeds of Steinem's activism were planted during the civil rights and antiwar movements of the 1960s. But it was not until the women's liberation movement began in the late 1960s that she felt empowered enough to become a national leader. She linked with fellow feminists such as Betty Friedan and Shirley Chisholm in 1971 to form the National Women's Political Caucus, which urged women to vote for candidates who supported causes such as legalized abortion and equal employment opportunities. A year later she challenged Democrats at their convention to seat more women and adopt a proabortion plank.

Steinem continued to throw her energy into the burgeoning women's rights movement, founding *Ms.* in 1972, the preview issue of which sold out. By 1977, the magazine boasted a half-million subscribers. Although her work as editor was time-consuming, she remained in the political arena, helping plot out the women's agenda for the 1976 Democratic National Convention.

Steinem remained quite active after the women's liberation movement of the 1970s. She recounted her days as a Playboy bunny, as well as her own experiences and those of other prominent 20th-century women in her 1983 book, *Outrageous Acts and Everyday Rebellions*. She followed it up three years later by penning a book about the tragic life of film actress and sex symbol Marilyn Monroe titled *Marilyn: Norma Jean*. In 1992, she delved into the subject of self-worth in her book *Revolution from Within: A Book of Self-Esteem*. She came out strongly against American involvement in Iraq after the attack on the World Trade Centers on September 11, 2001. Steinem also spoke out against the qualifications and views of Republican vice-presidential candidate Sarah Palin in 2008.

Ironically, Steinem was inducted into the American Society of Magazine Editors Hall of Fame along with Hefner in 1998, five years after she had been inducted into the Women's Hall of Fame.

Steinem has undergone at least one notable change. Once espousing the view that marriage was demeaning to women, she wed South African human rights activist David Bale in 2000. However, she did wear jeans and a flower in her hair at the ceremony.

See also Women's Movement.

FURTHER READING

Marcello, Patricia Cronin. *Gloria Steinem: A Biography*. Westport, CT: Greenwood Press, 2004.

Steinem, Gloria. *Outrageous Acts and Everyday Rebellions*. New York: Holt, Rinehart and Winston, 1983.

T

TALK SHOW REVOLUTION Many Baby Boomers who watched with great or little interest the sophisticated news and staid entertainment talk shows viewed by their parents in the 1950s and 1960s have been horrified by the revolution experienced by the genre in recent years. Baby Boomer offspring have grown up on the new wave of confrontational talk programming in which unusual characters off the streets of the United States do battle verbally and even physically over personal disagreements.

The television talk show can be separated into two categories—news and entertainment. Guests on news shows over the years such as *Meet the Press, Face the Nation*, and *Nightline* discussed the topics of the day. Livelier banter was provided by such entertainment venues as *The Today Show, The Merv Griffin Show*, and *The Tonight Show with Johnny Carson* (and later Jay Leno). Although both formats and even many of those programs still exist and remain strong in the ratings, new shows that Baby Boomers and others claim target the lowest common denominator in American society such as *The Maury Povich Show* and *The Jerry Springer Show* have permeated the television landscape. Live audiences react with cheers, jeers, and chants as guests wrangle over such personal issues such as pregnancies, love affairs, homosexuality, and even transsexuality.

The talk show genre was launched in the early 1950s. The first and most popular was hosted by Joe Franklin, but it was highly respected newscaster Edward R. Murrow who gave impetus to the news talk format with his show *Small World* in the late 1950s. In later years newscasters such as Mike Wallace, Barbara Walters, Tom Brokaw, Ted Koppel, William Buckley, Bill Moyers, and several cable news show hosts have kept the journalistic tradition and news talk show genre alive. *Meet the Press* and *Nightline* have remained staples of the television lineup for more than a generation.

Although *The Tonight Show* and later *Late Night with David Letterman* have dominated the post-primetime hours for decades, several entertainment-based television talk show hosts earned tremendous popularity and acclaim during the formative years of Baby Boomers in the 1960s and 1970s. Included were Merv Griffin,

Mike Douglas, Steve Allen, Joey Bishop, David Frost, Tom Snyder, Dick Cavett, Phil Donahue, Larry King, and Charlie Rose. Frost, Snyder, Cavett, King, and Rose have been considered a bit worldlier in their formats and often embarked on intriguing interviews with newsworthy guests of the political world whereas Griffin, Allen, and Bishop spoke almost strictly to those in the entertainment industry.

The talk show revolution of the 1980s seemed to be a natural extension of those programs. Such hosts as Phil Donahue and Oprah Winfrey emerged to discuss in a sophisticated, but livelier tone, a myriad of topics involving human relationships and societal issues. But networks encouraged verbal and even physical confrontation in later shows that were hosted by Ricki Lake, Geraldo Rivera, Maury Povich, and Jerry Springer.

The advent of expanded cable programming has allowed all formats to thrive. Cable news talk shows have learned a ratings lesson from the confrontational entertaining programs and encouraged heated exchanges between guests about political and moral issues. Such occurrences were rare when Baby Boomers were growing up, although they might recall archconservative William Buckley threatening to punch author and playwright Gore Vidal in the face during coverage of the 1968 Democratic National Convention for calling him a "Crypto Nazi" as they argued about the Vietnam War.

Many Baby Boomers believe the popularity of confrontational entertaining programming represents a "dumbing down" of the United States, although more sophisticated shows in the same realm such as those hosted by Winfrey and, in more recent years, Phil McGraw (*Dr. Phil*), remain highly rated. The same Baby Boomers hope, for the sake of their children and grandchildren, that such programs as *The Jerry Springer Show*, which invite physical fights among those representing the lowest intellectual and educational tiers in the United States, are merely a passing phase in television entertainment.

See also Carson, Johnny; Television.

FURTHER READING

Grindstaff, Laura. *The Money Shot: Trash, Class, and the Making of TV Talk Shows*. Chicago: University of Chicago Press, 2002.

Shattuc, Jane M. *The Talking Cure: TV Talk Shows and Women*. New York: Routledge Publishing, 1997.

TEAM SPORTS When all but the last wave of Baby Boomers were kids, most professional athletes earned salaries akin to those of a typical accountant or shoe storeowner. Young Boomers in middle-class suburban neighborhoods often passed by the home of an athlete from one of their town's sports teams on the way to and from school.

Until the early 1970s, athletes were generally bonded to the teams on which they played. The reserve clause, which was legal and standard in the contracts of athletes in all major professional sports (e.g., baseball, football, basketball, and hockey), stated that the teams retained the rights to its players upon the expiration of their deals. Each league boasted different provisions that eliminated the freedom of its athletes, thereby markedly curtailing salaries. The freedom of movement enjoyed by the rest of the American workforce was not afforded the professional athlete. For instance, the minimum annual salary in Major League Baseball until the late 1960s was $7,000.

Although several significant changes and astounding achievements have occurred in the world of sports since the first Baby Boomers were born in the late 1940s, the greatest impact revolved around the advent of free agency and the resulting skyrocketing salaries since the mid-1970s.

The Baby Boomer era began with baseball as the United States' most popular sport. The first major change occurred in the late 1950s when the storied Brooklyn Dodgers franchise moved to Los Angeles and the New York Giants relocated to San Francisco, giving rapidly growing California its first two teams and leaving just one in New York. The woeful New York Mets ended that problem by joining the National League in 1962. Major League Baseball also placed a National League team in Houston after adding American League teams in Los Angeles and Washington a year earlier. Further expansion in 1969 brought franchises to San Diego, Montreal, Kansas City, and Seattle, which lost its team to Milwaukee in 1970.

Americans, particularly young Baby Boomers, began to lose interest in watching professional baseball because of its slow pace and low scores. Pitching dominated the game in the 1960s and early 1970s to the point in which 1-0 finals became commonplace. The problem became so acute in 1968, when St. Louis right-hander Bob Gibson lost nine games despite setting a major league record with a 1.12 earned run average, that the sport's rules committee had the mound lowered before the 1969 season to give hitters a fighting chance.

The stripping of the reserve clause in the early 1970s not only resulted in multi-million dollar contracts, but also launched a period of labor strife and greatly broadened the financial gap between small-market and large-market teams such as the New York Yankees and Los Angeles Dodgers, who could now afford to offer the most lucrative contracts to premier free agents.

Meanwhile, the fight for freedom by the players and the vain attempt by the owners to place a salary cap on teams proved costly to baseball's popularity. A work stoppage in 1982 cost one third of the regular season and another in 1994 ended the season prematurely, wiped out the World Series, and threatened to kill the 1995 season as well. Fans were sickened by what they perceived as the greed of the now-rich players and the wealthy owners. The lack of a salary cap, which has been adopted by the National Football League (NFL) and the National Basketball Association (NBA) to maintain a competitive balance, remains a pressing issue in baseball and has continued to widen the gap between the haves and the have-nots to the point in which many small-market franchises have no chance of maintaining a contending team because they cannot afford to keep their best players once they become eligible for free agency.

Relative parity is one reason the NFL has long surpassed Major League Baseball in popularity among Baby Boomers, but particularly among those of younger generations, who also vastly prefer the speed and violence of football in comparison to the snail's pace and relative staid nature of baseball. Professional football was a secondary sport, even to its college brethren, until the late 1950s. The famed nationally televised 1958 NFL championship overtime classic between the Baltimore Colts and New York Giants thrust professional football into the spotlight, and its popularity has been on the rise ever since.

The creation of the Super Bowl in 1967 and the merger between the NFL and the upstart American Football League in 1970 played roles in the growth of the game. So did the launching of *Monday Night Football* in 1970, which proved to be one of the most successful media innovations in the history of American sport. Millions of young Baby Boomers throughout the country discussed the previous night's game with their coworkers every Tuesday morning.

The most significant shift on the field has been the increased use of the forward pass. Quarterbacks in the 1960s and 1970s often led the NFL with little more than 3,000 yards through the air during the course of a season. It is now unheard-of for the league passing champion to earn that title with fewer than 4,000 yards. The wide-open style of play has contributed to the growing popularity of professional football.

Massive expansion and a strong identity with the top players have fueled the growth of the NBA. The league has quadrupled in size since the 1960s, when only the presence of such superstar players as Bill Russell, Jerry West, Wilt Chamberlain, and Oscar Robertson could fill up arenas. The game itself has remained virtually the same over the years, although the advent of the three-point shot has placed a premium on long-distance shooting.

The popularity of the NBA increased slightly when it merged with the upstart American Basketball Association in the 1970s and more dramatically in the early 1980s when college antagonists Larry Bird of the Boston Celtics and Magic Johnson of the Los Angeles Lakers embarked on a heated on-court rivalry that resulted in the most intense basketball competition in league history. The addition several years later of the brilliant Michael Jordan, who led the Chicago Bulls to several championships and is still considered by many as the greatest player in the history of the NBA, created an attendance explosion. Current stars such as Kobe Bryant of the Lakers and LeBron James of the Miami Heat have ensured the continued interest in the sport.

Despite expansion into many American cities, hockey has remained far more popular in Canada than it has in the United States. Yet millions of Baby Boomers and others have stayed loyal to the sport and have maintained a keen interest throughout the years as such stars as Gordie Howe, Bobby Orr, Wayne Gretzky, and Sidney Crosby have, in chronological order, helped keep the National Hockey League in the public eye.

The loyalty to local teams in all major sports was an important and soothing bridge in the generation gap between Baby Boomers and their parents in the 1960s and early 1970s. In an era in which many of them rarely agreed on anything, particularly in regard to politics, fashion, and lifestyle, a shared fondness and even passion for particular teams often provided moments of friendly communication. Millions of Baby Boomers still fondly recall accompanying their parents to sporting events that occurred during their childhood.

See also Aaron, Hank; Jordan, Michael; Namath, Joe; Television.

FURTHER READING

Michener, James. *Sports in America*. New York: Fawcett Books, 1987.

Oriard, Michael. *Brand NFL: Making and Selling America's Favorite Sport*. Chapel Hill: University of North Carolina Press, 2007.

Ward, Geoffrey, and Ken Burns. *Baseball: An Illustrated History*. New York: Knopf, 1996.

TELEVISION The children and grandchildren of the first decade of Baby Boomers are often taken aback when informed by their parents and grandparents that there were three channel choices until the mid-1960s: NBC, CBS, and ABC.

It seems remarkable in this age of expanded cable programming that Boomers had such a limited selection. But what the younger generations do not always understand is that the Boomers did not mind. It was all they had, and they never questioned it. In addition, there always seemed to be something good to watch.

Television programming has generally reflected American society. The oldest Baby Boomers in their preteen years recall the spate of family shows that gained popularity throughout the 1950s. Most were set in suburbia, to which millions of families had flocked after World War II. Sitcoms such as *Father Knows Best, The Danny Thomas Show, Ozzie and Harriet*, and *Leave It to Beaver* depicted the American family as virtually problem-free. Quite tame by today's standards, most episodes would spotlight a silly complication, most often stumbled into by one of the children, from which one and all were painstakingly extricated.

A more popular genre among young Baby Boomers in the 1950s, especially boys, was the western. *Gunsmoke, Bonanza, Wagon Train, Maverick, The Rifleman, Cheyenne*, and *Rawhide* were just a few of the dozens of westerns that hit the airwaves, mostly late in the decade. Many of them lasted well into the 1960s and even 1970s. *Gunsmoke* and *Bonanza* remain two of the most revered programs in television history.

Game shows were also highly rated in the 1950s, although generally less geared for Baby Boomers than their parents. A 1954 Supreme Court ruling that game shows were not a form of gambling paved the way for the genre to be shown on television. Programs such as *Twenty-One, The $64,000 Question, The Price Is Right, You Bet Your Life* (hosted by comedian Groucho Marx), and *I've Got a Secret* remained near the top of the ratings. Game shows were temporarily disgraced when it was revealed in 1958 that the highly popular quiz show *Twenty One* was fixed. The scandal gave many young Baby Boomers the first taste of adult dishonesty.

Also highly rated, but far less popular among young Baby Boomers, were variety shows starring Ed Sullivan, George Gobel, Perry Como, Jackie Gleason, Bob Hope, and Jack Benny that dotted the evening lineups.

Escapism from the turmoil of the 1960s played a huge role in the programming of that decade, particularly in regard to sitcoms. Television executives concluded that people deluged with news about assassinations, riots in the inner cities, and the Vietnam War wanted to travel as far away from reality as possible, so shows about a witch (*Bewitched*), genie (*I Dream of Genie*), Martian (*My Favorite Martian*), talking horse (*Mr. Ed*), strange families (*The Munsters, The Addams*

Family), caped superhero (*Batman*), flying nun (*The Flying Nun*), and bumbling hillbilly Marine (*Gomer Pyle*) peppered the television landscape. All were highly rated and popular among the growing Baby Boomer population.

Although *Bonanza* and *Gunsmoke* remained favorites and the imaginative *Wild, Wild West* hit the scene, running westerns fell out of vogue by the mid-1960s whereas cop and detective programs such as *I Spy, The Untouchables, Man From U.N.C.L.E.*, and *Mission Impossible* gained favor among Baby Boomers.

After the quiz show scandal of the late 1950s died down, a new generation of game shows that inundated the weekday morning lineups earned popularity, including *Jeopardy, Password, Let's Make a Deal, The Match Game, Hollywood Squares, The Newlywed Game*, and *The Dating Game*. Baby Boomers now in their teenage years were more likely to tune in to game shows and still-popular variety shows. One variety show that proved far more controversial in the late 1960s and was a favorite among antiwar Baby Boomers was *The Smothers Brothers Comedy Hour*, which featured humor criticizing government policies in regard to the Vietnam War. Although it was one of the most highly rated programs of its era, it was abruptly cancelled because of its refusal to slip out of the political arena.

Soon the sitcom *All in the Family* was revolutionizing television. It was the first socially relevant fictional series and it spearheaded the CBS Saturday night lineup, arguably the most popular and critically acclaimed in television history, featuring *The Mary Tyler Moore Show, M*A*S*H*, and *The Bob Newhart Show*. Baby Boomers and their family members would often stay home on Saturday nights to tune in. *All in the Family* delved deeply into such issues as war, race, the growing women's liberation movement, and even homosexuality. After a slow start, it catapulted to number one in the ratings and remained there through most of the 1970s. After the launch of *All in the Family*, any issue was fair game.

Television headed in a different direction in the 1970s. Sitcoms such as *The Brady Bunch* and *The Partridge Family* continued to avoid controversial subject matter and remained popular. And although the *Sonny and Cher Comedy Hour* and the *Flip Wilson Show* attracted a large audience early in the decade, the variety show genre was dead and buried by the end of the 1970s. Several game shows remained on the air but were not as highly rated. Action detective programs such as *Kojak, The Rockford Files, Police Woman, Mannix, Starsky and Hutch, Charlie's Angels*, and *Baretta* ruled the night on television. Meanwhile, news magazine *60 Minutes* set a standard for that new genre that would result in the launching of many others and *The Tonight Show* made host Johnny Carson one of the most beloved personalities in American history.

Perhaps the most socially significant program of the 1980s was *The Cosby Show*, starring African American comedian Bill Cosby. Cosby portrayed a doctor married to a lawyer in a large black family. Previous sitcoms starring African Americans, such as *Good Times, Sanford and Son*, and *The Jeffersons*, featured lowbrow humor and portrayed them as poor or deceptive with little moral character. *The Cosby Show* raised the level of black parenting on television to that of the most noble white mothers and fathers. Other popular shows of the 1980s included sitcoms such as the highly acclaimed *Cheers* and *Family Ties*, which featured former hippies parenting a conservative teenage boy, and detective show *Hill Street Blues*.

A new genre—the nighttime soap opera—also became highly popular in the 1980s. It kicked off with the premiere of *Dallas* in 1978 and was followed by *Knots Landing, Dynasty*, and *Falcon Crest*.

Although network programming still ruled the ratings roost, the advent of cable television in the 1980s had an immediate impact and gave viewers far more choices. Music Television (MTV), the ESPN sports network, and such general programming networks as USA and WTBS were established and continued to grow in popularity. But it would be quite a while before any cable shows worked their way anywhere near the top spot in the ratings.

Cable began making more of an impact in the 1990s with such popular programs as the animated *South Park* and gangster drama *The Sopranos*. More sophisticated network programs such as *Frasier* and *Northern Exposure* also garnered high ratings, but sitcoms *Seinfeld, Friends*, and *Everybody Loves Raymond* were the most wildly popular shows on television. In fact, many consider *Seinfeld* as the funniest and most well-written sitcom in history.

The 2000s were dominated by the explosion of reality television. American viewers became engrossed in the real-life challenges presented to their fellow Americans in such programs as *American Idol, Lost, Survivor, Dancing with the Stars*, and *The Amazing Race*. Meanwhile, taboos were being broken in the network sitcom *Two and a Half Men*, in which the characters discussed previously avoided subjects regarding sex and relationships.

Television has grown exponentially since the staid shows of the 1950s and socially irrelevant programming of the following decade. The events of those decades and the changing tastes of the growing Baby Boomer population paved the way for more sophisticated and controversial television offerings.

See also All in the Family; Carson, Johnny; *M*A*S*H*; Moore, Mary Tyler; *Saturday Night Live*; Talk Show Revolution.

FURTHER READING

Barnouw, Erik. *Tube of Plenty: The Evolution of American Television*. New York: Oxford University Press, 1990.

Edgerton, Gary. *The Columbia History of Modern Television*. New York: Columbia University Press, 2009.

Waldron, Vince. *Classic Sitcoms: A Celebration of the Best in Prime-Time Comedy*. Los Angeles: Silman-James Press, 1998.

TERRORISM Terrorism is defined by the U.S. Department of Defense as "the calculated use of unlawful violence or threat of unlawful violence to inculcate fear; intended to coerce or intimidate governments or societies in the pursuit of goals that are generally political, religious, or ideological."

Although the attacks on the nation perpetrated by Islamic extremists on September 11, 2001, brought terrorism to the United States from outside of the country for the first time, Boomers can recall terrorist actions taken by foreign elements involving Americans outside of its borders and by its own citizens inside of its borders.

Methods of terrorism changed after World War II, during which German air raids in Poland and other countries before the French campaign could certainly be placed into that category. In the postwar world, terrorism was most likely to be used for ideological reasons or to attain political goals by factions within nations that were not world powers.

One example of American terrorism that was fueled by political and ideological philosophies was the short-lived but violent actions spearheaded by the far left-wing Weather Underground in the late 1960s and early 1970s. Otherwise known as the Weathermen, the group consisted of a few Baby Boomers who morphed into the radical faction of the Students for a Democratic Society (SDS). The Weather Underground set out on a mission to create a violent revolution, destroy the capi-talist system, and overthrow the U.S. government. It was wholly unsuccessful, but it did create terror through a series of bombings, including one that killed a student at the Mathematics Research Center on the campus of the University of Wisconsin in 1970.

Modern terrorism has generally centered on the Middle East and has sometimes targeted Americans and U.S. interests because of their support for Israel and the perceived decadence of Western culture. The first modern terrorist attack is con-sidered to be the 1968 hijacking of an El Al plane heading from Israel to Rome by members of the Popular Front for the Liberation of Palestine (PFLP). It was not the first hijacking, but it was the first instance in which terrorist hijackers took passen-gers as hostages and made demands of a government, in this case that of Israel.

Until 2001, the most memorable and heart-wrenching terrorist attack younger and older Baby Boomers recall occurred during the Munich Olympics in September 1972. Although it did not directly involve the U.S. team, Americans sat stunned when 8 Palestinian terrorists seized 11 Israeli athletes and eventually killed them all as West German authorities bungled a rescue attempt.

Another hostage crisis that falls into the category of terrorism hit home with far greater force and turned some Baby Boomers who had been calling for peace-ful solutions to world problems throughout their adult lives to demand a swift, violent response. That was the seizing of 66 American diplomats from the U.S. Embassy in Tehran by Iranian student radicals in November 1979. The tense situ-ation figuratively held the American people hostage for more than a year before the diplomats were released in early 1981.

However, by that time terrorist activity had become frighteningly common-place in much of the world, particularly in the Middle East, Africa, parts of Asia, and even Ireland. Terrorist activity often involved Americans. Examples include the suicide truck-bombing on a U.S. Marine compound in Beirut, Lebanon, that killed 242 Americans in 1983 and the bombing of Pan American Flight 103 over Lockerbie, Scotland, five years later by what was believed to be Libyan terrorists in which all 259 passengers, including 179 Americans, perished.

The first in a series of terrorist attacks in the United States occurred in February 1993 when a bomb left in an underground garage at the World Trade Center in New

York exploded, leaving 6 dead and 1,000 injured. Taking credit for the attack were followers of Egyptian cleric Umar Abd al-Rahman. But the tragedy of that event paled in comparison to that of the bombing of the Federal Building in Oklahoma City in 1995 perpetrated by right-wing extremists Timothy McVeigh and Terry Nichols. The largest terrorist attack on American soil at that time killed 166 and injured hundreds more. Even Baby Boomers who were raised in the 1960s in the shadow of race riots, violent antiwar demonstrations, and assassinations were taken aback by the knowledge that terrorist attacks could take place inside of American borders.

They were more than taken aback on September 11, 2001, when two hijacked planes crashed into the twin towers of the World Trade Center and another struck the Pentagon, leaving more than 3,000 dead. The attacks were the first to prompt strong American military action.

Baby Boomers and other Americans learned grave lessons about terrorism and the proper response to it after the invasion of Iraq in 2003. Many believed that the war was akin to responding to terrorism with a knee-jerk reaction. The connection between the Iraqi government and the Al-Qaeda terrorists, led by Osama Bin Laden, was strongly questioned. By the end of President George W. Bush's term in office in early 2009, the war was hugely unpopular, Bin Laden was still free, and the threat of terrorism remained. Many from the Baby Boomer generation who had protested against the Vietnam War, yet advocated the use of force against Iraq in 2003, reverted to their past inclinations to be cynical of the intentions and truthfulness of corporate, government, and military leaders and came to believe that the war was being fought for such capitalist gains as oil rather than to combat terrorism. Some believed that the Bush administration terrorized the American public through false reports of threat levels and sending thousands of soldiers to their death unnecessarily and terrorizing the Iraqi people.

See also Radicalism.

FURTHER READING

Emerson, Steven. *American Jihad: The Terrorists Living Among Us*. New York: Free Press, 2003.

Fouskas, Vassilis, and Bulent Gokay. *The New American Imperialism: Bush's War on Terror and Blood for Oil*. Westport, CT: Praeger, 2005.

THOMPSON, HUNTER S. (1937–2005) "Gonzo" journalist Hunter S. Thompson epitomized the transition from conservative upbringing to ultraliberalism and even radicalism that millions of Baby Boomers experienced. Thompson made his mark in the late 1960s and early 1970s by creating what became coined as "gonzo journalism," which placed the reporter as a prime character into the story in a first-person narrative.

Thompson was born in Louisville, Kentucky, on July 18, 1937, the son of Virginia and Jack Thompson, who worked as an insurance agent. Thompson received a rather typical public school education before joining the Air Force, where he exhibited a love for writing and a penchant for preposterous behavior. He received a dishonorable discharge in 1958 for allegedly flouting the military dress code and disregarding authority to the point in which he was a poor influence on his fellow airmen.

Author Hunter S. Thompson, right, speaks on the influence of the news media on the recent national elections during a panel discussion at Yale University in New Haven, Connecticut, on December 7, 1972. Frank Mankiewicz, center, who was campaign director for Democratic presidential candidate George McGovern, is also a member of the panel, which is moderated by Yale Political Science professor Robert Dahl, left. (AP Photo)

Thompson was fired from jobs at a New York newspaper and *Time* magazine, and he moved to Puerto Rico and began writing for a bowling publication. He returned to the United States in 1960 and settled in Big Sur in California, where he penned a book that failed to be published. He then traveled to South America, where he wrote for *The National Observer*, a magazine owned by Dow Jones. He continued working for that magazine upon returning to the United States in 1963, covering such topics as Native American fishing rights in Washington State. Thompson quit his job when his request to cover the burgeoning Free Speech Movement at the University of California at Berkeley was refused.

Thompson soon settled in San Francisco, where the hippie culture and political radicalism were beginning to flourish. He received an opportunity to write about the left-wing student movement at Berkeley for *The Nation* magazine, which then assigned him a story about the Hell's Angels. His work garnered national attention and piqued the interest of publisher Random House, where an editor asked him to do an inside investigative piece on the Hell's Angels. Thompson spent a year riding and living with the noted and sometimes notorious motorcycle gang before writing his first book, *Hell's Angels: The Strange and Terrible Saga of the Outlaw Motorcycle Gang.*

In 1968, after experiencing what has been described as a police riot against Vietnam War protesters outside of the Democratic National Convention in Chicago, Thompson returned to Aspen, Colorado, to run unsuccessfully for sheriff of that town on a "Freaks" platform. As Thompson became further intrigued by the counterculture in the late 1960s, he wrote extensively for *Ramparts* and *Scanlan's Monthly* magazines, but it was his story on the Kentucky Derby in 1970 that ushered in a new form of journalism. Drunk and struggling with writer's block and an approaching deadline, he submitted to *Scanlan's* a disorganized set of notes that focused more on himself than on the Derby. Titled *The Kentucky Derby Is Decadent and Depraved*, it was published word-for-word and began gonzo journalism.

The unconventional writing style landed Thompson work at *Rolling Stone* magazine, which assigned him to cover a motorcycle race and national drug law enforcement convention in Las Vegas. His two-part story titled *Fear and Loathing in Las Vegas: A Savage Journey to the Heart of an American Dream* (1971) became an instant classic and was trumpeted as the launching of a new wave in journalism. Thompson focused on himself experiencing drug-induced outrageous adventures in a wild, humorous style that millions of young Baby Boomers who embraced change in traditional writing lapped up.

Thompson also covered the 1972 presidential campaign for *Rolling Stone*, which became *Fear and Loathing on the Campaign Trail '72* (1973). The first to predict a George McGovern nomination as the Democratic candidate, Thompson was criticized for a lack of objectivity and a writing technique that mocked traditional style. He was again the star of his writing.

Thompson maintained his reputation as an iconoclast journalist, but his influence waned in the later 1970s, particularly during the conservative wave that swept across the United States late in that decade. He was dispatched to Zaire in 1974 to cover the heavyweight title fight between Muhammad Ali and George Foreman for *Rolling Stone* but contracted malaria and never wrote the story. The magazine sent him to Vietnam at the end of the war, but he managed to produce just one short dispatch. His last article for *Rolling Stone* was a story on future president Jimmy Carter in 1976.

Thompson announced upon the release of a collection of his early work titled *The Great Shark Hunt* (1979) that he had killed off the literary persona that had made him famous. A year later, he toiled on a film titled *Where the Buffalo Roam* about his adventures with attorney Oscar Zeta Acosta. In 1984, *The Curse of Lono*, a book about his trip to Hawaii, was published. During the latter half of the 1980s, he landed work as a columnist for the *San Francisco Examiner* that gained further attention through syndication. He released two more collections of his writings during that time, admitting at one point that he was lazy and that making money as a journalist was much easier than earning a living in the literary world because the former allowed him to get paid simply to cover events.

Thompson became a bit of a recluse at his 100-acre farm near Aspen, and he remained a hard drinker and fond of motorcycling and shooting off gongs with his .44 Magnum gun. He remained quite unconventional in his lifestyle into his fifties and was charged with five felony counts of possessing drugs and owning and storing illegal explosives, although the charges were later dropped.

His autobiographical *Fear and Loathing in Las Vegas* was released again in 1996 to commemorate its 25th anniversary. A movie adaptation of the work, which starred noted actor Johnny Depp and was directed by Terry Gilliam of Monty Python fame, flopped at the box office. In 1998, Thompson released a book titled *The Rum Diary: The Long Lost Novel by Hunter S. Thompson*, which was based on his experiences in Puerto Rico about four decades earlier.

Thompson committed suicide on February 20, 2005, at age 67. He died of self-inflicted gunshot wounds to his head. His 32-year-old wife Anita was talking to him on the phone when he killed himself.

See also Ali, Muhammad; Antiwar Movement; Conservatism; Drinking; Free Speech Movement; Vietnam War.

FURTHER READING

Thompson, Hunter S. *Fear and Loathing in Las Vegas: A Savage Journey to the Heart of the American Dream*. New York: Vintage Books Publishing, 1997.

Thompson, Hunter S. *The Great Shark Hunt: Strange Tales from a Strange Time*. New York: Simon and Schuster, 2003 (reprint).

Thompson, Hunter S. *Fear and Loathing on the Campaign Trail '72*. New York: Grand Central Publishing, 2006 (reprint).

u

U2 The oldest Baby Boomers fervently embraced several iconic rock-and-roll art-ists and bands as symbols of their generations, including Bob Dylan, the Beatles, and the Rolling Stones. By the time millions of the first wave of Baby Boomers were in college, such groups as the Doors and Led Zeppelin could be added to the list.

The youngest Baby Boomers born in the mid-1960s enjoyed several rock acts in their teenage years, although few that many consider among the all-time greats. But one that rivaled some of the premier bands of the late 1960s was U2. The Irish quartet not only achieved tremendous artistic and commercial success in the 1980s and 1990s, but they also gained favor among Baby Boomers of all ages for their politically and socially oriented messages.

U2 was founded in Dublin in the fall of 1976 by drummer Larry Mullen, who placed a notice on a bulletin board seeking band mates. Soon lead singer and gui-tarist Paul Hewson, who became better known as Bono, joined with guitarist and keyboardist Dave Evans (the Edge), Dik Evans, and bass guitarist Adam Clayton. The departure of Evans to join another group left four members who adopted the name Feedback. They changed their name to the Hype before settling on U2.

The band received encouragement when it won a local St. Patrick's Day talent contest in 1978. Although Bono later admitted that other bands in the competition boasted greater musical talent, he claimed the triumph was due to his group's elec-trifying stage presence. CBS Records executive Jackie Heyden was so impressed that he arranged a demo session for U2, but a lack of experience and studio time prevented them from making a strong impression.

However, U2 built a dedicated fan base that enjoyed their live shows. Among those who saw potential in the band was Irish journalist Bill Graham, who intro-duced them to future manager Paul McGuinness. U2 signed a three-year contract with CBS Ireland and released a few singles before inking a worldwide deal with Island Records in 1980. Their first two albums, *Boy* and *October,* gained greater critical acclaim than they did sales.

In 1983, U2 broke through as a mainstream act with their third LP titled *War*. The record featured two huge hits in "Sunday Bloody Sunday" and "New Year's Day." Both cemented U2 as a band boasting not only tremendous musical talent, but also thoughtful and even powerful lyrics. "Sunday Bloody Sunday" decried the ongoing violence in their native country by harkening back to a 1972 civil rights protest in Northern Ireland in which 26 protesters were shot and killed. The iconic video of that song featuring Bono carrying a large white flag on stage remains one of the most memorable moments in music video history. "New Year's Day" was a hopeful song about dreaming of a time in which the Irish could live without fearing for their safety. Bono also stated that he wrote the song with the current struggles against tyranny in Poland in mind. Martial law in that country had been declared by the Soviet Union, and Solidarity union leader Lech Walesa had been imprisoned.

Although follow-up album *The Unforgettable Fire* was not as well received by the public, it did include the hit "Pride (In the Name of Love)" and also earned critical acclaim. In April 1985, *Rolling Stone* magazine named U2 "The Band of the Eighties." That summer the group electrified a huge crowd at the Live Aid concert in Wembley Stadium in London. U2, which had by that time established itself as one of the most politically and socially relevant bands in the world, played a benefit for Ireland's unemployed in 1986 and joined the Conspiracy of Hope Tour for Amnesty International.

The youngest generation of Baby Boomers, who could not remember the political activism of the 1960s and early 1970s, embraced U2 as a group that cared about more than simply gaining fame and selling records.

In 1987, U2 released the album *The Joshua Tree*, which proved to be their greatest commercial success, reaching number one in 22 countries, including the United States. The accompanying tour included more than 100 shows and captured the attention of *Time* magazine, which declared it as rock's hottest ticket. Tour stops in the United States, particularly those in Denver, Colorado, and Tempe, Arizona, were captured on tape and released as part of a film and album titled *Rattle and Hum*. The most successful song from the LP was "Desire," which proved to be one of their top hits.

At the end of the decade, U2 played four concerts in Dublin, the last of which, on New Year's Eve, was broadcast around the world. In November 1991, the band released the album *Achtung Baby*, which was criticized by some for its heavy emphasis on studio electronics. The subsequent ZooTV tour featured huge video screens and created a giant spectacle. At the end of each show, Bono attempted to call a famous person such as President Bill Clinton, opera star Luciano Pavarotti, or Princess Diana.

A foray into greater experimentation musically culminated in 1993 with the release of the album *Zooorapa*, which was not well received commercially. Four years later, they submitted the soundtrack for the movie *Batman Forever*. However, by that time the band members were busily working on collaborations and solo projects. However, the 2000 album *All That You Can't Leave Behind* did spawn the hit single "Beautiful Day."

Although U2 are rarely placed in the same category as the Beatles, the Rolling Stones, or Led Zeppelin in regard to their influence and commercial success in the music industry, they are one of the finest and most important bands from the last era in which Baby Boomers were experiencing their teenage years.

See also The Beatles; Diana, Princess of Wales; Led Zeppelin; Rock-and-Roll; The Rolling Stones.

FURTHER READING

Bordowitz, Hank. *The U2 Reader: A Quarter Century of Commentary, Criticism, and Reviews*. Milwaukee, WI: Hal Leonard Corporation, 2003.

U2, and Neil McCormick. *U2 by U2*. New York: It Books, 2006.

V

VIETNAM WAR No event in history has banded Baby Boomers together for a common cause with greater passion than the Vietnam War. The cause was to save the lives of fellow Baby Boomers who were dying in droves in a conflict antiwar activists and millions of others considered immoral.

The seeds of American involvement in the war halfway around the world and in a nation many never heard of were planted in 1956 when the U.S. Military Assistance Advisor Group took over for the French in training South Vietnamese troops who were attempting to repel forces from North Vietnam and a group of their own countrymen called Viet Cong, who were trying to unite the nation under a Communist government.

The decision by President John F. Kennedy in the early 1960s to send military advisors to Vietnam was met with little resistance. But a firestorm of protest ensued when successor Lyndon B. Johnson began dispatching ground forces and continued to increase troop levels throughout his presidency.

The war and reaction to it established four separate factions of Baby Boomers. Many from the rapidly growing middle and upper middle class suburban areas, particularly those who were raised in liberal households, developed an immediate mistrust of American policies and that feeling grew into a passionate hatred with time.

They were joined by inner city Baby Boomers, many of them black, who detested the war, could not understand why billions of dollars were being spent in Vietnam when many of them lived in abject poverty, and became further disgusted by the fact that most troops who were sent to fight and die represented the lower economic strata of American society.

Baby Boomers from small towns and rural areas tended to support the war effort, particularly at first, although many turned against it by the time most Americans had done so in the late 1960s.

The fourth group was the Baby Boomers who fought the war, more than 50,000 of whom were killed. Many veterans came to the conclusion during their stint or after returning home that American involvement was wrong, although others angrily claimed that poor support on the home front and a lack of commitment to the troops wrecked any opportunity to bring the war to a successful conclusion.

The protest movement began on college campuses as young Baby Boomers such as those who had formed the Students for a Democratic Society (SDS) in 1962 and others on such traditionally politically active campuses as the University of California at Berkeley started a grassroots campaign against the growing American presence in Vietnam around 1965. The students had initially responded to Johnson opening up the war to U.S. ground troops after a supposed incident in the Gulf of Tonkin, in which a North Vietnamese PT boat allegedly fired upon an American destroyer. The Congress and Senate passed the Gulf of Tonkin Resolution, which gave Johnson the freedom to wage war without a declaration of war.

During the next four years, hundreds of thousands of Baby Boomers were sent to Vietnam with the number peaking at about 550,000 in 1969. The intensity of the protest movement coincided with the increased troop levels and death count. The first major demonstration was the March on the Pentagon in 1967, which attracted 50,000 protesters. Throughout the late 1960s, some youth burned their draft cards in protest and others fled to Canada to avoid military service.

Until 1968, a great discrepancy existed between the views of Baby Boomers and their parents on the righteousness of American involvement in Vietnam. Unlike the older generations, most of the younger generation believed the troops should return. But in January 1968, the North Vietnamese and Viet Cong launched the Tet Offensive, which proved to millions of Americans that the Communists were far from subdued. It was at that point that overall public opinion turned against U.S. war policy. When renowned and highly respected newscaster Walter Cronkite claimed on his nightly broadcast his view of the war was unwinnable, Johnson reportedly lamented that he had lost Middle America. By 1969, after successor Richard M. Nixon had assumed the office, the protests had grown in scope and numbers. Several demonstrations attracted 500,000 or more.

Two incidents intensified Baby Boomer and overall American disenchantment with the war effort. The first was the 1969 revelation that in March of the previous year a company of U.S. troops massacred approximately 300 unarmed Vietnamese men, women, and children in the village of My Lai. The second was the killing of four Kent State University students by Ohio National Guardsmen during a May 4, 1970, demonstration against the announced expansion of the war into Cambodia, which set off protests by Baby Boomers on college campuses throughout the country.

In 1969, Nixon launched what he termed a "Vietnamization" program in which the war effort would be slowly turned over to South Vietnamese troops as American soldiers began coming home. By the end of 1970, the number of U.S. troops had been sliced in half to approximately 280,000, although protests against the war continued well into 1971. It was in that year that the *New York Times* published the Pentagon Papers, which revealed theretofore secret information about a history of deception in regard to war policy, including the questionable Gulf of Tonkin incident and exaggerated enemy casualty counts. Nixon attempted to squelch the publication of the Pentagon Papers, but his request was denied by the U.S. Supreme Court.

Although only 70,000 American troops remained in Vietnam in 1972, Nixon escalated the bombing of the North Vietnamese capital of Hanoi. In early 1973, a cease-fire was called and the last American troops left the country. In 1975, a Communist takeover in South Vietnam officially made it the first defeat in American military history.

It has been debated whether the antiwar movement, which was spearheaded by Baby Boomers and particularly college students, played a major role in ending American involvement in Vietnam. Baby Boomers were certainly involved in all facets of the war, aside from its planning and managing. They fought for it, against it, and in it.

See also Antiwar Movement; Kennedy, John F.; Racism; War.

FURTHER READING

Lind, Michael. *Vietnam: The Necessary War: A Reinterpretation of America's Most Disastrous Military Conflict.* New York: Free Press, 2002.

Mailer, Norman. *The Armies of the Night.* London: Weidenfeld and Nicolson, 1968.

Sheehan, Neil, Hedrick Smith, E.W. Kenworthy, and Fox Butterfield. *The Pentagon Papers.* New York: Bantam Books, 1971.

W

WAR The Baby Boomers' attitudes about war have shifted over the years. The two main reasons for that change are a transition from idealism to realism and the particular events of the last half-century.

The first wave of Baby Boomers grew up with the notion that war is sometimes a necessary evil. The aggression of Nazi Germany in launching World War II was still fresh in the minds of Americans in the 1950s. In fact, the fathers of millions of Boomers during that era had played roles in subduing Germany and Axis allies Japan and Italy during that conflict. Many Boomer boys received war-related birthday and holiday presents such as toy guns and soldiers.

Many Baby Boomers from small towns and rural areas throughout the country have maintained the same outlook on the necessities or even glory of war throughout their lives, but a huge segment of inner city blacks and suburban whites from that generation changed their view of war, including its causes and effects, as the 1960s progressed.

Growing American involvement in Vietnam by the mid-1960s prompted some young Boomers to believe that their own government was to blame. That was not a well-accepted concept during previous wars of the 20th century; citizens were generally gung-ho behind the military in World War I, World War II, and even Korea. But some in the early 1960s began to question the pragmatism in such anti-Communist actions as those being taken in Vietnam, as well as the motivations of what former president Dwight D. Eisenhower had termed the military-industrial complex.

Millions of Baby Boomers and a smattering of those from older generations began to embrace an idealistic ideology in the 1960s. They believed peace could be achieved among all countries if greedy world leaders ended their struggles for power inside and outside of their national boundaries. Idealistic Boomers viewed war as the result of a militaristic mindset rather than a peaceful one, disregarding the argument that it was most often started by an aggressor nation, which, in turn, required other nations to step in and stop the aggression.

The righteousness of American involvement in Vietnam was questioned in the 1960s. Many Boomers believed it was a civil war in which the United States had no business interfering. Antiwar activists claimed that the fear of a "domino effect" in which other capitalist countries would fall to Communism if Vietnam did was unfounded. They furthermore stated that maintaining corporate interests in that Southeast Asian country and creating a profitable business relationship between the manufacturers of war materials and the military were the primary motivations for American involvement. Meanwhile, young black Baby Boomers during that era decried the comparatively high number of their own people being sent to and killed in Vietnam.

Baby Boomers who were against the war in the 1960s have generally maintained that opinion about that particular conflict. But future events served to wear away the idealistic sentiment that war can become obsolete simply through a peaceful mindset adopted by world leaders.

Disturbing trends in the Middle East in more recent years changed the thinking of many once-idealistic Baby Boomers. The revolution in Iran that resulted in the taking of American hostages had some Boomers calling for a military response. The Iraqi invasion and takeover of a weaker Kuwait in 1990 did the same. Boomers generally joined other Americans to praise President George H. W. Bush for leading a United Nations effort to kick Iraqi leader Saddam Hussein's forces out of Kuwait.

By that time, most Boomers were judging potential U.S. war involvement on a case-by-case basis. In addition, those who protested against policies that resulted in more than 58,000 American deaths in Vietnam pointed out that that 1960s war was greatly condemned internationally. Desert Storm, the operation that successfully and quickly defeated Iraqi forces, was not achieved alone. It was indeed an international effort that was even lauded and aided by the governments and military of other Islamic Middle Eastern countries.

Although criticized for a lack of activism in comparison to that of the Vietnam era, many Baby Boomers spoke out privately or publicly after the war in Iraq perpetrated by President George W. Bush after the terrorist attacks on the United States in September 2001. Boomers angered by the attacks in New York and Washington, D.C., and who not only backed Bush's claims that Iraqi terrorists supported by Hussein spearheaded the attacks, but also believed the contention that Iraq boasted weapons of mass destruction and was a clear and present danger to the United States, voiced agreement with the invasion of 2003. When it became clear that there were no such weapons in Iraq, many of those same Baby Boomers turned against the war and Bush, who they claimed lied to the country. They began to think that the United States was not achieving anything positive for its own nation in Iraq and decried the effort that resulted in several thousand American deaths and more of civilian Iraqis.

Polls indicated that the percentage of Americans against the war in Iraq grew to rival that of Vietnam, but there was a major difference in the relationship between antiwar Boomers and U.S. soldiers. During the Vietnam War, some in the antiwar movement condemned their fellow Baby Boomers who had participated in the conflict, going so far as to calling them "baby killers." But even those strongly against future wars from the Boomer generation tended to blame the government and military leaders rather than the soldiers for what they perceived as unwarranted involvement in overseas conflicts.

See also Antiwar Movement; Idealism; Vietnam War.

FURTHER READING

Buzzell, Colby. *My War: Killing Time in Iraq.* New York: Putnam Adult, 2005.

WATERGATE By the late 1960s, young Baby Boomers who had been critical of the American government and cynical about the honesty of politicians had been joined in their disillusionment by millions of other Americans.

Although many from older generations sided with Boomers who argued against U.S. involvement in Vietnam, most disagreed with their more radical teenage sons and daughters who were more than skeptical of the intentions of those in office. Even most Baby Boomers who disagreed with policy could not have imagined their leaders engaging knowingly in criminal activity.

The Watergate scandal that followed, toppling the presidency of Richard M. Nixon in the process, sent American trust in their government plummeting to arguably its lowest ebb in the nation's history. The tumultuous events served to prolong the country's agony in the wake of the 1960s, the most divisive era in the history of the country since the Civil War.

The scope and importance of the controversy affected Baby Boomers of all ages. Even the youngest of the generation who had yet to reach their teenage years understood enough about the implications of the events to grasp their importance.

The seeds of discontent within the high offices of the American government were planted in September 1971, when White House operatives burglarized a psychiatrist's office to secure files on patient Daniel Ellsburg, a former defensive analyst who had leaked inside since-published information about the handling of the Vietnam War to *the New York Times*. Nixon hoped to discredit Ellsburg in the process.

The Watergate scandal began during the 1972 presidential campaign in which Nixon was running against antiwar Democrat George McGovern. On June 17, five men, including one former CIA agent, were arrested attempting to bug the offices of the Democratic National Committee at the Watergate hotel in Washington, D.C. Shortly thereafter, *The Washington Post* reported that a cashier's check for $25,000, earmarked for the Nixon campaign, had been deposited into the bank account of one burglar.

Post reporters Bob Woodward and Carl Bernstein continued to push forward on their investigation, eventually earning nationwide acclaim and a movie titled *All the President's Men* (1976) about their persistence and achievements. The two reported in late September that Attorney General John Mitchell had controlled a secret Republican Party fund to finance extensive intelligence-gathering operations against the Democrats. Two weeks later, the *Post* tied the Watergate burglary directly to the Committee to Re-Elect the President.

The allegations were not enough to derail Nixon in 1972. Many Baby Boomers scoffed at the timing when Secretary of State Henry Kissinger announced the end of American troop involvement in Vietnam just days before the election, but the announcement helped make the result of the election a foregone conclusion. Nixon won all but one state in one of the biggest landslide victories in the history of American presidential elections.

Soon after Nixon began his second term in office, the Watergate scandal intensified when presidential aides G. Gordon Liddy and James McCord were convicted of conspiracy, burglary, and wiretapping. Exactly three months later, top Nixon staffers H.R. Haldeman and John Ehrlichman and Attorney General Richard Kleindienst resigned, and White House counsel John Dean was fired.

The firing of Dean came back to haunt Nixon. Two weeks after the Senate Watergate committee began nationally televised hearings, the *Post* reported that Dean told investigators that he discussed a cover-up of the affair at least 35 times. On July 13, 1973, former presidential appointments secretary Alexander Butterfield revealed that Nixon had taped all conversations and telephone calls, including those regarding the alleged cover-up.

The refusal of Nixon to turn over the tapes to the Senate committee marked the beginning of the end of his presidency. He attempted to quash the investigation on October 20, 1973, by firing special prosecutor Archibald Cox, Attorney General Elliott Richardson, and Deputy Attorney General William Ruckelshaus in what became known as the "Saturday Night Massacre," which led to calls for Nixon's impeachment.

In mid-November, Nixon made perhaps his most famous utterance to the American people, stating, "I am not a crook" in maintaining his innocence in the Watergate affair. But after an 18.5-minute gap was found in one of the tapes that had been subpoenaed, suspicions about his guilt grew in intensity.

On April 30, 1974, Nixon released 1,200 pages of edited transcripts of his tapes to the House Judiciary Committee, but the committee insisted that he turn in the tapes. Three months later, the U.S. Supreme Court concurrred, rejecting Nixon's claim of executive privilege. On July 27, the committee passed the first of three articles of impeachment. On August 8, Nixon became the first president to ever resign from office.

The controversy continued. Some were disappointed when Gerald R. Ford, who assumed the presidency, pardoned Nixon of all charges related to Watergate. Many Baby Boomers who believed that justice should be meted to all people who committed crimes regardless of position thought that Nixon should have been put on trial and even served a prison term if indeed found guilty of criminal activity. However, others contended that the nation had suffered through a difficult period and that putting Nixon on trial would serve no purpose and would simply extend the embarrassment and misery heaped upon the American people.

Millions of once-liberal or even radical Baby Boomers have moved to the center or right politically since Nixon was in office, but most still regard him with disdain and believe that they were justified in their mistrust of him. They believe that he earned the derisive nickname "Tricky Dick" well before the Watergate scandal began.

See also Conservatism; Elections; Idealism; Political Participation; Vietnam War.

FURTHER READING

Bernstein, Carl, and Bob Woodward. *All the President's Men*. New York: Simon and Schuster, 1994 (revised).

Kutler, Stanley I. *The Wars of Watergate: The Last Crisis of Richard Nixon*. New York: W.W. Norton and Company, 1992.

THE WHO Through one iconic song, British Invasion rock quartet the Who established a connection with Baby Boomers around the free world. That song, ironically enough, was titled "My Generation."

The Who, perhaps more than any rock band aside from the Beatles, best expressed the feelings, ideals, and rebelliousness of young Baby Boomers as they grew into adults and challenged the establishment in the 1960s and early 1970s through songs such as "I Can't Explain," "The Kids Are Alright," and "Won't Get Fooled Again."

The London-based quartet was formed by singer Roger Daltrey, guitarist and singer Pete Townshend, whose parents were professional musicians, and bassist John Entwistle. Townshend played banjo and Entwistle played trumpet in a Dixieland band when they were teenagers. They also worked in a rock band until

Singer Roger Daltrey (left) and guitarist Pete Townshend, of English rock group the Who, performing at the Manchester Apollo, March 1, 1981. (Kevin Cummins/Getty Images)

Entwistle left in 1962 to join a group called the Detours, which featured Daltrey on lead guitar, then vocals. Townsend was added soon thereafter, as was drummer Keith Moon, who had been performing in a surf band called the Beachcombers and eventually earned a reputation as arguably the greatest drummer in the history of rock-and-roll. By early 1964, the Detours had changed their name to the Who and Townshend had established what would become a longstanding tradition by smashing his guitar on stage.

By that time, Baby Boomers in the United States were embracing Beatlemania and the British Invasion had begun. However, the Who created a better-dressed "Mod" image. They played covers of established blues and early Motown songs but changed drastically when Townshend and Daltrey began writing their own music. "I Can't Explain," a pure rock-and-roll song that expressed the frustrations of youth who did not know how to explain their feelings, earned the band its first record deal and hit the charts in 1965. It was ignored until the Who appeared on the British television show *Ready, Steady, Go*. When audiences watched the band's performance, which included Townshend smashing his guitar and Moon overturning his drum set, the song soared to number eight in the United Kingdom.

By the end of the year, the group would also place "Anyway, Anyhow, Anywhere" into the British Top 10 and release "My Generation," which would catapult to number two in the United Kingdom and make a dent in the American charts. Such hit songs as "Substitute" and "Happy Jack" would follow. So would their coming-out party in the United States at the 1967 Monterey Pop Festival. The American audience sat spellbound and shocked by the Who's violent stage act, but the group quickly became stars across the Atlantic. By the following year, "I Can See for Miles" had reached the Top 10 in the United States. The Who never had a number one song in the United States, primarily because they grew into an album-oriented hard-rock band with little motivation to soar in the pop charts.

During the late 1960s, Townshend began working on a 90-minute rock opera called *Tommy*, which was the story of a deaf, dumb, and blind boy who became a pinball champion. Its first single, "Pinball Wizard," was a hit, as was "See Me, Feel Me," and the now-iconic rock opera was performed in the late spring of 1970 at the Metropolitan Opera House in New York City.

The Who gained tremendous commercial and critical success with their 1971 album *Who's Next*, which featured anthems of Baby Boomer rebelliousness and FM radio rock standards "Baba O'Riley" and "Won't Get Fooled Again." Two years later, the double-album rock opera *Quadrophenia*, which expressed the tortured lives of the early British Mods, reached number two in the U.S. charts. The hit single "Squeeze Box" emerged from the 1975 album *The Who by Numbers*, but by that time the group had lost much of its impact and personality clashes and personal problems were beginning to take a toll. The 1978 album *Who Are You*, which featured a hit song of the same name, did go double platinum. This was the last album for the original band.

Tragedy struck on September 7 of that year when Moon, who had returned to the United Kingdom to battle alcoholism, died of a prescription drug overdose. The other three band members remained together for three more years, but the Who was never the same. A year later, 11 fans were trampled to death or asphyxiated at the Cincinnati Riverfront Coliseum during a stampede for prime seating at a Who concert. The band was not informed of the tragedy until after the show.

After Moon's death, Townshend and Daltrey embarked on solo work. The former performed a U.S. Top 10 hit in "Let My Love Open the Door," stunned his bandmates by admitting that he had had homosexual experiences, and nearly overdosed on heroin and the tranquilizer Ativan, prescribed for alcoholism.

The Who released the hit single "You Better You Bet" in 1981 before embarking the next year on what they claimed at the time would be their last tour. But they reunited for the legendary Live Aid concert in 1985 and a long American tour in 1989. The Who's legacy grew in 1993 when a Broadway production of *Tommy* won five Tony Awards, including one for Townshend for Best Original Score. In 1994, the three remaining original band members reunited for a concert at New York's Carnegie Hall to celebrate Daltrey's 50th birthday. The show was filmed for cable television and included a 65-piece orchestra and such musical guest stars as Sinead O'Connor, Eddie Vedder, and Lou Reed. In 1996, the group recruited Zak Starkey, son of former Beatle Ringo Starr, to play drums on a series of tour dates.

The band remained active well into the new millennium. They embarked on another reunion tour in 2000, issued a live album, and even began considering returning to the studio. They appeared at the Concert for New York City to benefit those affected by the tragedy of the September 11, 2001, terrorist attacks and even toured again in the summer of 2002 after Entwistle died of a heart attack brought on by cocaine abuse.

The Who has remained in the public eye and received an acknowledgement of their place among the greats of rock-and-roll when they were invited to perform at halftime of the 2010 Super Bowl in Miami. However, their performance disappointed many Baby Boomers, who believed the band sounded old. Even the band members admitted that a lack of practice time and the fact that they were forced to play mini-versions of their songs in a short period of time took a toll on their performance.

The longevity of the Who has allowed them to remain a favorite of younger and older Baby Boomers, although the earliest of the generation is more likely to appreciate them for what they represented and for what they achieved musically.

See also The Beatles; Drinking; Rock-and-Roll.

FURTHER READING

Fletcher, Tony. *Moon: The Life and Death of a Rock Legend.* New York: It Books, 2000.
Marsh, Dave. *Before I Get Old: The Story of The Who.* Medford, NJ: Plexus Publishing, 2003.
Wilkerson, Mark. *Who Are You: The Life of Pete Townshend.* London: Music Sales, 2008.

WILL, GEORGE (1941–) George Will followed the trend toward intellectual conservatism started by William F. Buckley and became its most respected voice.

His writing helped turn some Baby Boomers into conservatives and supporters of Ronald Reagan as a candidate and president in the late 1970s and early 1980s.

Will has also proven critical of what he perceives as populist conservatism before and after the presidential election of Barack Obama in 2008. He lashed out at Republican vice-presidential candidate Sarah Palin as being woefully lacking in credentials and claimed that she could never win the presidency.

Will was born in 1941 in Champaign, Illinois. One might believe he inherited his intellectualism from his father, Frederick, who was a philosophy professor at the University of Illinois. The younger Will eventually earned his Ph.D. in politics from Princeton University. He worked with Colorado Republican senator Gordon Allott in the early 1970s.

Bypassing a career in politics, Will joined the staff of the *National Review* in 1972 and served for six years as an editor of that conservative political publication, which was founded by Buckley. He became a contributing editor with *Newsweek* magazine in 1976 and began writing a syndicated column twice a week in 1979 after joining *The Washington Post* Writers Group. He continued to serve in both capacities well into 2010.

Despite his relative lack of experience at the time, Will won a Pulitzer Prize for Commentary in 1977 for his writing on various subjects. He has been known to pepper his work with references to baseball, a sport about which he is passionate and has written two books, including the bestseller *Men at Work: The Craft of Baseball* (1990).

Will earned a reputation for open-mindedness and unbending morality in regard to his conservative thought. He refused to support President Richard M. Nixon after wrongdoing was revealed during the Watergate scandal and was highly critical of President George W. Bush's handling of the war in Iraq in the mid-2000s. He has remained pragmatic while taking opposing stands to those of traditional conservatives, proposing a withdrawal of troops from Afghanistan, praising the Democrat Obama's response to the 2009 post-election uprisings in Iran, and criticizing Bush for the treatment of prisoners at Guantanamo Bay, as well as his policies during the Iraq War, which Will deemed as unrealistic. Will criticized Bush for a perceived lack of truthfulness in reporting the difficulties of maintaining order in that strife-torn Middle Eastern country.

Particularly conservative on social and economic issues, Will has taken a stand against the landmark *Roe v. Wade* Supreme Court decision that paved the way for legalized abortions, came out in favor of private gun ownership as a constitutional right, and expressed his skepticism over the effectiveness of affirmative action programs. He has also fallen in line with traditional conservative thinking that lower taxes spur economic growth and has questioned the existence of global warming.

Will was also angered by the presidential campaign of Republican John McCain in 2008, particularly his selection of Sarah Palin as his vice-presidential candidate. He blasted her qualifications for that position and criticized McCain as careless for making that choice.

Although Will is regarded as scrupulous in his honesty, he has fallen victim to controversy on occasion. He has been criticized by those who perceive that he has purposely shed his objectivity. During the 1980 presidential campaign, he helped Reagan prepare for his debate against incumbent Democrat Jimmy Carter, and then appeared on the ABC late-night news talk show *Nightline* after the debate to discuss the event as ostensibly an independent journalist. In 2005, Will admitted that his role in helping Reagan prepare for the debate was inappropriate.

The events of 1980 had no long-term effect on Will's career as a television journalist. He has been providing commentary for ABC since the early 1980s and was among the first members of the panel on that network's popular news talk show *This Week with David Brinkley*. He also served in the 1970s as a regular panelist on the long-running NBC news talk program *Meet the Press*.

Although millions of Baby Boomers have disagreed with most of Will's views for decades, others have embraced them. Many conservative and liberal Boomers respect Will for his intellect and journalistic integrity.

See also Conservatism; Reagan, Ronald; Talk Show Revolution; Watergate.

FURTHER READING

Will, George. *Men at Work: The Craft of Baseball*. New York: Macmillan, 1990.

Will, George. *One Man's America: The Pleasures and Provocations of Our Singular Nation*. New York: Three Rivers Press, 2009.

WOMEN'S MOVEMENT The second wave of the women's movement, which overhauled all aspects of gender relations in society, began in the late 1960s and was aided greatly by young Boomers imbued with the spirit of change that helped define their generation.

Although later activists have been credited for spurring what was then known as the women's liberation movement of the late 1960s and early 1970s, a little-recognized name was responsible for planting the seeds for it a decade earlier. Women's Bureau of the Department of Labor Director Esther Peterson encouraged government leaders to address issues regarding discrimination against women in the early 1960s and motivated President John F. Kennedy to convene a Commission on the Status of Women, which was headed by former first lady Eleanor Roosevelt. Its 1963 findings reported discrimination against women in every facet of American life. The report prompted the establishment of state and local commissions to research situations in their areas and recommend changes.

The first leader of the women's movement of that era was Betty Friedan, whose landmark book *The Feminine Mystique* (1963) registered the complaint that middle-class educated women were being intellectually and emotionally oppressed because they had been placed in servitude as housewives or were unable to maximize their professional potential. The book became a runaway best seller and inspired millions of women, including some young female Baby Boomers, to examine their current lives or futures.

Although the sweeping 1964 Civil Rights Act is known mostly for attempting to end racial discrimination, the last-minute inclusion of women in the bill motivated the Equal Employment Opportunity Commission to investigate complaints in regard to sexual injustice. By 1969, it had received 50,000 sex discrimination

Women gather to protest the Miss America pageant in Atlantic City, New Jersey, on September 7, 1968. Marching along the city's famous boardwalk, they denounced male oppression and racism, which they considered blatant in the way the pageant treated women as objects and discouraged nonwhite contestants. *Time* used the phrase "women's liberation" in reference to the demonstration. (AP/Wide World Photos)

complaints. In 1966, Friedan and other feminists created the National Organization for Women (NOW), a civil rights group inspired by and built along the same lines as the National Association for the Advancement of Colored People (NAACP).

Among those showing particular interest in the burgeoning women's movement were Baby Boomers on college campuses who had been involved in groups fighting racial inequities and American involvement in Vietnam. Frustrated and angered by a perceived blocking of advancement into leadership roles in those efforts by men, many of the young female Boomers began organizing on-campus women's liberation movements.

The movement had captured the hearts and minds of millions of American women by the late 1960s and early 1970s. Many of the most passionate took action, joining or organizing marches, opening women's bookstores from which they delivered messages about women's equality, and protesting such events as the Miss America Pageant. Others quietly vowed to work toward equality in their own professional and personal relationships. Their voices and deeds began to change the direction of gender relations in all aspects of American society.

Among the first major changes was the implementation of Title IX into the Education Codes of 1972, which guaranteed equal access to higher education and professional schools. The result was a huge increase in the number of female Baby Boomers attending graduate school and forging careers as doctors and lawyers and other prestigious and high-paying professions. That same year, the Equal Rights Amendment (ERA), which had been introduced a half-century earlier, passed through Congress and was placed into the state legislatures for ratification. However, the 1982 deadline to ratify passed, and the ERA remains a topic for debate among those who are concerned with how its passage would affect certain such issues as abortion and women's roles in the military.

The most significant area in which the women's movement has affected society has been in the financial realm. Until the 1970s, married women could not get credit cards in their own name, and to get a bank loan they needed a male co-signer. Full-time women workers earned 59 cents for every dollar earned by men.

Backlash against the women's rights movement occurred during the wave of conservatism that swept the country in the late 1970s and early 1980s. Such far right-wing conservatives as Phyllis Schlafly railed and campaigned against passage of the ERA, claiming it would deteriorate family structure in the United States, force women to serve as combat soldiers during wartime, and even result in unisex bathrooms.

By the mid-1980s, much of what the women's movement had fought for during the previous decade had been generally accepted, including the right to pursue lofty educational and professional goals and the notion that household chores should be shared.

However, not all women, including Baby Boomers now approaching middle age, embraced the views supported by feminists on various topics. In the 1990s, women faced several thorny questions that became a matter of conscience regarding controversial social and political issues. Among them was abortion, which had been legalized in 1973. Some who supported other women's rights issues came to believe that abortion should be illegal or that it should not be performed after the fetus had reached a certain stage of development.

Several other questions regarding women's rights and equality have faced Americans in recent years. Should women serve in combat? Is pornography degrading to women or is it a matter of free speech? Where does flirting end and sexual harassment begin? How much paid time off should pregnant women receive from employers?

Some see that the so-called Third Wave of feminists in the 1990s and beyond has taken the gains of the Second Wave for granted and do not show the intellectual and ideological weight of their mothers' generation.

See also Civil Rights Movement; Equal Rights Amendment; Kennedy, John F.; Steinem, Gloria; Vietnam War.

FURTHER READING

Baumgardner, Jennifer. *Manifesta: Young Women, Feminism, and the Future*. New York: Farrar, Straus and Giroux, 2010 (reprint).

Faludi, Susan. *Backlash: The Undeclared War Against American Women.* New York: Three
   Rivers Press, 2006.

WOODSTOCK The Woodstock Music Festival earned legendary status less for
the on-stage performances of the premier rock-and-roll acts of the era than for the
spirit exuded by a concert-goers despite monumental logistical challenges.

Billed as "Three Days of Peace and Music," the concert was held August 15–18,
1969, on the property of farmer Max Yasgur in upstate New York. An estimated 500,000
patrons—mostly young Baby Boomers—streamed in from throughout the country to
witness what became known as the quintessential event of their generation.

The influx of humanity converging into the area shut down the New York State
Thruway and overwhelmed organizers, who gave up on taking tickets, thereby
turning Woodstock into a free festival. The result was an expected economic disaster, although a profit was eventually realized through money earned from the film
documentary. Baby Boomer organizers stated during the event that although they
anticipated a financial bloodbath, the pride and joy they felt playing a role in bringing together a half-million people to display the spirit of their generation meant
far more to them than any loss of money. Boomers cheered their favorite bands,
rollicked in the mud, smoked marijuana, skinny-dipped in nearby lakes, and congregated peacefully throughout to make Woodstock a symbol of their generation.

Protest acts began the proceedings on August 15, and the festival kicked off
with African American folk singer Richie Havens, who closed his set with antiwar
tunes "Handsome Johnny" and "Freedom." The contentious war in Vietnam was
addressed specifically by the next band, Country Joe and the Fish. Lead singer
Country Joe McDonald urged the crowd to sing along to "I-Feel-Like-I'm-Fixing-
to-Die-Rag," a black-humor poke at the military and those of the older generation
who were sending young Baby Boomers halfway around the world to die for what
most of those at Woodstock perceived as an unworthy cause.

Indian sitar player Ravi Shankar, who had been embraced by the Beatles and
other bands of the day, performed early in the event as well, as did Arlo Guthrie,
whose father Woody Guthrie was among the most famous folk singers in American history. The highlight of the younger Guthrie's set was "Coming into Los
Angeles," which told the story of a young man bringing a shipment of marijuana
into the country and hoping to slip by customs. The folk music continued when
Joan Baez brought back memories of the union movement early in the century
with "Joe Hill" and the civil rights struggles of the late 1950s and early 1960s with
"We Shall Overcome."

The focus shifted on Saturday when Carlos Santana displayed his talents and
placed himself among the guitar greats of his generation such as Jimi Hendrix
and Eric Clapton by performing "Soul Sacrifice." Although Canned Heat and
Creedence Clearwater Revival were California bands, neither provided rock
sounds prevalent in that state in the 1960s. The former sang "Going up the Country," which gained popularity later when it was featured in the Woodstock movie.
Creedence, which was at the height of its popularity that summer, regaled the

crowd with a set that included "Born on the Bayou," "Green River," "Bad Moon Rising," and "Proud Mary."

Hippie favorite the Grateful Dead and emerging funk band Sly and the Family Stone ("Dance to the Music") also performed on Saturday, as did soulful Janis Joplin, who belted out "Piece of My Heart" and "Ball and Chain." The Who, arguably the most accomplished band at Woodstock, sang early hits "I Can't Explain" and "My Generation" as well as current songs such as "Tommy, Can You Hear Me" and "Pinball Wizard." The soaring vocals of Jefferson Airplane lead singer Grace Slick performing the psychedelic classics "Somebody to Love" and "White Rabbit" as well as antiwar counterculture favorite "Volunteers" concluded the Saturday session.

The crowd was given a wide array of music on Sunday, from the hard-core raspy blues of Joe Cocker ("Delta Lady") to guitar-dominated Ten Years After featuring Alvin Lee ("I'm Going Home") to the country rock sounds of the Band ("The Weight") to the folk rock of newly formed Crosby, Stills, and Nash ("Suite: Judy Blue Eyes"). The latter admitted their nervousness on stage because they were playing together for only the second time.

By Monday morning, just 35,000 fans remained, but they were awakened to the National Anthem as played by Hendrix, arguably the finest rock guitarist in history. Hendrix also treated the remaining fans to one of his most famous songs, "Foxy Lady."

As Woodstock progressed, the more traditional media portrayed it as a colossal mess and financial disaster. But the word of mouth from those who attended, as well as the documentary movie that followed, changed the perception. By the early 1970s, Woodstock had become accepted with pride by Baby Boomers and others as the event in which the spirit of a generation was defined.

See also Antiwar Movement; Hippie Movement; Marijuana; Rock-and-Roll; Vietnam War; The Who.

FURTHER READING

Fornatale, Pete. *Back to the Garden: The Story of Woodstock.* New York: Touchstone, 2009.

Landy, Elliott. *Woodstock Vision: The Spirit of a Generation.* San Francisco: Backbeat Books, 2009.

Lang, Michael. *The Road to Woodstock.* New York: Ecco Press, 2009.

Selected Bibliography

Adler, Jerry, and Julie Scelfo. "Boomers, Religion and the Meaning of Life." *Newsweek*. September 18, 2006. http://www.newsweek.com/id/39530.

Allyn, David. *Make Love, Not War: The Sexual Revolution: An Unfettered History*. New York: Routledge, 2001.

Bailey, Beth L. *From Front Porch to Back Seat: Courtship in Twentieth Century America*. Baltimore: Johns Hopkins University Press, 1989.

Barnouw, Erik. *Tube of Plenty: The Evolution of American Television*. New York: Oxford University Press, 1990.

Bonilla-Silva, Eduardo. *Racism Without Racists: Color-Blind Racism and the Persistence of Racial Inequality in America*. Lanham, MD: Rowman & Littlefield, 2006.

Brackett, David. *The Pop, Rock and Soul Reader: Histories and Debates*. New York: Oxford University Press, 2008.

Brandt, Allan M. *The Cigarette Century: The Rise, Fall, and Deadly Persistence of the Product That Defined America*. New York: Basic Books, 2007.

Brokaw, Tom. *Boom! Voices of the Sixties: Personal Reflections on the '60s and Today*. New York: Random House, 2007.

Bugliosi, Vincent. *Four Days in November: The Assassination of President John F. Kennedy*. New York: W.W. Norton and Company, 2008.

Bumpass, Larry. "The Changing Contexts of Parenting in the United States." Parenthood in America. 1999. http://parenthood.library.wisc.edu/Bumpass/Bumpass.html.

Cadbury, Deborah. Space Race: *The Epic Battle Between America and the Soviet Union for the Dominion of Space*. New York: HarperCollins, 2006.

Cohen, Robert, and Reginald E. Zelnick, eds. *The Free Speech Movement: Reflections on Berkeley in the 1960s*. Berkeley: University of California Press, 2002.

Coleman, Marilyn, Lawrence H. Ganong, and Kelly Warzinik. *Family Life in 20th-Century America*. Westport, CT: Greenwood Press, 2007.

Cosgrove-Mather, Bootie. "Baby Boomers Take to Internet: Boomers More Active Than Younger Americans in Some Online Tasks." CBS News. November 13, 2002. http://www.cbsnews.com/stories/2002/11/13/tech/main529232.shtml.

Cott, Jonathan. *Bob Dylan: The Essential Interviews*. New York: Wenner Publishing, 2006.

DeBenedetti, Charles. *An American Ordeal: The Antiwar Movement of the Vietnam Era*. Syracuse, NY: Syracuse University Press, 1990.

DeGrandpre, Richard. *The Cult of Pharmacology: How America Became the World's Most Troubled Drug Culture*. Durham, NC: Duke University Press, 2006.

Dicker, John. *The United States of Wal-Mart*. Portland, OR: Powell's Books, 2005.

Duberman, Martin Bauml. *Stonewall*. New York: Plume, 1994.

Edgerton, Gary. *The Columbia History of Modern Television*. New York: Columbia University Press, 2009.

Elbaum, Max. *Revolution in the Air: Sixties Radicals Turn to Lenin, Mao and Che*. New York: Verso Books, 2002.

Epstein, Edward Jay. *The Assassination Chronicles*. New York: Carroll & Graf, 1992.

Feagin, Joe R., and Melvin P. Sikes. *Living with Racism: The Black Middle-Class Experience*. Boston: Beacon Press, 1995.

Fornatale, Pete. *Back to the Garden: The Story of Woodstock*. New York: Touchstone, 2009.

Friedman, Lester, ed. *American Cinema of the 1970s: Themes and Variations*. New Brunswick, NJ: Rutgers University Press, 2007.

Grindstaff, Laura. *The Money Shot: Trash, Class, and the Making of TV Talk Shows*. Chicago: University of Chicago Press, 2002.

Harris, John F. *The Survivor: Bill Clinton in the White House*. New York: Random House, 2005.

Hine, Thomas: *I Want That: How We All Became Shoppers*. New York: Harper Perennial, 2003.

Huber, Adam, Chris Lemieux, and Marlin Hollis. "The Hippie Generation: A Brief Look into the Hippie Culture." http://users.rowan.edu/~lindman/hippieintro.html.

Hurley, Dan. "Divorce Rate: It's Not as High as You Think." *New York Times* online. April 19, 2005. http://www.divorcereform.org/nyt05.html.

Kaplan, David. "Baby Boomers Set to Revolutionize Retirement." *Houston Chronicle*. August 21, 2005. http://www.chron.com/disp/story.mpl/business/3318326.html.

King Jr., Martin Luther. *The Autobiography of Martin Luther King, Jr.* Lebanon, IN: Grand Central Publishing, 1998.

Kutler, Stanley I. *The Wars of Watergate: The Last Crisis of Richard Nixon*. New York: W.W. Norton and Company, 1992.

Lang, Michael. *The Road to Woodstock*. New York: Ecco Press, 2009.

Lee, Martin A., and Brian Shlain. *Acid Dreams: The Complete Social History of LSD, the CIA, the Sixties, and Beyond*. New York: Grove Press, 1994.

Leland, John. *Why Kerouac Matters: The Lessons of On the Road (They're Not What You Think)*. New York: Viking, 2007.

Lewis, John. *Walking with the Wind: A Memoir of the Movement*. Fort Washington, PA: Harvest Books, 1999.

Lipschultz, Jeremy Harris, and Michael L. Hilt. *Mass Media, an Aging Population and the Baby Boomers*. Mahwah, NJ: Lawrence Erlbaum Associates, 2005.

Macunovich, Diane. "'The Baby Boomers'" Macmillan Encyclopedia of Aging." October 2000. http://newton.uor.edu/Departments&Programs/EconomicDept/macunovich/baby_boomers.pdf.

Mansbridge, Jane J. *Why We Lost the ERA*. Chicago: University of Chicago Press, 1987.

Markoff, John. *What the Dormouse Said: How the Sixties Counterculture Shaped the Personal Computer Industry*. New York: Viking, 2005.

Melzer, Scott. *Gun Crusaders: The NRA's Culture War*. New York: New York University Press, 2009.

Miller, Timothy. *The 60's Communes: Hippies and Beyond*. Syracuse, NY: Syracuse University Press, 2004.

Moschis, George, and Anil Mathur. *Baby Boomers and Their Parents*. Ithaca, NY: Paramount Market Publishing, 2007.

Parlett, David. *The Oxford History of Board Games*. New York: Oxford University Press, 1999.

Pepper, William F. *An Act of State: The Execution of Martin Luther King*. New York: Verso, 2003.

Peterson, Amy T., and Ann T. Kellogg, eds. *The Greenwood Encyclopedia of Clothing through American History, 1900 to the Present*. Westport, CT: Greenwood Press, 2008.

Riley, Glenda. *Divorce: An American Tradition*. Lincoln, NE: University of Nebraska Press, 1997.

Roberts, Selena. *A Necessary Spectacle: Billie Jean King, Bobby Riggs, and the Tennis Match That Leveled the Game*. New York: Crown Publishers, 2005.

Rolling Stone. *The Rolling Stone Illustrated History of Rock and Roll: The Definitive History of the Most Important Artists and Their Music*. New York: Random House, 1992.

Roof, Wade Clark. *Spiritual Marketplace: Baby Boomers and the Remaking of American Religion*. Princeton, NJ: Princeton University Press, 2001.

Schlesinger, Arthur M. *Robert Kennedy and His Times*. New York: Mariner Books, 2002.

Schor, Juliet B. *The Overspent American: Upscaling, Downshifting and the New Consumer*. New York: Basic Books, 1998.

Shabecoff, Philip. *A Fierce Green Fire: The American Environmental Movement*. Washington, DC: Island Press, 2003.

Smead, Howard. Excerpt from "Don't Trust Anyone Over Thirty: A History of the Baby Boom." http://www.howardsmead.com/boom.htm.

Stone, Skip. *Hippies from A to Z: Their Sex, Drugs, Music and Impact from the Sixties to the Present*. Buffalo, NY: High Interest Publishing, 1999.

Szatmary, David P. *Rockin' in Time: A Social History of Rock-and-Roll*. Upper Saddle River, NJ: Prentice Hall, 2009.

Taylor, Robert Joseph, James S. Jackson, and Linda Marie Chatters. *Family Life in Black America*. Thousand Oaks, CA: Sage, 1997.

Tervalon, Jervey, and Gary Phillips. *The Cocaine Chronicles*. New York: Akashic Books, 2005.

Thomas, Pauline Weston. "1960–1980 Fashion History." http://www.fashion-era.com/1960-1980.htm.

Thompson, Hunter S. *Fear and Loathing on the Campaign Trail '72*. New York: Grand Central, 1973.

Trynka, Paul. *The Beatles: Ten Years That Shook the World*. New York: DK Publishing, 2004.

Tyner, James. *The Geography of Malcolm X: Black Radicalism and the Remaking of American Space*. New York: Routledge, 2005.

Waldron, Vince. *Classic Sitcoms: A Celebration of the Best in Prime-Time Comedy*. Los Angeles: Silman-James Press, 1998.

Weiss, Jessica. *To Have and to Hold: Marriage, the Baby Boom, and Social Change*. Chicago: University of Chicago Press, 2000.

Williams, Juan. *Eyes on the Prize: America's Civil Rights Years, 1954–1965*. New York: Penguin, 1988.

Wolfe, Tom. *The Electric Kool-Aid Acid Test*. New York: Farrar, Straus and Giroux, 1968.

The Women's Rights Movement. "Living the Legacy: The Women's Rights Movement 1848–1998." http://www.legacy98.org/.

Index

About the Author

MARTIN GITLIN is a prolific writer and sports journalist based in Ohio. He is the author of such books as *Diana, Princess of Wales: A Biography* (Greenwood, 2008), *The Ku Klux Klan* (Greenwood, 2009), and *Wounded Knee Massacre* (Greenwood, 2010).